Anonymous

Sutherland and McEvoy's Indianapolis City Directory

and business mirror for 1860-61

Anonymous

Sutherland and McEvoy's Indianapolis City Directory
and business mirror for 1860-61

ISBN/EAN: 9783337291471

Printed in Europe, USA, Canada, Australia, Japan

Cover: Foto ©Andreas Hilbeck / pixelio.de

More available books at **www.hansebooks.com**

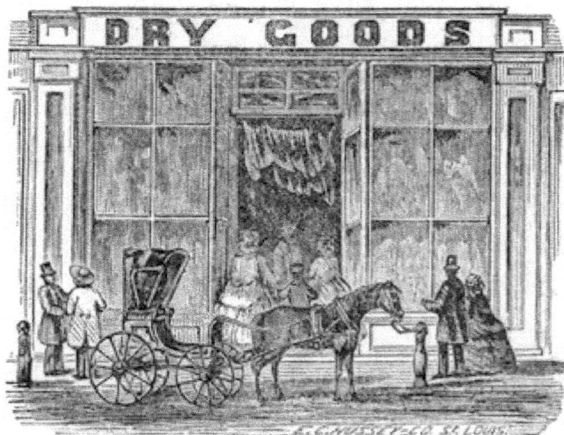

SUTHERLAND & McEVOY'S

Indianapolis City Directory

AND

BUSINESS MIRROR,

FOR 1860-61.

PUBLISHED ANNUALLY.

SUTHERLAND & McEVOY,
Publishers and Compilers.
1860.

BINGHAM & DOUGHTY, STEAM PRINTERS.

TO THE PUBLIC.

Our second edition of the Indianapolis City Directory is herewith presented to the public.

As we have had the advantage of two distinct and separate canvasses of the city, which were diligently compared together, we feel confident that it will be found reliable in an unusual degree.

We respectfully call attention to the statistics of our city, which, it will be observed, form a new and highly interesting feature. On page 287 will be found a business summary, showing the number of citizens engaged in each separate branch of trade, and in the various professions.

To those gentlemen who have kindly furnished us with information relating to the various societies, institutions, &c., we tender many thanks.

To all who have had the kindness *and good sense* to advertise in the Indianapolis Directory, we would say: may you soon have to extend the dimensions of your store-houses and incur the expense of employing additional clerks to wait upon your thronging customers.

We have to congratulate our advertising patrons upon the favorable circumstances which gives them the benefit of the circulation of both editions. Our friends have done nobly by us. "As ye have sown, *so* may ye reap."

Respectfully,
SUTHERLAND & McEVOY.

INDEX TO ADVERTISEMENTS.

INDEX TO CINCINNATI ADVERTISEMENTS.

INDEX TO RAILROADS.

CONTENTS.

JASON DAME,
MARBLE WORKER

AND

Monument Builder

No. 67 East Washington St.,

OPP. TOUSEY AND BYRAM'S STORE,

INDIANAPOLIS, IND.

Keeps on Hand and Manufactures to Order all kinds of

Monumental & Tombstone Work

Of the finest designs and best Patterns used in the business.

Persons wanting anything in my line will consult their interest by calling at my Establishment, before buying elsewhere, as I possess every facility for getting up works as good and cheap as anywhere in the city, and therefore defy competition.

PLEASE GIVE ME A CALL.

Indianapolis City Directory

FOR 1860-61.

ABBREVIATIONS.

Bds., *boards;* cor., *corner;* res., *residence;* col., *colored;* wid., *widow;* opp., *opposite;* bet., *between;* ave., *avenue;* E., W., N., S., *East, West, North, South.* The word *street* is implied.

A

ABBETT LAWSON, physician and surgeon, res. 20 Virginia ave.

Abbett William A., clerk Hausman & Co., bds. 20 Virginia ave.

Abrams John, clerk P. S. Birkenmeyer & Co., res. 55 E. Ohio.

ACHEY AMERICUS, carpenter and builder, res. 79 Vermont.

ACHEY COL. HENRY, retired, Kentucky ave.

ACHEY JOHN, Club House, 13 N. Illinois.

ADAMS EXPRESS CO., (John H. Ohr, agent,) 12 E. Washington.

Adams George H., book-keeper Witness office, res. 70 N. Pennsylvania.

ADAMS HARRY E., clerk Palmer House.

Adams H. S., policeman, res. 274 S. Delaware.

Adams John M., bds. 149 N. Delaware.

Adams Reuben, clerk Bradshaw & Glazier, res. 71 S. New Jersey.

Adams William L., clerk H. A. Fletcher & Co., res. 26 E. Market.

Adkins Mrs. Mary, bds. 91 S. Tennessee.

ÆTNA BUILDINGS, 14 N. Pennsylvania.

2

ÆTNA INSURANCE CO., Wm. Henderson, agent, 14 N. Pennsylvania.
Agerett John, res. St. Clair.
Alaire P. A., bricklayer, bds. 138 N. Alabama.
Albert Lawson, blacksmith, 66 Indiana ave.
Albertsmearchan S. M. Donald, Union.
Albertsmeyer Henry, saw miller, res. 152 N. Noble.
Albrecht George, varnisher, Spiegel, Thoms & Co., res. 95 N. Davidson.
Albro Henry, moulder, res. 252 S. Delaware.
Aldag August, shoemaker, res. 50 N. Liberty.
Aldag C. L., shoemaker C. Aldag, res. 50 N. Liberty.
ALDAG CHARLES, boots and shoes, 133 E. Washington, res. 32 N. Liberty.
Aldag Louis, shoemaker, res. 30 N. Liberty.
ALDENE MADAME, dress maker, &c., 118 N. Illinois.
Aldene Miss Lizzie, bds. 118 N. Illinois.
Aldland Hiram, baker, bds. 150 N. New Jersey.
Alexander John, conductor J. and I. Railroad, bds. American House.
Alford Thomas G., (Mills, A. & Co.,) res. 79 N. Alabama.
Allaire Andrew B., blacksmith, bds. 138 N. Alabama.
Allaire James P , brick mason, res. 138 N. Alabama.
Allaire Peter A., brick mason, bds. 138 N. Alabama.
Allamon Samuel, (Osgood, Smith & Co.,) res. cor. Maryland and Pennsylvania.
ALLEN CHARLES F., civil engineer, 8 Blake's Block, bds. American House.
Allen Emery, (col.,) teamster, 133 N. Alabama.
Allen Henry, (A. & Hinesley,) res. 68 W. Vermont.
ALLEN & HINESLEY, livery stable, rear of Palmer House.
Allen James R., student, bds. James.
Allen James S., gas fitter, bds. 121 Maryland.
Allen Joseph, (col.,) res. 186 W. North.
Allen Miss Mary, weaver, Ohio P. W. Factory, bds. W. Maryland.
Allen Robert, moulder, 117 W. Maryland.
ALLEN STEPHEN, grocer, cor. Illinois and Indiana ave., res. 49 Indiana ave.
Allen William, machinist Bellefontaine Railroad shop, res. 105 Meek.
Allison J. E., plasterer, bds. 21 N. Alabama.
Allison L. L., engineer I. and C. Railroad, bds. 70 S. Noble.
Allred G. M., sexton grave yard, res. 103 South.
Altland Samuel T., carpenter, res. 171 N. New Jersey.
Alvord E. S., U. S. mail contractor, res. 54 N. Pennsylvania.

AMERICAN EXPRESS CO., H. W. Daniels, agent, S. E.
cor. Washington and Meridian.

AMERICAN HOUSE, Wiggim & Morrow, proprietors,
Louisiana, opp. Union Depot.

AMES RIGHT REV. EDWARD R., Methodist Episcopal,
res. N. Pennsylvania, E. S., bet. First and Second.

AMES JAMES, agent for Gilbert's piano fortes and Grover
and Baker's sewing machines, cor. W. Washington and
Kentucky ave.

Amos James, spinner, res. 201 W. Washington.

Amos Mrs. Nancy, res. 143 N. Noble.

Amos Thomas D., policeman, 1st ward, res. 75 N. Spring.

Anderson Charles, carpenter, bds. 53 E. Market.

Anderson David, carpenter, 52 Indiana ave.

Anderson George, carpenter, bds. 53 E. Market.

Anderson George P., miller, res. 140 E. Market.

Anderson Henry, carpenter, res. 53 E. Market.

Anderson J., res. 147 E. New York.

Anderson Jacob, laborer, res. E. St. Marys.

Anderson James, coachman, 54 N. Pennsylvania.

Anderson James W., messenger American Express Co., res.
96 N. East.

Anderson J. A. P., proprietor Bates City Mills.

ANDERSON JOHN HOWELL P., superintendent Bates
City Mills, res. 36 N. Delaware.

Anderson Robert J., brick mason, res. 15 E. North.

Anderson Samuel, (col.,) wood sawyer, res. 63 S Noble.

Anderson Thomas, laborer, 97 N. Mississippi.

ANDRA JOHN, saddler and harness maker, 196 E. Washington, res. 152 E. New York.

Andrews Henry, (col.,) express man, bds. 149 N. Alabama.

ANDREWS L. N., general freight agent P. & I. Railroad ;
office at Depot, res. 73 S. Delaware.

Angevine E. G., painter and paper hanger, res. 134 N. East.

Ankanbrock Henry, drayman, S. Delaware.

Antee Jacob, blacksmith, res. 199 S. Delaware.

Anthony David, carpenter, res. 14 N. West.

Anton Charles, draftsman, bds. Pyle House.

Appleton Mrs. Eliza, (col.,) res. 141 N. East.

APPLETON JAMES R., foreman press room Sentinel
office, res. 46 Indiana ave.

Archey David, (col.,) porter Bates House.

Archey Edward, (col.,) cook, Little's Hotel.

Arevels Rev. Willis, (col.,) Meth. Episc., res. 119 N. West.

Armanenk Christian, laborer, res. 13 N. Railroad.

Armstrong Geo. A., res. 53 S. Mississippi.

Armstrong Geo. F., deliverer American and U. S. Express
Co.'s.

Armstrong John, 165 W. Washington.
Armstrong J. K., tailor, res. South.
Armstrong Miss M., 139 W. Washington.
Arnholter Henry, harness maker, bds. 152 E. New York.
ARNOLD & DAVIS, cancer doctors, 40½ Louisiana, up stairs.
Arnold Edward, carpenter, bds. Farmers' and Drovers' Hotel.
Arnold Mrs. Jane, res. 10 N. West.
Arnold John W., (A. &. Davis,) bds. Tremont House.
Arnold Lewis, laborer, res 277 East.
Arnold Peter, laborer, 143 E. Washington.
Arnold wid. Sallie, res. 283 S. East.
Arnold Thomas, brick moulder, res. 283 S. East.
Arnold William, brick moulder, res. 283 S. East.
Arnold Willis, brick maker, res. 147 S. Mississippi.
Arthur Thomas, moulder, res 240 W. Washington.
Ash Frank, laborer, res. 14 S. Georgia.
ASH ISAAC N., Deputy Auditor of State, res. 16 California.
ASHER & CO., publishers and booksellers, Odd Fellows' Hall, up stairs.
Asher John R., (A. & Co.) bds. 11 Madison ave.
Askin Patrick, peddler, res. 56 Massachusetts ave.
Asmos Charles, clerk, bds 151 Indiana ave.
Asmus Frederick, weaver, 158 N. Noble.
Askren David, carpenter, res. 114 W. Ohio.
Aterbrook, Henry, drayman, res. 269 S. Delaware.
ATHON JAMES S., M. D., Superintendent Indiana Hospital for the Insane.
ATKINS ELIAS C., saw manufacturer, 155 S. Illinois, res. East, S. of Georgia.
Atkinson Joseph, engineer I. P. & C. R. R., bds. Ray House.
Atkinson Samuel, machinist I. P. & C. R. R., bds. Ray House.
Atkinson Thomas, painter, res. 116 N. Mississippi.
Atkinson Joseph B., law student with N. B. Taylor, bds. 22 W. Maryland.
ATLAS, daily, weekly and tri-weekly, John D. Defrees publisher, 18 S. Meridian.
Austin James, res. 28 S. Meridian.
AVERY LEONARD S., groceries and provisions, 24 W. Washington, res. N. Tennessee, bt. Michigan and Vermont.
Avery John L., carpenter, 124 N. Alabama, res. 104 N. Alabama.
Avery John P., 104 N. Alabama.
Averill V. B., bookbinder, bds. 61 W. New York.
Avels Joseph, carpenter, 255 S. Pennsylvania.

Avels Mrs. Margaret, groceries and provisions, 277 S Delaware.
Ayres Milton, wagon maker, 56 S. East.

B

BABCOCK H., wholesale grocer, 75 E. Washington, res. 169 Delaware.
Babcock M. D., manager H. Babcock, res. 75 E. Washington.
Babbitt wid. A., res. 78 S. Illinois.
Babbitt Alonzo P., printer, res. 78 S. Illinois.
Back Clemmens, cigar maker, bds. Union Hall.
Back John, porter Tremont House.
Backes Thomas, blacksmith, bds. E. Market.
Backman William, laborer Central Depot, res. 208 S. Alabama.
BACON DANIEL, superintendent Bates House Saloon, bds. Bates House.
Bacon E. W., painter, res. 131 N. Alabama.
Bacon John L., blacksmith, bds. 131 N. Alabama.
Bacon Robert D., silver smith, rear of 21 E. Washington, bds. Mrs. Kirk.
Bacon Theodore L., book keeper, bds. 127 Massachusetts ave.
Bacon William M., painter, res. 158 N. Delaware.
Bade Anthony, laborer, res. 129 S. Alabama.
Bader Henry, currier J. Fishback, res. Bluff Road.
Baer Henry C., marble cutter W. A. Keys, bds Pyle House.
Balirmann John, laborer, 112 S. Noble.
Baier C., agent Zeitung, Delaware.
Baier Jacob, tailor, bds. Union Hall.
Bailey wid. John, res. 18 N. East.
Baine Thomas, physician, 68 Blackford.
Bair Leonidus, harness maker, bds. Kentucky ave., bet. Maryland and Georgia.
Baker Albert C., (B. & Kelly,) res. Huron.
BAKER MRS. ANNA, milliner, 20 S. Illinois, res. same.
Baker Miss Evaline, 20 S. Illinois.
Baker Frederick, plasterer, 203 N. Illinois.
Baker Henry, res. cor. North and Blake.
Baker Henry, helper, res. 302 N. Illinois.
Baker Isaac W., laborer, Blake opp. Mill.
Baker Jacob, tailor, res. 113 E. New York.
BAKER JAMES M., salesman Hickok & Starr, res. 16 S. Illinois.
Baker John, porter Tremont House, res. 243 S. Pennsylvania.
Baker John, jr., harness maker, bds. Mrs. Smith.

Baker & Kelly, painters, cor. of Washington and Meridian, up stairs.

BAKER MISS SARAH A., dress maker, 20 S. Illinois.

Baker S. W., salesman New York Store, bds. Macy House.

Baker Thomas, bar tender T. B. Dunn, 68 E. Washington.

Baker W. I., passenger agent B. R. R., res. 108 E. South.

Baker William, teamster, res. Blake, bet. Washington and New York,

BALCKE CHARLES, saloon and billiard table, 175 E. Washington.

BALCKE CHARLES, Secretary German Mutual Insurance Co., 95 E. Washington.

Baldwig wid. Levi, res. 183 N. East.

Baldwin Mrs. Emma R., res. 183 N. East.

Baldwin J. H., (H. Hausmann &Co.,) res. 41 E. Michigan.

Ball Miss M. J., teacher Indianapols Female Institute, bds. 34 E. Michigan.

Ballard Austin, seal engraver, res. 5 Circle.

Ballard Charles E., carriage painter, bds. 5 Circle.

BALLARD GRANVILLE M., principal teacher Indiana Institute for the education of the Blind.

Ballard J., clerk, bds. 21 S. Delaware.

Ballard W. G., clerk A. D. Wood, bds. S. Beck.

Balls Christian, carpenter, bds. 51 Union.

Ballweg Ambrose, machinist, 57 Madison ave.

BALLWEG FREDERICK, State House Saloon, 95 W. Washington.

Bals Charles, (Ruschhaupt & B.,) res. 56 E. St. Joseph.

BAMBERGER H. & CO., hats, caps and furnishing goods, 16 E. Washington.

Bamberger Herman, (H. B. & Co.,) bds. Bates House.

Bandy Peter, carpenter, res. California.

Banghart Aaron W., laborer, res. 189 N. New Jersey.

BANK OF THE STATE OF INDIANA, H. McCulloch, president; James M. Ray, cashier, cor. Illinois and Kentucky ave.

Banks Francis R., engineer B. R. R., res. cor. Broadway and Strawberry alley.

Bannon James, at Bellefontaine R. R. shop, res. Virginia ave.

Banse William, wagon maker, 306 Virginia ave.

Banstroke Mrs. Anna, 18 W. Maryland.

Barahmanan John, laborer, 112 S. Noble.

Barbee Robert B., constable, res. 165 N. East.

Barbee Sampson, moulder, res. 201 S. Delaware.

BARBOUR & HOWLAND, attorneys at law, 19 E. Washington.

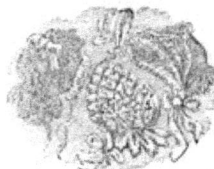

Barbour Lucian, (B. & Howland.) res. Alabama, S. E. cor. Michigan.

BARBOUR SAMUEL, Deputy U. S. Marshal, res. 37 W. Maryland.

Barbs Mrs. Elizabeth, res. 81 N. Pennsylvania.

Bare B., bds. 152 W. Georgia.

Bare Dewitt, bds. 152 W. Georgia.

Bare Leonidus, bds. 152 W. Georgia.

Bare Mrs. Sidney, res. 152 W. Georgia.

Bark Henry, 63 Bluff Road.

BARKER THOMAS D., County Treasurer, office Court House, res. 117 N. Delaware.

Barks James A., painter, res. 279 S. Delaware.

Barlow Thomas, baggage master B. R. R., bds. American House.

Barlow Thomas, carver, bds. 37 South.

Barneclo John M., shipping clerk I. C. R. R. Depot, res. 45 E. Louisiana.

Barneclo Orlando, laborer, bds. 45 E. Louisiana.

Barnes A., Meridian, bet. Maryland and Washington.

BARNES ELLIS, foreman job room Journal Co., res 20 S. Meridian.

Barnes Patrick, laborer, 245 S. Pennsylvania.

Barnes William, rope maker, res. S. West.

Barnham William, blacksmith, cor. W. Vermont and California.

BARNITT & BRO., groceries and provisions, 170 E. Washington.

Barnitt Isaac, (B. & Bro.,) res. 68 N. East.

Barnitt Thomas, sr., (B. & Bro.,) res. 83 E. Market.

Barnitt Thomas, jr., (Hanlin & B.,) bds. 83 E. Market.

Barr B. J., tailor, bds. Railroad ave.

Barr Jacob, venitian blinds, res. 86 N. Alabama.

Barr Joseph, tailor, res. 127 Railroad ave.

Barr Mrs. Nancy, res. 134 N. East.

Barret Patrick, laborer, res. 76 S. Noble.

BARRINGER GEORGE L., conductor I. & C. R. R., bds. Bates House.

Barrows H. W., machinist, bds. Galt House.

Barry wid. Richard, 306 S, Delaware.

Barry Thomas, clerk Wm. Hannaman.

Bars L., (col.,) oyster saloon, Washington, cor. of Meridian.

Barth George, laborer, 198 Virginia ave.

Barth Rev. John H., res. 121 N. Alabama.

BARTLETT JOSEPH L., groceries &c., 133 S. Tennessee, res. 121 Tennessee.

Bartlett L. B., bds. 58 W. Vermont.

Bartz Charles, res. 148 N. Illinois.

BASSETT HORACE, clerk U. S. Circuit Court, office Masonic Hall, res. 20 E. Ohio.
Bassett William J., mason, res. 31 Indiana ave.
BATES' CITY MILLS, J. A. P. Anderson proprietor, 282 E. Washington.
Bates Edward, jr., shoemaker, res. 8 McOuat's Block.
BATES HERVEY, Sr., res. 66 E. Market.
BATES HERVEY, Jr., res. 73 N. Delaware.
BATES HOUSE, William Judson, proprietor, cor. Illinois and Washington.
Batty Edwin, carpenter, res. Broadway ave.
Batty John H., grocery and provisions, 21 N. Alabama, res. Broadway ave.
Bauer Mrs. Mary, 63 N. Illinois.
Baugh Casper, butcher, 14 Garden.
Baumann Andrew, proprietor Pennsylvania House, cor. Washington and East.
Baumeister A. E., clerk C. Meyer, res. 16 W. Georgia.
Baumeister Herman, clerk Klotz & Pfafflin, bds. 16 W. Georgia.
Bavington Albert, plasterer, bds. W. H. Lingenfelter.
Bayles E., bds. 58 W. Vermont.
BAYMILLER CHARLES P., bds. 90 Massachusetts ave.
Bayton William (col.,) currier, 139 West.
Bazzell Mrs. Sarah, res. 79 Vermont.
BEACH WILLIAM B., clerk Supreme Court, office State House, res. 106 N. West.
Beak John, blacksmith, res. 119 E. South.
BEAL JOHN A., attorney, 6 Glenns' Block, res. 82 N. East.
Beal M. S., res. 82 N. East.
BEALE JOSHUA, painter and glazier, 133 Virginia ave., res. 19 Bates.
Beam David, (Byrkit & B.,) res. 125 S. Tennessee.
Beam Mary, res. 125 S. Tennessee.
Bean John, bar tender Tremont House.
BEATY DAVID S., sec'y Gas Co. and Central Plank Road Co., office 3 W. Washington, res. 80 E. Michigan.
BEARD & SINEX, agricultural implements, N. E. cor. Washington and Tennessee.
Beasley Mrs. Ann, res. 105 N. Tennessee.
Beasley John, boot maker A. Knodle & Son, res. 105 N. Tennessee.
Beaty Mary, res. 122 N. Illinois.
Beaver Elisha, carpenter, res. 182 Massachusetts ave.
Beaver Joseph, (col.,) cook Little's Hotel.
Becher Conrad, cigar box maker, res. 215 N. Alabama.
BECK ANDREW J., conductor T. H. & R. Railroad, bds. Palmer House.

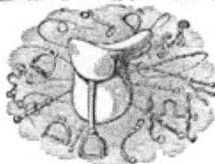

BECK CHRISTIAN, gunsmith, 15 S. Meridian, res. 80 N. New Jersey.

BECK EDWARD, Crystal Palace Saloon and Restaurant, 44 W. Washington.

Beck George L., carriage painter, bds. Macy House.

Beck Jacob, gunsmith, 76 Fort Wayne ave.

BECK JACOB, gunsmith, 86 E. Washington, res. 79 E. St. Clair.

BECK JOHN A., watch maker C. G. French, bds. 51 S. Delaware.

BECK & MOFFITT, Western Paint and Color Works, 87 E. Washington.

Beck Samuel, (B. & Moffitt,) res. 21 S. Delaware.

BECKER H., trunk manufacturer, 30 W. Washington, res. 76 N. Tennessee.

Becker Jacob, (Tapking & B.,) 113 E. New York.

Beckett Wm., on Indiana Central Railroad, bds. Ray House.

Beckner Henry W., carpenter, res. 23 McCarty.

Beckner Samuel R., mail agent, res. 34 E. Market.

Bedford W. R., attorney at law, 35½ E. Washington.

BEEBE R., Empire Saloon, 23 W. Washington.

Beezley Louisa C., bds. 132 S. Delaware.

Beezley Nathaniel, boarding, 132 S. Delaware.

Behie Frederick, shoemaker, 130 S. Delaware.

BEHYMER DANIEL, sash and blind manufacturer and carpenter, 6 N. Delaware, res. 110 E. Market.

Belhaus John, apprentice Dumont & Sinker.

Bell Miletus & Co., grocers, 46 Fort Wayne ave.

Bell Miletus, physician, res. 124 N. Delaware.

Bell Peter, moulder, bds. 258 S. Delaware.

BELL THADDEUS D., auction and commission, jewelry, &c., 15 W. Washington, bds. Tremont House.

Bell William, teamster, res. 74 Blackford.

BELLEFONTAINE RAILROAD OFFICE, cor. Meridian and Louisiana.

Bellows E., blacksmith, res. 57 N. Delaware.

Beltzner Michael, teamster, res. 116 E. Market.

Belzer George, foundryman, 213 N. Alabama.

BENDER DAVID, proprietor National Hotel, 217 W. Washington.

Bender Tobias, currier J. Fishback, res. E. Market, near New Jersey.

Bennett Mrs. Julia, 161 S. Tennessee.

Bennett William H., (Root, B. & Co.,) res. 80 N. Meridian.

Benson Henry C., cooper, 51 Benton.

Benson H. C., clerk, res. 68 Noble.

3

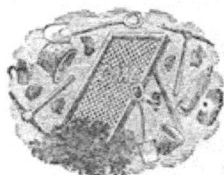

BENTON A. R., professor of languages, N. W. cor. University, res. N. E. of city limits.

BEOCHER & WERTHER, butchers, 175 S. Delaware.

Beocher Henry, (B. & Werther,) res. 1 mile on Madison R.R.

Berg Mrs. Frederica, res. 105 E. South.

Berg Henry, stone mason, res. 276 S. Delaware.

Berg Henry, carpenter, res. 141 S. Alabama.

Berger John, clerk J. A. Heidlinger, bds. California House.

Berger Leander, cigar maker J. A. Heidlinger.

BERGNER GUSTAV, clerk Indianapolis Branch Banking Co.

Bernauer Joseph, laborer, res. 52 S. Huron.

Berner Charles, clerk, res. 36 Indiana ave.

Berner Gottlieb, huckster, res. 90 N. Davidson.

Bernhammer Henry, waiter Crystal Palace Saloon.

Berringer Joseph, cabinet maker, bds. Kentucky ave.

Berry Elizabeth A., bds. 52 S. Delaware.

Berry I. N., last maker, bds. Mrs. Kinder's, 79½ E. Washington.

Berry John, 266 N. Indiana ave.

BERRY JOSEPH A., printer, Sentinel office, bds. Farmers' Hotel.

Berry Michael, stone cutter, res. 46 N. Spring.

Berryman Eli, cabinet maker, res. 160 S. Alabama.

Berryman Ezekiel, cabinet maker, res. 46 S. Noble.

Berryman John, blacksmith and wagon maker, E. Washington, near limits, res. 50 S. Noble.

Berryman William, blacksmith, 46 S. Noble.

Beynon Thomas, laborer, res. 241 E. Massachusetts ave.

BIBLE DEPOSITORY, Mrs. E. Wilkins, agent, 34 E. Market.

Biche Frederick, shoemaker, 130 S. Delaware.

BIDDLE & COOPER, boots and shoes, 79 E. Washington.

Biddle Sylvanus, (Eldridge, McMillin & B.,) res. 50 S. Mississippi.

Biddle Wm., (B. & Cooper,) res. 52 E. Market.

Bier Jacob, tailor, bds. Union Hotel.

Bigelow Ira, plasterer, res. 182 E. New York.

Biggy Thomas, laborer, res. 178 East.

Bilger Joseph, carpenter, res. 154 E. New York.

Billingsworth John, confectioner, 45 Union.

Bina Timothy, laborer, 108 Wabash, bet. East and Liberty.

BING SIMON, Jr., fancy goods, notions, toys, &c., 32 W. Washington.

BINGS BAZAAR, 32 W. Washington.

BINGHAM & DOUGHTY, proprietors Indiana State Sentinel, office 16, 18 and 20, Sentinel Buildings, E. Washington.

Bingham J., stone cutter S. C. Jones.
BINGHAM JOS. J., editor State Sentinel, E. Washington, res. 88 W. Maryland.
BINGHAM W. P. & CO., watches and jewelry, 20 E. Washington.
Bingham Wheelock P., (W. P. B. & Co.,) res. 7 E. Ohio.
Binkley Samuel, (Wilson Jones & Co.,) res. 205 N. Illinois.
Bippus Frederick, laborer, bds. 137 N. Mississippi.
Bippus John, tailor, 137 N. Mississippi.
Birch James C., res. cor. Market and Alabama.
Bird Henry, (col.,) barber, bds. 145 W. Washingtion.
BRINKENMAYER P. S. & CO., dealers in agricultural and horticultural implements, 74 E. Washington.
Birkenmayer P. S., (P. S. B. & Co.,) res. 145 N. Pennsylvania.
Boinbaum Joseph, salesman S. Bings, jr.
Bisbing Charles, machinist, bds. 124 N. West.
Bisbing Jacob I., deputy city marshal, res. 124 N. West.
Bishop George, cabinet maker, bds. 255 S. Delaware.
Bishop widow John, res. 193 N. New Jersey.
Bishop Lewis P., laborer, res. 193 N. New Jersey.
Bissett S. A., baggage master J. and I. Railroad, bds. American House.
Black George H., carpenter, 81 N. East.
Black John, conductor Indiana Central Railroad, bds. American House.
Black William M., tanner, 22 W. Maryland.
Blaes Nicholas, ale and beer agent, 66 S. Delaware, res. same.
BLAIN JAMES W., house and sign painter, 31 S. Delaware, res. same.
Blain Thomas M., cupola tender, res. 95 W. New York.
Blair B., painter, 129 Blake.
BLAIR JAMES M., harness and collar manufacturer, 87 W. Washington, res. same.
BLAKE JAMES, off. Blake's Building, res. 186 N. Tennessee.
Blake James R., clerk Rolling Mill, bds. 186 N. Tennessee.
Blake John, (Kregelo, B. & Co.,) res. 134 N. West.
Blake Margaret C., washing and ironing, res. Huron, bet. Ohio and New York.
Blake Walter A., bds. 186 N. Tennessee.
Blake William M., 201 N. Tennessee.
BLAKE'S BUILDING, cor. Washington and Illinois.
Blanc Francis, (H. Tilly & Co.,) res. S. Pennsylvania.
Blanc John, butcher, 101 N. Meridian.
Blanch Anthony, clerk C. Vonnegut, bds. 142 E. Washington.

Bland Hiram, carpenter, res. 155 N. New Jersey.
Blausteg V., stone mason, 162 Liberty.
Blauvelt David C., bds. 74 N. Tennessee.
Blessing Benj., watchman at Depot, res. 229 S. Alabama.
Bloom Francis, res. 190 S. Pennsylvania.
Blovelt Charles, teamster, res. 33 S. Liberty.
Blue Cyrus B., carpenter, res. 69 Fort Wayne ave.
Blumer John, laborer, 23 McAllister.
Blunk Andrew F., carpenter, res. 269 Massachusetts ave.
Bly Oliver H. P., switchman Union Railroad Co., 32 N. East.
Blythe Samuel, machinist, res. 15 E. Lord.
Blythe William, fireman, bds. 56 S. Noble.
BOAZ W, T., treasurer I. and C. Railroad Co., bds. 20 W. North.
BOAZ WILLIAM, deputy sheriff, res. 261 S. Pennsylvania.
Bocart Frederick, coppersmith, res. N. Meridian.
Bock Christian, carpenter, res. 140 N. Alabama.
Bockstahler Martin, baker, res. 50 South.
BOBBS J. S., physician, 172 E. Washington, up stairs, res. outside Corporation.
Bock Christopher, carpenter, 140 N. Alabama.
Bodantz Henry, merchant tailor, 158 W. Washington.
Bodcar Conrad, cigar box maker, res. 215 N. Alabama.
Boek John S., plumber, bds. National Hotel.
Boerum Joseph S., carpenter, 204 N. Illinois, res. 200 N. Illinois.
BOETTICHER JULIUS, publisher of Indiana Volksblatt, 132 E Washington.
Boetticher Otto, printer Indiana Volksblatt, bds. 132 E. Washington.
Bogert Charles, teamster, bds. cor. Missouri and Merrill.
Bogert Cornelius, watchman Peg Factory.
Boging Hiram, laborer, bds. 38 S. Alabama.
BOHLEN D. A., architect Ætna Buildings, N. Pennsylvania, res. 41 Huron.
Bohme Christian, carpenter, 22 S. Alabama.
Bohme Mrs. Mary, midwife, 22 S. Alabama.
Bolinger Madison, carpenter, res. 18 N. West.
Bollman Frederick, baker, 91 E. Washington, res. same.
Bolton Ezra, res. 71 Madison ave.
Bolton Mrs. James, bds. 55 S. Illinois.
Bolton James P., checkman Bellefontaine R. R. Depot.
Bolton Sarah, candy maker, bds. 55 S. Illinois.
Bomer Nicholas, laborer, 64 Bluff Road.
Bond A. V., shoemaker, bds. Mrs. Ferguson.
Bonner Mrs. Mary, res. cor. Meridian and North.
BONTH REV. J. H., (Ger. Meth.,) res. 121 N. Alabama.

Bookter Geo., weaver, res. cor. California and Maryland.
Boon Daniel, (col.,) teamster, res. 97 Massachusetts ave.
Boots D. S., traveling agent, res. 44 Pennsylvania.
Borgman Frederick, laborer, res. 190 N. Davidson.
Bornorden Charles, laborer, res. Fletcher's add.
Borst Frederick, (Pouder & B.,) 15 Indiana ave.
Boston James, (col.,) barber, bds. Macy House.
Bott Frederick J., clerk, bds. 109 E. Washington.
BOTT HENRY, Union Saloon and billiards, 109 E. Washington.
BOUCHET ED., dyeing and scouring, 174 W. Washington, res. same.
Bouvgheart Watson, laborer, 189 N. New Jersey.
Boury Adrain, tinner, res. 153 N. Liberty.
Bovard James, livery, res. 18 W. Ohio.
Bow Benjamin, blacksmith, bds. Meridian.
Bowen Silas T., (Stewart & B.,) 87 N. Illinois.
Bowles Geo. A., clerk Wm. Y. Wiley, bds. Mrs. Smith.
BOWLES THOS. H., attorney at law and notary public, office 10 E. Washington, bds. Bates House.
Bowman A., clerk H. A. Fletcher & Co., bds. 50 W. Vermont.
Bowman Miss E. W., teacher Indiana Institute for the Education of the Blind.
Bowman Henry, brick moulder, res. 74 S. Noble.
Bowroff Samuel, baggage master L. and I. Railroad, bds. American House.
BOYD DAVID M., salesman patent rights, res. 37 S. Meridian.
Boyd E. C., clerk post office, bds. 21 S. Delaware.
Boyd John, clerk Carlisle & Dixon.
BOYD JOSEPH F., general ticket agent Bellefontaine Railroad, office cor. Meridian and Louisiana, bds. Bates House.
BOYD J. T., physician, cor. Meridian and Maryland, res. 12 Indiana ave.
Boyer Martin, fruit stand, cor. Pennsylvania and Washington, res. Noble.
Boyles Michael W., clerk J. C. Yohn, bds. 22 Virginia ave.
Boykink Christ, drayman, Union.
BRACKEN CAPT. JAMES R., local editor Indiana State Sentinel, res. 128 N. Alabama.
Badchope Detrich, teamster, res. 115 E. New York.
Brademier Christ, laborer, 113 E. South.
Brademier Frederick J., teamster, 69 N. Spring.
Brademier Henry, saloon, 312 Virginia ave.
BRADEN DAVID, dealer in agricultural implements, 84 W. Washington, res. 208 N. Illinois.

Braden William, (Sheets & B.,) bds. Palmer House.
BRADLEY J. & J., dry goods and groceries, &c., 81 E.
  Washington.
Bradley James W., (J. & J. B.,) bds. 78 S. Pennsylvania.
Bradley Jeptha W., (J. & J. B.,) res. 78 S. Pennsylvania.
BRADLEY JOHN H., Superintendent Columbus and Piqua
  R. R., res. 69 N. Pennsylvania.
Brado Charles, grocer, cor. North and N. Alabama, res. cor.
  Ohio and East.
Brado Thomas, grocer, res. 134 E. Ohio.
BRADSHAW & GLAZIER, produce and commission mer-
  chants, 16 Meridian, cor. Pearl.
BRADSHAW J. & J., groceries and provisions, 25 W. Wash-
  ington.
Bradshaw James, (J. & J. B.,) res. 149 N. Illinois.
Bradshaw John A., (J. & J. B.,) res 15 E. Ohio,
Bradshaw Oliver L., machinist, bds. 46 S. Noble.
Bradshaw Wm. A., (B. & Glazier,) res. 160 S. New Jersey.
Bradshaw William, retired, res. 161 S. Alabama.
Brady Patrick, laborer, res. National Road.
Braetoff Henry, laborer, Union.
BRAES PHILLIP, professor of languages and painting,
  17 Indiana ave.
Bragunier William, teamster, bds. 142 E. New York.
Bramwell John M., book keeper Rob't. Browning, res. 48 S.
  Mississippi.
BRANCH OF THE BANK OF THE STATE OF IN-
  DIANA, N. E. cor. Washington and Meridian, George
  Tousey, president; C. S. Stevenson, cashier.
Brandon John, res. 25 S. Georgia.
Brandt Herman H., telegraph operator I. & C. R. R., bds.
  Ray House.
Branham John C., bds. 149 N. Delaware.
Branham L., railroader, res. 91 S. Illinois.
Branham Preston E., clerk L. Street & Bro., bds. 91 S. Illi-
  nois.
Branham John, res. Ohio, bet. Meridian and Pennsylvania.
Brannan Donald, laborer, res. 33 E. Market.
Brannan John, porter Post Office, res 356 Virginia ave.
Brannan Patrick, porter American House.
Braun Henry, bar keeper J. C. Brinckmeyer, 75 E. Wash-
  ington.
Braun John, laborer, bds. Union House.
Bray John S., carpenter and joiner, res. 149 N. West
Brademeyer C., laborer, 105 E. South.
Breh Leopold, baker, res. 102 E. New York.
Bremmerman Caston, carriage maker, res. 42 E. Pratt.
Bremmerman Fred., carriage maker, res. 115 N. Alabama.

Brenck Frederick, teamster, res. 184 E. Vermont.
BRENKER AUGUST, groceries and provisions, 94 E. New York
Brenker William, cooper, 169 N. New Jersey.
Brensill Henry, laborer, Madison ave.
Bretney William, butcher, 58 W. Louisiana.
BRETZ ADAM, groceries and provisions, cor. Illinois and Louisiana, res. 60 S. Illinois.
BREWNIG REV. GEORGE A., (Ger. Meth.,) res. University ave.
BREUNINER AUGUSTUS, groceries and provisions, 168 Virginia ave.
Brick Daniel, laborer, 14 S. Georgia.
Bricket Mrs. E. A., res. 135 W. Market.
Bridge Albert R., turner Osgood, Smith & Co., bds. Pyle House.
Brigham Charles E., compositor Locomotive Office, bds. 69 W. South.
Briggs Charles H., clerk, bds. 30 S. Illinois.
Briggs George, carpenter, bds. 72 W. Maryland.
Briggs James, butcher, res. 152 N. Mississippi.
Bright Amos L., printer, bds. 27 Indiana ave.
Bright Mrs. Eliza, boarding house, 27 Indiana ave.
Bright Major, boarding, 27 Indiana ave.
Brighton James, brick mason, 100 N. Tennessee.
Brinckmeyer Frederick, laborer, res. 127 N. Davidson.
Brinckmeyer George, clerk, res. 129 N. Davidson.
Brinckmeyer John, sr., 152 N. Liberty.
BRINCKMEYER JOHN, saloon keeper, res. 152 N. Liberty.
BRINCKMEYER JOHN C., saloon, 75 E. Washington, res. same.
Brinker William, cooper, res. 163 N. New Jersey.
BRINKMAN & BUCKSOT, livery and boarding stable, 17 S. Delaware.
Brinkman Charles, (B. & Bucksot,) res. 67 N. New Jersey.
Brinkman Frederick, carpenter, res. 191 N. Noble.
Brinning Frederick, carpenter, res. 295 S. Delaware.
Brison Miss Annie, tailoress, bds. 118 N. Alabama.
Bristor Samuel M., carriage maker, res. 51 N. Delaware.
Brodemeyer Charles, runner Little's Hotel.
Brodemeyer Christian, laborer, 53 Union.
Broden James, moulder, res. 119 E. New York.
Broden John, millwright, res. 117 E. New York.
Broden Michael J., printer Locomotive Office, res. 117 E. New York.
Broden Patrick, moulder, res. 54 Benton.
Broderick T. P., bar tender Bates House Saloon.

BRONSON GEORGE W., assistant teacher Commercial College, res. 50 S. Mississippi.
Bronson Robert, joiner, bds. 31 Indiana ave.
Brookman S., general business agent, bds. Tully House.
BROOKS REV. A. L., (Presb.,) res. 89 E. Ohio.
Brooks Bennet, carpenter, res. 175 N. New Jersey.
Brooks Mrs. Hannah, res. 146 W. Market.
Brother John, blacksmith, 3 N. Noble, res. E. Washington, E. of Bates' City Mills.
Brough George, butcher, res 32 N. Davidson.
BROUGH JOHN, President and Superintendent I., P. & C. R. R., office cor. Meridian and Louisiana.
Brough John W., clerk B. R. R., office S. Meridian.
BROUSE ANDREW & SONS, carpenters and builders, 56 E. New York.
Brouse Andrew, (A. B. & Sons.) res. 60 E. New York.
Brouse Charles W., salesman Tousey & Byram, bds. 38 E. Market.
Brouse David, (A. B. & Sons,) bds. 60 E. New York.
BROUSE REV. JOHN A., (Meth.) res. 38 E. Market.
Brouse O. R., res. 38 E. Market.
Brouse Thomas, (A. B. & Sons,) bds. 60 E. New York.
Brower John, laborer, bds. 184 S. East.
Brower Wm., res. 184 S. East.
Brown Albert, laborer, res. 149 S. New Jersey.
BROWN C. F., Superintendent Indianapolis Gas Light & Coke Co., res. cor. Pennsylvania and Market.
BROWN CLAY, physician, office 23 S. Meridian, res. 66 N. Delaware.
Brown Cyrus W., well digger, bds. 193 N. New Jersey.
Brown Ernst, laborer, 168 N. Noble.
Brown Frederick, body maker, res. 115 Alabama.
Brown Geo. P. C., machinist, res. 167 N. Alabama.
Brown Harry, baggage master J. & I. Railroad, bds. American House.
Brown Henry, bar tender, res. 13 N. Alabama.
BROWN IGNATIUS, attorney at law and notary public, 19½ E. Washington, res. 151 E. South.
Brown James D., plasterer, res. 135 N. Alabama.
BROWN JAMES T., traveling agent Indiana State Sentinel Bindery, res. 66 N. Delaware.
Brown Jason B., law student, McOuat's block, bds. Mrs. Smith.
Brown Jerry, (col.,) engineer Locomotive Office, res. 151 N. Alabama.
Brown J. W., clerk, B. R. R. office, res. 22 N. Meridian.
BROWN REV. JOHN, (Christian,) res. 130 N. New Jersey.
Brown John, plasterer, res. 182 N. Liberty.

Brown John, tinner, bds. cor. Alabama and St. Clair.
Brown John, carpenter, res. 231 W. Washington.
Brown Jown G., laborer, bds. 144 N. New Jersey.
BROWN JOHN L., patent right emporium, 12 S. Pennsylvania, res. 227 N. Tennessee.
Brown John W., bakery, 150 N. New Jersey
Brown John W., laborer, bds. 144 N. New Jersey.
Brown Mrs. Mary, Garden, bet. Tennessee and Illinois.
Brown wid. Mary, res. 159 S. Delaware.
Brown Mrs. M. C., 144 N. New Jersey.
Brown Phillip, laborer, bds. 144 N. New Jersey.
Brown Phillip, lumber dealer, res. 275 Massachusetts ave.
Brown Richard T., machinist, res. 46 N. East.
BROWN R. T., Professor Natural Science, N. W. C. University.
Brown Samuel (col.,) eating saloon, cor. Tennessee and W. Washington.
Brown Stephen, bds. 87 N. Pennsylvania.
Brown Willis, (col.,) farmer, 160 W. Georgia.
Browning Edmund, bds. 88 Virginia ave.
BROWNING GEO. T., wholesale grocer, 6 Bates House, res. 134 N. Tennessee.
Browning M. H., clerk, bds. E. Browning.
BROWNING ROBERT, drugs and medicines, 22 W. Washington, res. 162 N. Illinois.
Browning Wood, clerk Robert Browning.
Bruchman John, cigar maker C. C. Hunt.
Brueggemann William, tailor, res. 192 E. Ohio.
BRUENING E. & J., photographers and painters, 6 E. Washington, up stairs.
Bruening Edward, (E. & J. B.)
Bruening Joseph, (E. & J. B.)
Bruhning John F., carpenter, 295 S. Delaware.
Brummer Charles, music teacher, res. 33 N. Alabama.
BRUNDAGE E. C., general agent for G. W. Hawes.
Brunger James, weaver, bds. 91 Indiana ave.
BRUNNER CHARLES, boots and shoes, 38 W. Washington, res. 112 S. New Jersey.
Bryan Jerry, tinner, res. 4 N. New Jersey
BRYANT ALEXANDER C., general freight agent B. R. R., res. 105 S. New Jersey.
Bryant Benjamin, surveyor and insurance agent, res. 111 W. South.
Bryant B. F., salesman New York store.
BRYANT'S COMMERCIAL COLLEGE, Thomas J. Bryant, principal, Ramsay's block, S. Illinois.
BRYANT JAMES R., State Librarian, office State House, res. 111 W. South.
4

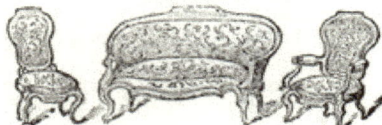

Bryant McClure H., painter, bds 111 W. South.
BRYANT THOMAS J., principal Bryant's Commercial
College, cor. Maryland and Illinois.
Bryant Washington L., at Bryant's Commercial College.
Bryns Patrick, 3 Willard.
Buchanan A.. peddler, res. 218 S. Alabama.
Buchanan Cyrus F., carpenter, res. 14 S. West.
Buchanan George W., carpenter, res. 83 S. East.
Buchanan Ignatius, laborer, res. 218 S. Alabama.
Buchanan James M., (Richman & B.,) res. E. Washington,
bet. Liberty and Noble.
Buchanan John, teamster, res. N. West.
Buchanan Thomas, res. 262 E. Washington.
Buche Frederick, boot and shoe maker, 93 S. Illinois, res.
Delaware, bet. South and Louisiana.
Buck Christian, carpenter, 140 N. Alabama.
Buck Clark, moulder, bds. National Hotel.
Bucker John, marble polisher, res. 57 E. St. Joseph.
Buckley John, brakeman I. & C. R. R., res. alley, bet. Ohio
and New York.
Buckley Timothy, laborer, res. 22 S. Liberty.
Buckhart Jackson, ice dealer, res. 146 N. Mississippi.
Buckingham Charles, chair maker, bds. 79 S. Illinois.
Bucksot William, (Brinkman & B.,) res. 84 E. Market.
Budd Milton, brick maker, res. N. Winston.
Buddenbaum Henry, carpenter, res. 206 E. Ohio.
Budence Henry, tailor, 158 Wahsington, res. 190 Pennsyl-
vania.
Buecher Frederick, blacksmith, bds. near I. & C. R. R. car
shops.
BUEHRIG HENRY E., proprietor Farmers' Hotel.
Buehrig William, bell-boy Farmers' Hotel.
BUELL CHESTER H., patent medicine, 5 N. Meridian,
res. 151 N. Pennsylvania.
Buff Louis, clerk Moritz & Bro., bds. Farmers' Hotel.
Bugby L. M., (B. & Smithers,) res. Michigan Road.
BUGBY & SMITHERS, State soap and candle works, office
9 W. Washington.
Bugg Nathan, (col.,) cook Bates House.
Buhnegal Frederick, baker, bds. 134 S. Illinois.
Buhring Charles, boot and shoe maker, 176 E. Washington,
res. same.
BUIST THOMAS, dealer in hardware, stoves and iron, 70
W. Washington, res. 156 N. Tennessee.
Bullen W. S., carriage trimmer, res. 92 N. East.
Bullard Charles G., cabinet finisher, res. 35 Hosbrook.
BULLARD TALBOT, physician and surgeon, office 23 S.
Meridian, res. 87 E. Ohio.

Bullard W. R., physician with Dr. T. Bullard.
Bumbarger David, res. 207 Indiana ave.
Bundy John, carpenter, 156 E. New York.
Bunte John, carpenter, res. New York, bet. Libery and
Noble.
Bunty William, wagon maker, res. 136 East.
Bard James, laborer, 266 Railroad.
Burdgledink Hermon, cabinet maker, bds. John Jones.
Burges Cornelius N., printer, res. 112 N. East.
Burgess Lloyd A., saddler, res. 89 E. Market.
BURGTORF FREDERICK, undertaker and cabinet ma-
ker, 129 E. Washington, res. same.
Bark Elisha, well digger, res. 141 N. West.
Burk George, carpenter, res. 133 S. Tennessee.
Burk Henry, stone mason, res. 274 S. Delaware.
BURK JOHN, coal dealer, res. 148 N. Tennessee.
Burk William C., bds. 148 N. Tennessee.
Bark William, pattern maker, res. 44 Pennsylvania.
Burke H., currier, bds. Meridian Saloon.
Burks James M., painter, res. 279 S. Delaware.
Burmer Andrew, res. Elizabeth.
Burnam George, lime dealer, Central Depot, bds. Pyle
House.
Burnett J., teamster, res. corporation line, bet. New Jersey
and Alabama.
Burns James, laborer, res. 46 Massachusetts ave.
Burns John, blacksmith, bds. E. Market, bet. Noble and
Davidson.
Burr William, clerk Boston Store, bds. Mrs. Kinder.
BURROWS G. W., auction and commission, 6 W. Wash-
ington, res. cor. New York and Spring.
Burt Gabriel, (col.,) res. N. West.
Burton G. H., cooper, res. 78 N. Mississippi.
Burton John C., res. 221 N. New Jersey.
Burton Martin, laborer, res. 219 N. New Jersey.
BUSCH CHRISTIAN, dealer in boots and shoes, 138 W.
Washington.
BUSCHER & CO., dealers in foreign and domestic liquors,
140 W. Washington.
Buscher Henry, saloon, 51 E. South, res. same.
Buscher Henry, liquor store, res. 14 S. Alabama.
Buser Geo., switch tender on T. H. and R. Railroad, bds.
Tully House, S. Illinois.
Buser Samuel, engineer Bellefontaine Railroad, bds. Tully
House.
BUSH JACOB, City Bowling Saloon, 248 E. Washington,
res. 246 E. Washington.
Bushman William, clerk, bds. 247 N. New Jersey.

Bushworth George, res. 162 Indiana ave.
BUSSELL E. T., president White River Valley Insurance
Co., 2 Glenns' Block.
BUSSELL DR. E. T., solicitor of patents, res. 19 S. Mississippi.
BUSSEY JOHN, Verandah Saloon and billiards, 38 Louisiana. res. same.
Buster Samuel M., carriage maker, 38 Kentucky ave , res.
51 N. Delaware.
Buswel John, carpenter, N. W. cor. Ohio and Delaware.
Butler George, clerk Billiard Saloon, bds. American House.
Butler Mrs. Margaret, res. 114 N. Alabama.
BUTLER OVID, res. E Forest Home ave.
BUTSCH GEO. M., grocer, 173 S. Delaware, res. same.
Butsch P., laborer, res. 73 S. Illinois.
BUTSCH VALENTINE, dealer in lime, coal and cement,
N. of the M. and I. Railroad Depot, res. 24 South.
Butscha Jacob. laborer, res. 36 Union.
Butterfield C. S., printer Journal office, bds. Tully House.
Butterfield J. W., pressman Atlas office, res. 67 N. New
Jersey.
Butterfield M., patentee, res. 176 N. East.
Butts Joel R., shoemaker, res. 269 Massachusetts ave.
Butts M. R., student N. W. C. University, bds. 149 N. East.
Buzzard John, baker, res. 165 S. Delaware.
Byer Jacob, tailor J. & P. Gramling.
Byggs L. C., conductor P. and I. Railroad, bds. American
House.
Byram N. S., (TOUSEY & B.,) res. 119 N. N. Jersey.
Byrd Abram, res. 95 N. Illinois.
BYRKIT & BEAM, planing mill, sash, doors, and carpenters. 60 S. Tennessee.
Byrkit Martin, (B. & Beam,) res. 68 S. Tennessee.
Byrkit Philip. carpenter, res. 81 N. New Jersey.
Byrkit Socrates, engraver Jno. Fahnestock, bds. 81 N. New
Jersey.

C

Cady Mrs. Abba A., res. 4 Circle.
Cahill Dudley, carpenter, 139 New York.
Cahill Hugh, weaver, 239 W. Washington.
Cahill John. carder, bds. 239 W. Washington.
Cahill Michael, laborer. 232 E. Washington.
Cahill John, laborer, bds. 232 E. Washington.
Cain George W.. bookbinder, bds. 135 W. Market.
CAIN JOHN, Exchange and Loan office, 8½ E. Washington, res. 49 S. Maryland.

Cain Michael, laborer, res. 177 S. New Jersey.
Caldhoff Henry, laborer, res. 141 N. Liberty.
Caldwell James, blacksmith, 201 S. Pennsylvania.
CALIFORNIA HOUSE, 136 S. Illinois.
Call Lewis, tailor, res. 206 N. Alabama.
Call Louis, tailor, res. 69 N. Alabama.
Callahan Dennis O., res. alley, bet. Ohio and New York.
Callahan Jeremiah, shoemaker, bds. 27 Ellsworth.
Callahan John P., cabinet maker, res. 255 S. Delaware.
Callahan Michael, res. 176 S. Alabama.
Callahan Michael, laborer, 23 St. George.
Calmyer Henry, boot and shoe maker, res. 155 S. Alabama.
Calvin Joseph, painter, res. 133 N. Davidson.
Cameron George, brick maker, res. 285 S. East.
CAMERON WM. S., job printing, 8 E. Pearl, res. 116 N.
    Alabama.
Campbell Andrew, tailor, res. Georgia, bet. Canal and
    West.
CAMPBELL W. H. & BRO., bookbinders and blank book
    manufacturers, 37 E. Washington.
Campbell Charles, res. 2 North.
Campbell C. C., U. S. Receiver, McOuat's Block, res. cor.
    Meridian and North.
Campbell Noah N., (W. H. C. & Bro.,) 92 N. New York.
Campbell Samuel, messenger Branch Banking Co., bds.
    Pyle House.
Campbell Samuel L., bookbinder, bds. 2 W. North, cor.
    Meridian.
Campbell Thomas, bookbinder, res. N. Meridian.
Campbell Wm. H., clerk post office, res. 102 N. Pennsyl-
    vania.
Campbell William H., (W. H. C. & Bro.,) res. 102 N. Penn-
    sylvania.
CAMPBELL WILLIAM L., clerk Sinking Fund, bds. 60
    N. Alabama.
Campbell William, sr., bds. 102 N. Pennsylvania.
Cane Dennis, blacksmith, cor. Georgia and Benton.
Cantrill Daniel M., compositor, bds. N. Tennessee.
Cantwell Michael, pattern maker, res. 61 N. Spring.
CARICO J. M., grocery and provision store, cor. Tennessee
    and Indiana ave, res. same.
Carl Mrs. ——, res. 74 W. Michigan.
Carle William H., res. South.
CARLISLE & DIXON, grocery and feed store, 208 W.
    Washington.
Carlisle Daniel W., clerk I. C. Railroad Depot, res. 55 N.
    Meridian.
Carlisle Hamilton, res. N. of Carlisle, S. old mill.

Carlisle John, (C. & Dixon.) res. 204 W. Washington.
CARMICHAEL JESSE D., proprietor Palmer House. cor. Illinois and Washington.
Carney John, gas fitter, res. 131 S. Alabama.
Carpenter John B., engineer M. and I. Railroad, res. 71 Merrill.
Carr Eugene, clerk, bds. 245 S. Delaware.
Carr George, fireman I. C. Railroad, bds. Davidson.
Carr Henry, laborer, res. 166 N. East.
Carr Owen J., moulder, res. 264 S. Delaware.
Carroll H., res. N. West.
Carroll Mrs. Michael, res. N. West.
Carroll Patrick, res. 241 S. Pennsylvania.
Carter Charles E., watchman, res. 89 N. Illinois.
Carter Charles F., carpenter, bds. E. Knight.
Carter E. B., carpenter, res. 98 W. Maryland.
Carter George, student N. W. C. University, bds. E. Clarke.
Carter Henry C., carpenter, Georgia, W. of Canal.
Carter Hugh F., carpenter, res. cor. W. Georgia and Missouri.
Carter John, res. 147 N. Delaware.
Carter Joshua, carpenter, bds. 98 W. Maryland.
Carter William, porter Galt House.
Cartright Thomas, res. at State Fair Ground.
Case David H., carpenter, 64 Louisiana.
Case D. H., engineer, bds. cor. New York and Noble.
Case John B., engineer, res. 79 N. Noble.
Case John L., engineer, res. 250 E. Washington.
Cassady Isaac N., trader, 14 N. West.
Casselberry Mrs. M., dress maker, bds. 181 Massachusetts ave.
Cathcart Andrew, res. 162 S. New Jersey.
Cathcart Robert, clerk Merrill & Co., bds. A. Cathcart.
Cathing Edward, house mover, W. Maryland.
Catterson A., grocer, 147 S. Alabama.
Catterson Cyrus W., carpenter, res. 91 N. Meridian.
Catterson Henry, harness maker, bds. 89 E. Market.
Catterson James B., farmer, 241 Indiana ave.
Catterson James W., 67 S. Pennsylvania.
Catterson Robert F., tinner. bds. Palmer House.
Caufman Jacob, carpenter, 173 S. New Jersey.
Cautt Geo., shoemaker, 260 S. Delaware.
Cavanaugh Matthias, laborer, res. S. Missouri.
CAVEN JOHN, attorney and counselor at law, over 19 E. Washington, bds. Bates House.
Cawdell Dr. ——, res 180 S. Pennsylvania.
Caylor Jacob, butcher, res. 125 E. Market.
Caylor Otho, butcher, res. 125 E. Market.

Challan Jas. R., professor of English language N. W. C. University.

Chambers Abraham, engineer, res. 152 N. Meridian.

Chambers Caleb S., salesman, bds. Macy House.

Champion Wm., newspaper agent, res. 152 N. New York.

Chanley Thomas E., res. 258 W. Washington.

Chanley William G., res. 258 W. Washington.

Chapin Sewell, broom maker, res. 69 Maryland.

Chapman D. C., painter, bds. Tully House.

CHAPMAN GEORGE H., attorney at law and notary public, College Hall, E. Washington, res. 32 N. Meridian.

Chapman William, moulder, bds. 258 S. Delaware.

Charles John, res. 102 N. Meridian.

Charles John P., agent Pennsylvania Central Railroad, res. 91 W. Maryland.

Charles Thomas, hackman, 75 S. Georgia.

Chase Fred, carpenter, res. 215 S. Delaware.

Chase James, conductor Bellefontaine Railroad, res. 235 S. Delaware.

Chase Joseph, switchman M. & I. Railroad, res. 223 S. Delaware.

Cheney Joel, machinist, bds. E. Louisiana.

Cherry Thomas R., clerk Tousey & Byram, 36 E. Market.

Cherry Wm. B., tinner, bds. Massachusetts ave., bet. Tennessee and Delaware.

CHESTER A. A., stair builder, cor. Pennsylvania and Union, res. 23 S. Liberty.

CHILDERS JOHN P., pump maker, res. 151 S. Noble.

Childers Mrs. Lavina, washer woman, res. 257 S. Delaware.

Chipman L., clerk B. F. Tuttle, res. 132 N. Tennessee.

Chism Robert, (col.,) res. 190 W. North.

Cholett Henry I., speculator, res. 22 N. Mississippi.

Choudler Thos. E., res. 258 W. Washington.

Choudler W. G., carpenter, res. 258 W. Washington.

Christie Albert, carpenter, res. 87 S. Illinois.

CHRISTIE SAMUEL K., foreman Sentinel newspaper office, res. Capital House.

Chuppel Hermon, at B. F. Tuttle, bds. Macy House.

CHURCH A. B., author of Church's Simplified Book-Keeping, bds. Alvord's Block.

Churchman F. M., clerk Fletcher's Bank, res. S. E. Michigan.

CINCINNATI HOUSE, Delaware, bet. South and Louisiana.

Circhoff Frederick, Union.

CITIZENS' LIVERY STABLE, William Wilkison, proprietor, 10 Pearl.

CRYSTAL PALACE

RESTAURANT,

No. 44 W. Washington St.,

INDIANAPOLIS, IND.

EDWARD BECK, - - Prop.

CLEMENS VONNEGUT,

DEALER IN

LEATHER,

Hides, and Shoe Finding,

NO. 142 EAST WASHINGTON STREET,

One Square East of the Court House,

INDIANAPOLIS, IND.

☞ Orders by letter will receive prompt attention. Cash paid for Hides.

City Greys' Armory, 24½ E. Washington, up stairs.
City Guards' Armory, Ætna Building, 14 N. Pennsylvania.
CITY HARDWARE STORE, A. D. Wood, proprietor, 12 W. Washington.
Claffey Mrs. Ellen, 96 E. McCarty.
Clancy Joseph, at Rolling Mill, bds. 184 S. Tennessee.
Clark A. M., res. 164 W. N. York.
Clark Absalom, res. 95 W. Market.
CLARK EDMUND, president Indiana and Illinois Central Railroad, 64 E. North.
Clark Hamton, carpenter, res. 158 W. Vermont.
Clark Hugh, carriage maker, res. 49 N. New Jersey.
Clark James B., tailor, res. 95 W. Vermont.
Clark Reuben, carpenter, res. 152 W. Michigan.
Clark Stephen A., carriage maker, N. Pennsylvania, bds. 109 N. New Jersey.
Clark W. T., clerk Bellefontaine Railroad office, bds. Mrs. Kinder's.
Clarke Alfred D., salesman Stewart & Bowen, bds. 164 W. New York.
Clarke John N., book-keeper Witness office, bds. N. E. cor. Vermont and Meridian.
CLARKE REV. MINOR G., editor of the Witness, res. N. E. cor. Vermont and Meridian.
Clarridge Daniel, plasterer, res. 59 N. Mississippi.
Cleaver Jefferson, brick mason, res. alley, bet. Ohio and New York.
Cleaver John, brick mason, res. 170 N. New Jersey.
Cleary Patrick, res. Fletcher's addition.
Cleary Patrick, porter Bates House.
CLEM A. & BRO., grocery, 118 Virginia ave.
Clem Aaron, (A. C. & Bro.,) res. 86 S. East.
Clem Frederick, brewer, bds. 135 W. Maryland.
Clem Wm. F., (A. C. & Bro.,) res. 110 N. Alabama.
Cleveland William, (Kile, Cleveland & Co.,) res. 123 N. Delaware.
Clifton Joseph B., foreman Patterson's livery stable, res. 73 S. Tennessee.
Cline Henry, res. 120 W. New York.
Cline Joel, carpenter, res. 166 S. Alabama.
Cline William, carpenter, res. 104 McCarty.
Clines Peter, teamster, res. in Drake & Mayhew's. add.
Clinton J. H., student Hayden's College.
Clinton John, blacksmith I. and C. machine shop, res. 149 Virginia ave.
Clinton Wharton, blacksmith, 252 E. Washington, res. 32 Georgia.
Cobal George R., carpenter, James, near Indiana ave.

Coburn Mrs. Ann, res. 159 N. Noble.
Coburn Henry, (C. & Lingenfelter,) res. 47 N. Delaware.
COBURN & LINGENFELTER, groceries and provisions,
     lumber, &c., S. E. cor. Delaware and New York.
Coburn James F., machinist, res. 72 E. Louisiana.
COBURN JOHN, attorney at law, 15½ E. Washington, res.
     60 E. Ohio.
Coburn Mrs. Sarah, res. 47 N. Delaware.
Coen John, boarding, 107 S. Tennessee.
Coens Simeon, (col.,) cook Little's Hotel, res. 155 N. West.
Coffin Alpheus, salesman Coffin & Morton, bds. Little's
     Hotel.
Coffin Barnabas, (C. & Morton,) res. Economy.
Coffin Eleaser, cigar maker, res. 21 S. George.
Coffin Isaac, (Ketcham & C.,) res. 83 N. Meridian.
Coffin & Morton, dry goods, &c., 3 Odd Fellows Hall.
COFFIN NATHAN T., patent saws, E. of Union Depot,
     res. 239 S. Alabama.
COFFMAN JACOB, carpenter, S. New Jersey, near Mer-
     rill, res. 171 S. New Jersey.
Cogan Mrs. Mary, 64 Merrill.
Colby Henry, (col.,) 156 Canal.
Colburne William H., American Express messenger Belle-
     fontaine R. R., bds. Bates House.
Cole David G., mail agent I. & C. R. R., res. 135 N. East.
Cole Francis, bds. 14 N. New Jersey.
Coleman (col.,) barber, bds. W. Michigan.
Coleman Mrs., 27 Bluff Road.
Coleman Mrs. Catharine, res. 168 E. Michigan.
Coleman Martin, laborer, 175 S. New Jersey.
Colestock Edward B., book binder, bds. 150 N. Illinois.
Colestock Ephriam, carpenter, res. 150 N. Illinois.
Colestock Mrs. Hannah, res. 150 N. Illinois.
Colestock Wesley S., carpenter, bds. 150 N. Illinois.
Colgan Henry G., res. 27 E. Georgia.
Colgan William, clerk Witness Office.
Collalto T. C., painter, res. 154 N. New Jersey.
Colley Edmond, bds. 164 N. New Jersey.
Colley Sims A., (Ellsworth C. & Redstone,) res. 164 N. New
     Jersey.
Colley J. G., saloon, res. 117 Maryland.
Collins Cornelius, laborer, res. 100 E. Market.
Collins Elisha J., carpenter, 205 N. Noble.
Collins James, carpenter, res. 205 N. Noble.
Collins John, laborer, res. North.
Colterpeter William, tailor, 63 E. Washington.
Comegys Levi, carpenter, 62 N. Delaware.
     5

Compagne Louis, carpenter, bds. 200 N. Illinois.
Conaty James B., manufacturer of bonnet blocks, bleacher and presser, 22 S. Illinois.
Condell James, blacksmith B. R. R. Shop.
Cones Robert N., res. 98 W. Michigan.
Conklin Israel, conductor T. H. & R. R. R., res. 85 S. New Jersey.
Connard Charles, carpenter, bds. National Hotel.
Connel Daniel, bds. California House.
Connell Dennis J., printer, bds. California House.
Connelly George, boiler maker, S. Noble.
Conner Alexander H., (C.'& Fishback,) bds. Mrs. Dana.
CONNER & FISHBACK, attorneys at law, and notaries public, S. W. cor. Pennsylvania and Washington, up stairs.
Conner Michael, laborer, Wabash, bet. New Jersey and East.
Conner Morris, laborer, 38 S. Alabama.
Conner Patrick, laborer, 98 E. Maryland.
Conner Thomas, laborer, res. 210 S. Delaware.
Connor Mark, laborer, res. 186 N. Tennessee.
Connor Mrs. Nannie, bds. 38 S. Alabama.
Connord C. P., (C. & Wentz,) bds. Alabama.
CONNORD & WENTZ, bakers and confectioners, 144 W. Washington.
Conroy Patrick, tailor, 6 Willard.
Conter William, clerk Galt House.
Converse Joel, carpenter, res. 263 Massachusetts ave.
Conwell Jerome B., (Howard & C.,) res. 268 N. Illinois.
CONZELMANN CONRAD, grocer, W. Washington.
Conzelmann George, clerk C. Vonnegut, res. 142 E. Washington.
Cook Charles, clerk G. Krug, bds. S. Liberty.
Cook Miss E. A., tailoress, bds. 167 E. Ohio.
Cook Fred., laborer, res. 36 S. Liberty.
Cook Miss M. R., tailoress, bds. 167 E. Ohio.
Cook Mrs. Mary, res. 20 N. Chattam.
COOK M. R., house and sign painter, cor. Meridian and Maryland, res. 79 W. Maryland.
Cook Jesse M., carpenter, res. 176 E. Ohio.
Cook John M., student, bds. 44 N. Pennsylvania.
COOK MRS. JULIA, boarding, 44 N. Pennsylvania.
Cook Rev. Peter S., (United Breth.,) res. 103 N. Noble.
COOK RICHARD, butcher, 5 N. Illinois, res. 22 Indiana ave.
COOK STEPHEN S., physician, office and res. 34 Ellsworth.
Cook Thomas, laborer, res. 181 S. New Jersey.
Cook William, (Koller & C.,) res. 38 S. Liberty.

Cook John, machinist Washington Foundry.
Cook Henry, brick mason, bds. N. Liberty.
Coons J., res. 125 E. New York.
Coon Peter, (Perkins & C.,) res. 11 E. North.
Cooney Dennis, laborer, res. 11 N. East.
Cooper Mrs. Jane, res. 111 N. Meridian.
Cooper John, machinist, res. 229 S. Delaware.
Cooper John, (Biddle & C.,) res. 81 Alabama.
Cooper Joshua, res. 81 N. Alabama.
Cooper William H., cooper, res. bet. Noble and Liberty.
Copeland Frank, carpenter, bds. Alvord's Block, S. Pennsylvania.
Copeland Jesse, carpenter and builder, 47 E. Market, res. 92 E. Market.
COPELAND JOSHUA W., bonnet bleacher and millinery, 7 S. Meridian, res. Alvord's Block, S. Pennsylvania.
Copeland S. P., clerk J. W. Copeland.
Corbaley Robert C., teacher and student Bryant's Commercial College, bds. Mrs. Cook.
CORLISS C. T., physician, 53 Maryland.
Corn Martin, carrier John Fishback, res. New Jersey, near Fort Wayne ave.
Cornelius Cassius, plasterer, res. Duncan.
Cornelius Mrs. Deborah, 237 S. Alabama.
Cornelius Edward, teamster, res. 237 S. Alabama.
Cornelius William, res. Duncan.
Cornell Joseph, laborer, res. 52 Liberty.
Corney John, laborer, res. 131 S. Alabama.
Cortepetre Ernst, teamster, res. 180 S. Alabama.
Cortright Charles, R. R. engineer, bds. Little's Hotel.
Cosby Richard M., carpenter, 58 Huron.
Cosler David W., carpenter, res. 131 N. Noble.
Costello John, shoemaker, 5 W. Washington, res. Blake's Building.
Costen Henry, laborer, res. 130 E. North.
COSTIGAN FRANCIS, architect and builder, Oriental House, S. Illinois.
Costin Henry, (col.,) teamster, 130 E. North.
Cottle James, ornamental painter, bds. Pennsylvania House.
Cottman John A., cutter, res. 195 W. Vermont.
COTTRELL & KNIGHT, coppersmiths, 94 S. Delaware.
Cottrell John, coppersmith, res. 104 S. New Jersey.
Cottrell Thomas (C. & Knight,) res. 102 S. New Jersey.
Coughlen William, (Merritt & C.,) res. 139 W. New York.
COULON CHARLES, attorney at law, and justice of the peace, 97 E. Washington, res. Cumberland, opp. brewery.
Covert Isaac, silver plater, 8½ W. Washington, res 136 N. Alabama.

Covert William T., engineer Osgood, Smith & Co., res. cor.
Union and Ray.
COVINGTON GEORGE B., agent Indianapolis Life In-
surance Co., office 14 and 16 S. Meridian, res. 154 W.
New York.
COVINGTON JOHN B., assistant secretary Indianapolis
Insurance Co., res. 154 W. New York.
COVINGTON SAMUEL F., secretary Indianapolis In-
surance Co., office 14 S. Meridian, res. 154 W. New
York.
Covington Mrs. Susan, res. 140 W. Market.
Cowgill John, carpenter, 110 S. Noble.
Cowles Dennis, laborer, 9 N. East.
Cox Andrew J., (Weeks & C.,) res. 205 S. Alabama.
COX CHARLES, tinware and stoves, 11 W. Washington,
res. 43 S. Meridian.
Cox Charles H., tinner C. Cox.
Cox Henry C. carpenter, res. 184 W. Washington.
COX JACOB, artist, 2 Blake's Building, res. 41 S. Meridian.
Cox Mrs. Sophia, res. 148 W. Market.
Cox William C., (Tomlinson &. C.,) res. 41 S. Meridian.
Coyner Martin L., contractor, 209 E. St. Clair.
Coyner Robert, clerk, bds. 149 N. Illinois.
Crabb Ezra, carpenter, cor. Ohio and Tennessee.
Craft Smith, blacksmith, res. 210 Indiana ave.
Craft William H., watch maker C. A. Ferguson, res. 40
New York.
Craighead Mrs. Mary J., res. 18 W. Maryland.
Crall A. B., (C. & Bros.,) bds. 71 Maryland.
CRALL & BROS., grocers, 55 W. Washington, Blake's
Commercial Row.
Crall F. H., bds. Mrs. Lawton's.
Crall H., (Crall & Bros.,) bds. 71 Maryland.
Crall L. H., (C. & Bros.,) bds. Pyle House.
Crane A. G., agent for New York House, bds. T. Park.
Crane Dennis, runner Farmers' Hotel.
CRANE E. C., agent for William N. Spinney, 10 W. Wash-
ington, bds. 44 N. Pennsylvania.
CRANE J. D., daguerrean artist, 19½ W. Washington, res.
Lafayette.
Crane Worth, bds. Mrs. Kinder's.
Crap Jonathan, showman, bds. 212 W. Washington.
Crap William H., engraver John Fahnestock, bds. Pyle
House.
Crape John, butcher, res. 184 S. Delaware
Crawford George, (col.,) barber, res. alley N. West.
Crawson Samuel, (col.,) wood sawyer, bds. Tennessee.
Creashaver Sabastian, boiler maker, res. 231 S. Alabama.

Creasser William, tanner, E. Washington, E. of Pogue's Run.
Creasser William, butcher, res. 180 E. New York.
Cremer Samuel, bds. 49 N. Alabama.
Creschal Chas., tailor, res. 135 Liberty.
Cressner Theodore, accountant W. Y. Wiley, res. 133 N. West.
CRIQUI MICHAEL, clothier, 158 E. Washington, res. 173 E. Ohio.
Crockett Robt., (col.,) grocery, res. N. Tennessee, bet. Illinois and Mississippi.
Crockett William J., student Hayden's Commercial College, bds. Judge Morrison.
Croas Ephriam, res. 280 Indiana ave.
Cropsey J. E., cabinet maker, res. 62 Missouri.
Crosier George, watchman Glenns' Block, 43 Tennessee.
Cross Henry, laborer, res. 166 N. East.
CROSSLAND JACOB A., wholesale dry goods merchant, 75 W. Washington, res. 75 N. Alabama.
Crowley Michael, waiter Bates House.
Crowley Patrick, laborer, 39 McCarty.
Crowley Timothy, laborer, res. 120 N. Mississippi.
Cruse Solomon, res. 72 E. Garden.
CRYSTAL PALACE SALOON, Edward Beck, proprietor, 44 W. Washington.
Csheck Frederick, carpenter, res. 215 S. Delaware.
Culbertson William H., policeman, res. 77 N. Noble.
Cullens Matthew, carpenter, res. W. Elizabeth.
Culley David D., printer, res. 13 E. Ohio.
Culley William B., boot and shoe maker, 198 E. Washington, res. 196 S. Illinois.
Culley Daniel B., on I. and C. Railroad, bds. 26 N. Illinois.
Culley David V., 13 E. Ohio.
Cuncoubman Conrad, grocer, W. Washington, near river, res. same.
Cunningham Charles G., bds. 56 N. Meridian.
Cunningham Frank, clerk Treasurer of State office, bds. 56 N. Meridian.
CUNNINGHAM FRED. P., confectionery and oyster saloon, 43 N. Illinois, res. same.
Cunningham George B., bds. 56 N. Meridian.
CUNNINGHAM NATHANIEL F., Treasurer of State, res. 56 N. Meridian.
Cunningham Rev. Thos., O. S. Presbyterian, bds. 170 N. Illinois.
Cunningham W. M., 56 Meridian.
Curran John, laborer, res. alley, bet. Ohio and New York.

Curry T. T., student Bryant's Commercial College, bds. 84 Virginia ave.
CURTIS ANDREW, justice of the peace, 39 E. Washington, res. 11 Fort Wayne ave.
Curtis Casper T., artist Hays & Runnion, bds. 275 S. Delaware.
Curtis Charles, engineer Sentinel office, res. 275 S. Delaware.
Curtis Joseph, (col.,) cook Bates House, res. 101 W. North.
Curtis T. M., engineer, res. 275 S. Delaware.
Curts H., blacksmith, res. 280 Indiana ave.
Currykendall Warren A., engineer, res. 100 E. Louisiana.
CURZON JOSEPH, architect, res. 218 N. Illinois.
Cusens Samuel, (col.,) 2d steward in steamboat, bds. 86 alley West.
Cussins William, plasterer, res. Harris.
Custer John, tailor, res. 19 N. East.
Custer L. N., doctress, res. 19 N. East.
Cutting Abel, basket maker, res. 177 N. Delaware.

D

Daary John, laborer, res. N. Wisconsin ave.
Dabebe Frank, cigar maker, South, bet. Delaware and Pennsylvania.
Daffin Mrs. Roda, bds. 266 Indiana ave.
DAGGETT W., confectionery and China teas, 22 S. Meridian, res. same.
Daine Frank, pattern maker, res. 184 S. Alabama.
Daine Thomas, painter, 51 S. Mississippi.
Daine William, laborer, res. 143 N. Liberty.
Dall Andrew P., laborer, 97 McCarty.
Dame Mrs. Jane M., res. 233 S. Delaware.
DAME JASON, marble yard, 67 E. Washington, res. 96 E. Market.
Dammeier Elton, laborer, res. 5 N. Railroad.
Dammeier Frederick, drayman, res. 146 E. Ohio.
Dana Mrs. Amos W., boarding house, 10 W. Market.
Danforth Albert J., (D. & Simpson,) res. 112 N. Pennsylvania.
DANFORTH & SIMPSON, wholesale and retail grocers, 3 and 5 Odd Fellows' Hall, N. Pennsylvania.
Daniels David G., painter, res. 95 S. East.
Daniels Henry W., clerk American and U. S. Express Co.'s, res. 35 W. New York.
Daniels Samuel P., mail agent B. Railroad, res. 63 S. New Jersey.
Darby John, bds. Mrs. Smith.

Darl Phillip, laborer, res. 135 N. Davidson.

Darnall Wm., carpenter, res. 55 N. Delaware.

Darragh William, tailor Moritz & Bro., res. Garden, cor. of Willow.

Darrach G. M., M. D., res. 41 N. New Jersey.

Dartenne Constantine, printer, bds. 132 E. Washington.

Daugherty Joseph F., grain dealer, res. 130 N. Pennsylvania.

Daugherty Michael, (McTaggart & D.,) res. in country.

Daugherty W. N., bds. Josh F. Daugherty.

Daumont Peter A., with S. H. Daumont, res. 114 N. Pennsylvania.

DAUMONT S. H., jeweler, 9 S. Meridian, res. 114 N. Pennsylania.

Davenport John, engineer Kregelo, Blake & Co.

David wid. William, 20 N. East.

DAVIDS & RIGGS, butchers, 67 S. Illinois.

Davids Thomas, (D. & Riggs,) res. 82 South.

Davidge Charles H., salesman L. Steet & Bro., bds. 44 S. Meridian.

Davidson John, collector Journal Co., res. 75 N. Noble.

DAVIS BENJAMIN F., road master T. H. and R. Railroad, res. 132 E. North.

DAVIS CHARLES B., insurance agent and attorney at law, Odd Fellows' Hall, 2d floor, res. 137 N. Pennsylvania.

Davis C. W., book keeper Chas. B. Davis.

Davis Daniel D., (Arnold & D.,) bds. Tremont House.

Davis Edward D., constable, res. 129 N. Pennsylvania.

Davis Elisha W., (G. Dietz & Co.,) 78 and 80 W. Washington.

DAVIS F. A. W., teller Branch Banking Co., bds. Mrs. Dana.

Davis George D., blacksmith, bds. Ray House.

Davis Halden, night police, res. 150 N. Delaware.

Davis Henry C., fireman Union Foundry.

DAVIS I. & CO., Union Foundry and Machine Shop, 98 S. Delaware.

Davis Ira, (I. D. & Co.,) res. 64 N. Meridian.

Davis James, teacher Deaf and Dumb Asylum, res. 60 N. East.

Davis James H., (J. W. Davis & Co.,) res. 26 N. Liberty.

DAVIS J. W. & CO., brass and bell founders, 96 S. Delaware.

Davis John, fireman Madison Railroad, bds. Ray House.

Davis John, laborer, 170 N. Liberty.

Davis Joseph S., messenger Adams' Express Co., res. 7 E. New York.

Davis Joseph W., (J. W. D. & Co.,) res. 129 Virginia ave.
Davis Robert F., saw maker E. C. Atkins, res. 151 S. Tennessee.
Davison Joseph K., printer, bds. 233 S. Delaware.
Dawes Adelbert C., salesman Mayhew & Co., bds. American House.
Dawson Daniel, blacksmith, res. 41 W. Georgia.
Dawson Daniel, bds. 161 N. East.
Dawson Miss E., dress maker, bds. 3 E. Michigan Road.
Dawson Mrs. Margaret, bds. 229 W. Washington.
Dawson wid. William, 161 N. East.
DAWSON WILLIAM, plow manufacturer, 250 E. Washington.
Day Elisha M., laborer, bds. 254 Indiana ave.
Day Jeremiah L., butcher, res. 196 E. St. Clair.
Day M. D. L., clerk Robert Browning, bds. 48 S. Mississippi.
Day Thomas, laborer, 254 Indiana ave.
Day William, butcher, res. 198 E. St. Clair.
Dearinger Simeon, plasterer, res. 35 E. St. Clair.
Deary Henry, laborer Kregelo, Blake & Co.
Deaver George W., clerk, bds. 92 N. New Jersey.
Decher Conrad, blacksmith, res. 231 Massachusetts ave.
Decher John, stone mason, res. 227 N. Alabama.
Deckinbrook Christ, res. 31 McCarty.
Deer John, laborer, res. 70 E. St. Mary's.
Deerberg Christopher, miller Bates City Mill.
Deffaubx Louis, carpenter, res. 159 N. Noble.
Defer John, Union.
Defning Daniel, peddler, at Depot, res. 73 S. Illinois.
Deford M. C., pressman Locomotive, bds. 113 Massachusetts ave.
DEFORD WM. R., attorney at law, notary public, real estate agent and stock broker, 35½ E. Washington, res. 113 Massachusetts ave.
De Forrest Daniel, laborer, res. alley, bet. Ohio and New York.
DEFREES JOHN D., editor and proprietor Daily and Weekly Atlas, 18 S. Meridian, res. 54 S. Meridian.
Defrees Rollin, book-keeper Atlas office, bds. Mrs. Ferguson's.
Degert Jacob, cabinet maker, 66 W. Ohio.
Deisler John, 31 South.
Deitz Henry, res. front National Hotel.
Deitz Peter, laborer, res. Blackford.
Deitzel Adam, laborer, res. 77 N. Davidson.
Deland Mrs. Sarah, res. 98 E. Maryland.
Delay Dennis, waiter Tremont House.
Delainey Peter, porter Ray House.

Delainey Michael, laborer, res. 143 E. New York.
Dell John, laborer, res. 120 N. Meridian.
Dell John, shoemaker, res. 89 N. Meridian.
Deller Frederick, painter, 102 N. Noble, res. same.
Delplane Samuel H., finisher woolen factory, res. W. Washington, near river.
Delzell Hugh, bds. Farmers' Hotel.
DELZELL & SMITH, real estate agents, 37 E. Washington, up stairs.
DELZELL SAMUEL, (D. & Smith,) res. 91 N. Alabama.
Demmy Martin, harness maker Jas. Sulgrove.
De Moss Leander, harness maker Hinesley & Hereth.
Demunn George, railroader, res. 12 N. Bates.
De Motte Wm. H., teacher D. and D. Institute, res. S. National Road.
Dena William, laborer, res. 143 N. Liberty.
Deneen Amenda, 157 N. Alabama.
Deneen James, tailor, res. 157 N. Alabama.
Denig J. Henry, printer Sentinel office, bds. 20 W. Michigan.
De Night wid. H., res. Georgia, bet. Illinois and Tennessee.
Deniuston Elizabeth A., dress maker, res. 84 N. Meridian.
Dennis Mrs. E. R., res. 78 N. East.
Dennis Peter, brick layer, bds. Cincinnati House.
Denny Austin F., res. on I. & C. Railroad, 2½ miles from city.
DERNHAM MAX., merchant tailor, 1 W. Washington, res. Alvord's Block, S. Pennsylvania.
Derr George, steward Tremont House.
Derr Jacob, yard man, Tremont House.
Dersh John, porter Root, Bennett & Co., bds. 139 N. Alabama.
Deshield Martin, cooper, res. 110 N. Missouri.
Despa Ernest, painter, res. 30 E. Lockerbie.
Dessar Adolph, (D. Bros.,) res. 73 W. Maryland.
DESSAR BROTHERS, clothing and furnishing goods, 4 E. Washington and 6 Meridian.
Dessar David, (D. Brothers,) bds. Bates House.
Dessar J. B., (D. Brothers,) res. Kentucky.
Dettert Wm., railroader, bds. 205 S. Delaware.
Detrick J. D., patent rights, Circle.
Devening Daniel, baker, 73 S. Illinois.
Devenish John, moulder, res. 138 S. East.
Devenport John, engineer, res. 58 Indiana ave.
Dewald Matthew, porter J. W. Holland, res. 55 E. Ohio.
Dexter George S., stencil cutter, 119 S. Tennessee.
Dickert Jacob, cabinet maker, 66 Ohio.

6

DICKINSON JAMES L., physician, (eclectic,) 241 S. Alabama.
Dickinson John C., res. 109 S. Alabama.
Dickmann Frederick, carpenter, res. 41 N. East.
Dickson Carlos, salesman Willard & Stowell, bds. 153 N. Illinois.
DIEKMANN CARL, lager beer saloon, 186 E. Washington.
Dieter Jacob, cigar maker G. F. Meyer.
Dietrich Mrs. M., millinery, 63 E. Washington, res. same.
DIETRICH WM., cigars and tobacco, 63 E. Washington, res. same.
DIETZ ADAM, proprietor Paradise Garden, res. 65 Fort Wayne ave.
Dietz F., clerk Geo. Dietz & Co., 78 W. Washington.
DIETZ GEO. & CO., Washington Hall Saloon, 78 and 80 W. Washington.
Dietz Geo., (G. D. & Co.,) res. 78 and 80 W. Washington.
Diever James, clerk post office, res. 44 Massachusetts ave.
Dill Ezekiel, blacksmith, South, near Delaware.
Dill Mrs. Gertrude, 20 W. St. Clair.
Dill Henry C., clerk, bds. 20 St. Clair.
Dill James, bds. 20 St. Clair.
Dill John P., bds. 20 St. Clair.
Dillon John B., Historian, 19 E. Washington, bds. E. Browning.
Dilly John, engineer Osgood, Smith & Co., res. S. Norwood.
Dilly Samuel, S. Norwood.
Dink Andrew, vinegar manufacturer, res. 135 Indiana ave.
Dipple Henry, laborer, res. 167 E. Michigan.
Dippell Henry, barkeeper John Bussey, 38 Louisiana.
Dipper Peter, laborer, res. 73 N. Noble.
Dipple Joseph, drayman, res. 111 N. Noble.
Dixon George, (col.,) res. 123 W. Ohio.
Dixon Jas. W., (Carlisle & D.,) res. S. Missouri.
Dobbs Cyrus J., harness maker Hinesley & Hereth, bds. Mrs. Kinder's.
Dobyns B. D., grocer, cor. St. Clair and Fort Wayne aves., res. 175 N. Alabama.
Dobyns Jno. L., student N. W. C. University, bds. 175 N. Alabama.
DODD HARRISON H., register of State, office 7 McOuat's Block, Kentucky ave, res. New York, near California.
DODD JOHN W., Auditor of State, office 7 McOuat's Block, Kentucky ave., res. 70 N. Illinois.
Dodds W. Harry, salesman Coffin & Morton, bds. American House.
Dodson Michael, engineer T. H. and R. Railroad, bds. 141 W. Market.

Dodge N. S., M. D. (D. & Scott,) 53 S. Illinois.
Dodge Warren C., master machinist M. & I. Railroad, res. 227 S. Delaware.
DODGE & SCOTT, physicians for lung and heart diseases, 3 Glenns' Block.
Doggett Richard, shoemaker, res. 69 Vermont.
Doherty Joab H., cabinet maker, bds. 11 Ellsworth.
DOMON EMILE, clerk California House, bds. 136 S. Illinois.
Donahan Mrs. Barbara, boarding, 74 N. Tennessee.
Donaldson Claiborne S., (D. Maxfield & Prine,) res. 42 W. Maryland.
DONALDSON, MAXFIELD & PRINE, wholesale dealers in teas, tobacco and cigars, also commission merchants, 71 W. Washington.
DONEGHY JOHN T., physician, 26 E. Washington, up stairs, res. 173 N. Tennessee.
Donnelly Francis, laborer, res. 22 Henry.
DONOUGH D. B., carpenter and builder, Vermont, near Alabama.
Donovan Andrew, laborer, Blake, bet. Washington and New York.
Donovan Daniel, laborer, bds. 38 S. Alabama.
Donovan Dennis, laborer, res. rear of 38 E. Market.
Donovan James, retired, res. 184 N. East.
Donovan Mrs. Margaret, res. E. Washington, cor. Benton.
Donovan Peter, well digger, res. 127 E. New York.
Dorsay Nicholas, physician, 46 and 48 N. Pennsylvania.
Dorsey Thomas, laborer, 72 N. Mississippi.
Dortz Emile, file cutter, Liberty, bet. New York and Michigan.
DOUGHERTY CHARLES, grocer, 245 S. Delaware, res. same.
Dougherty M., (McTaggart & D.,) 15 N. Illinois.
DOUGHERTY ZADOK, physician, California, W. side, near Market.
Dought Patrick, apprentice, bds. 14 and 16 N. Delaware.
DOUGHTY JOHN G., (Bingham & D.,) Indiana State Sentinel, res. 21 Indiana ave.
Douglas Benjamin W., machinist, res. 40 E. Hosbrook.
Douglass George, clerk, bds. 130 W. New York.
Douglass James, (D. & Palmer,) bds. 130 W. New York.
Douglass Mrs. Maria, res. 130 W. New York.
DOUGLASS & PALMER, bookbinders and blank book manufacturers, 36½ E. Washington.
DOUGLASS SAMUEL M., baggage master Union Depot, bds. 130 W. New York.
Dow Levi B., laborer, res. 55 McCarty.

Downey John, marble rubber, 11 S. Georgia.
Downey Jonah, bds. 39 McCarty.
Downey Mrs. M. E., res. 43 N. Pennsylvania.
DOWNEY MICHAEL, dealer in American and Italian
marble, cor. Washington and Alabama.
Downey Thomas, laborer, bds. Illinois.
Downey Robert, res. 82 N. Delaware.
Downs Charles, grocer, S. W. cor. Vermont and Massachu-
setts ave.
Doary Edward, laborer, res. N. Wisconsin ave.
DRAEGER CHARLES, watches, clocks and jewelry, 103
E. Washington.
Drake Edward B., (Root, Bennett & Co.,) res. 88 N. Ala-
bama.
Drayer Mrs. Hannah, res. W. Market.
Drechsel George, wagon maker, bds. E. Michigan, cor. Rail-
road.
Dreher Matthias, clerk Tousey & Byram, res. 48 Liberty.
Drew John A, carriage painter S. W. Drew, res. 59 E. Ohio.
DREW SAMUEL W., carriage manufacturer, E. Market
Square, res. same.
Drinkut William, watchman T. H. & R. Engine House,
res. 89 S. New Jersey.
Drum Mrs. E. J., bds. 60 Delaware.
Drum George, carpenter, res. 115 S. New Jersey.
Drum James J., with L. S. Avery, res. 144 N. Pennsyl-
vania.
Drum James S., clerk L. S. Avery, res. 21 Michigan.
Drum Miss Nettie, tailoress, bds. 48 E. New York.
Drum Robert, teamster, res. 203 N. Noble.
Duane William, laborer, 200 S. Delaware.
Dubach John, laborer, bds. Union House.
Duchene Charles, candy maker, bds. 15 N. Illinois.
Ducker John B., watch maker, res. 178 E. Market.
Duckwiler Jacob, engineer, res. E. Market.
Duffey James, laborer, res. 33 Ellsworth.
Duffey Mrs. Mary, res. 55 S. Illinois.
Duffey Michael, tailor Eli Hall, res. 55 S. Illinois.
Dugan P., tailor, bds. 25 S. Meridian.
Dugan Thomas, boot and shoe maker, 4th story Blake's
Row, res. 155 W. Michigan.
Dugan William, machinist, bds. Ray House.
DUKE & SMITH, auction and commission, 8 S. Me-
ridian.
Duke James, (D. & Smith,) res. 8 S. Meridian.
Dull C. C., res. 36 California.
Dummel Charles, laborer, S. W. cor. Meridian and Ohio.
Dumont Eugene A., res. cor. Louisiana and New Jersey.

DUMONT COL. E., (D. & Torbett,) President Sinking Fund, res. 60 N. Alabama.

Dumont John J., (D. & Sinker,) res. 23 E. Louisiana.

DUMONT & SINKER, engine, machine and boiler manufacturers, S. Pennsylvania, E. of Union Depot.

DUMONT & TORBETT, attorneys at law, junction of Pennsylvania and Virginia ave.

Dunbar Melzar, brick mason, 178 S. Pennsylvania.

DUNCAN R. B., attorney at law, office S. W. cor. Washington and Meridian, up stairs, res. Fort Wayne ave.

Duncan J. S., Fort Wayne ave.

Duncan John, grocer, 174 E. Washington.

Duncan Mrs. Mary, bds. 174 E. Washington.

Dunham Cyrus L., (D. & Tanner,) Secretary of State, bds. Bates House.

DUNHAM & TANNER, attorneys at law, 6 McOuat's Block.

Dunlap James B., artist, bds. Dr. Dunlap.

DUNLAP JOHN M., assistant physician Indiana Hospital for the Insane.

DUNLAP L., physician. 12 Virginia ave.

DUNLOP JOHN S., Jr., real estate and insurance agent, office Dunlop's Block, cor. Washington and Meridian, res. 116 N. Pennsylvania.

Dunlop John, sr., res. 72 N. Meridian.

Dunigan Edward, laborer, res. 79 E. Market.

Dunkam James, laborer, 163 S. Tennessee.

Dunn Edwin F., clerk Tousey & Byram, bds. H. Kellogg.

DUNN JOHN C., plumbing and gas fitting, shop 22 Kentucky ave., res. 67 N. Tennessee.

Dunn John P., director State Prison, bds. Col. H. Achey.

DUNN THOMAS B., saloon and restaurant, 7 N. Illinois, res. N. W. cor. New York and Illinois.

Dunn Wm. A., with Fitz Gibbon & Co., res. 20 N. Pennsylvania.

Dunning Thomas, carpenter, 140 N. Mississippi.

Dupuy James, res. 252 Indiana ave.

DURHAM GEORGE W., brick mason, res. 142 E. Ohio.

Durie Mrs. Margaret, res. alley, bet. Ohio and New York.

Dury John, engraver, bds. Mrs. Kinder's.

Duvall D. C., salesman Palmer & Talbott, res. 113 N. Illinois.

Duvall Mrs. Sarah, res. 112 Virginia ave.

Duzan William H., cabinet maker, res. 101 N. Noble.

Dwyer James, res. 105 E. South.

Dyer C. S., clerk U. S. Marshal, bds. Palmer House.

E

Eagan Patrick, watchman, res. 70 N. Mississippi.

Eagle Henry H., printer Journal office, bds. Pyle House.

Eagle John H., foreman Journal office news-room, res. 48 E. New York.

Eagle William, printer Indianapolis Journal, bds. Pyle House.

Earhrling John P., tailor, res. 173 E. Ohio.

EAST STREET HOUSE, Henry Hahn, proprietor, East, near Peru Depot.

EASTMAN HENRY, eating house, cor. Illinois and Louisiana.

Eaton William J., laborer, res. 191 E. St. Clair.

Ebert John, carpenter, res. 72 W. Maryland.

EDDY REV. AUGUSTUS, presiding elder M. E. Church, res. 143 N. Pennsylvania.

Eddy Morris R., book keeper Tousey & Byram, 143 W. Pennsylvania.

EDEN & COPELAND, carpenters and joiners, 27 E. Market.

Eden Charleton, (E. & Copeland,) res. Virginia ave, outside city limits.

Eden T. C., carpenter, bds. W. H. Lingenfelter.

EDGAR & FRAZEE, boots and shoes, Glenns' Block, E. Washington.

EDGAR JAMES W., attorney at law and notary public, 2 McOuat's Block, res. 37 E. Michigan.

Edgar Samuel A., (E. & Frazee,) res. 108 E. Ohio.

Edmunds William, salesman Hendrick & Co., res. 197 N. Illinois.

Edwards Nathan, carpenter, res. 93 W. South.

Elder Alexander, clerk post office, res. 95 N. Mississippi.

ELDER & HARKNESS, publishers of Locomotive and book and job printers, office 2 S. Meridian, 2d floor.

Elder John R., (E. & Harkness,) res. cor. New York and New Jersey.

Elder William G., laborer, res. 60 N. Delaware.

Eldridge Jacob, (E., McMillin & Biddle,) res. 50 S. Meridian.

ELDRIDGE, McMILLIN & BIDDLE, real estate and commission merchants, 39 W. Washington.

Elenby James, physician, bds. 21 S. Delaware.

Elering Deitre, laborer, res. 131 E. McCarty.

Elff Frank, (E. & Regenaur,) 25 S. Meridian.

ELFF & REGENAUR, saloon, 25 S. Meridian.

ELLIOTT BYRON, attorney at law, 24½ E. Washington, res. Maryland, one door west Illinois.

ELLIOTT C. A. & CO., wholesale grocers, 34 S. Meridian, cor. Maryland.

Elliott Calvin A., (C. A. E. & Co.,) res. 76 N. Illinois.

Elliott wid. John, res. 81 S. New Jersey.

Elliott J. H., baggageman I. & C. Railroad, res. 141 E. South.

Elliott J. W., with S. W. Elliott, bds. 67 N. Meridian.

Elliott R., bds. 81 S. New Jersey.

Elliott Russell, book keeper Boston Store, bds. 71 N. Meridian.

ELLIOTT SAMUEL W., boots and shoes, 28 E. Washington, res. 186 N. Illinois.

Elliott S. W., assistant ticket agent I. & C. R. R., bds. Maryland,

ELLIOTT THOMAS B., physician and surgeon, office 28 N. Illinois, res. Michigan.

ELLIOTT WILLIAM, general traveling agent, res. 59 Massachusetts ave.

Ellenbegg S., grocer, 180 S. Delaware, res. same.

ELLSWORTH, COLLEY, & REDSTONE, attorneys and solicitors of patents, office 10 S. Meridian.

Ellsworth Hon. Henry W., (E., Colley & Redstone,) res. 88 N. Meridian.

Elmer J. W., clerk Madison R. R. Depot, res. 140 E. McCarty.

Elstead Henry, foundryman, 168 S. Illinois.

Ely Joseph W., carpenter, 14 Willard.

Einatz Anthony, expressman, res. 283 S. Delaware.

Eska Christian, blacksmith, res. 344 Virginia ave.

Ettingbaugh Charles, grocers, 180 South, res. same.

Emery Phillip A., A. M., instructor in Deaf and Dumb Asylum, res. alley, bet. National Road and Michigan Road.

Emick Miss Ester, milliner, Mrs. Thomas, bds. Pyle House.

Emick Miss Rebecca, milliner, Mrs. Thomas, bds. Pyle House.

EMMENEGGER MATTHIAS, Union Hall saloon and billiards, 111 and 113 E. Washington.

EMMERICH & REESE, produce and liquor store, 91 and 93 W. Washington.

Emerich Henry, (E. & Reese,) res. 91 and 93 W. Washington.

Emmerson B. B., res. 141 W. Market.

Emmitt Robert, laborer, res. 98 N. Tennessee.

Ende Frederick, dyer, Ohio P. W. Factory, bds. W. Kolb.

Ende Hermon, weaver, Ohio P. W. Factory, bds. W. Kolb.

ENDERLINE C. AUGUSTUS, manager Crystal Palace Saloon, 44 W. Washington.

Engel John, butcher, res. 230 N. Alabama.
Engel John, carpenter, 9 E. Louisiana.
Engel Charles, shoemaker, bds. 164 W. Washington.
Engle Jacob, teamster, res. 35 N. Spring.
Engleking Frederick, employee Madison R. R., res. Bluff Road.
Engleking William, switchman T. H. & R. R. R., res. Bluff Road.
English Edward, waiter Little's Hotel.
English Joseph K., painter, res. 115 N. East.
English King, switch tender, res. 113 N. East.
ENNERS PHILLIP, at Washington Hall Saloon, W. Washington, res. 229 E. North.
Ennis Louis, butcher, res. 223 N. Noble.
Enos R. C., res. 94 N. Illinois.
Erick John, laborer, bds. Blackford.
Ernst Frederick, drayman, res. 23 Union.
Ernst Z., currier with J. Fishback, bds. California House.
Erwin Mrs., res. 137 Washington.
Eskew John D., printer Atlas Office, bds. 22 S. Meridian.
Espy Mrs. Margaret F., bds. 85 S. Tennessee.
Ethell N. F., local editor ATLAS, S. Meridian.
Etherton Samuel, carpenter, res. 129 E. North.
Etsler Loyd, wagon maker, res. 156 N. East.
Eudlay Elisha, res. 113 N. Tennessee.
Eudlay James E., teamster, res. 113 N. New Jersey.
EURICK JOHN L., Nebraska Saloon, 12 W. Louisiana, res. 21 Georgia.
Euwright Michael, laborer, bds. 306 S. Delaware.
Evans Henry W., carpenter, res. S. side National Road.
Evans Madison, Professor N. W. C. University, res. 125 Fort Wayne ave.
Evans Mrs. Maria J., res. 114 N. East.
Evans Owen F., salesman J. Fishback, res. 107 Virginia ave.
EVANS REV. THOMAS, (United Breth.,) res. 27 N. Liberty.
Evans Thomas, carpenter, res. 165 N. Liberty.
Everland William, bds. 25 W. Michigan.
Evers John, tailor, cor. East and Washington.
Everson George V., produce dealer, bds. 168 Tennessee.
Evert John, carpenter, 72 W. Maryland.
EWALD ROBERT de., Professor of Music, Little's Hotel.
EWING DR. J., eclectic, bds. 53 S. Pennsylvania.
Ewing Martin V., student Bryant's Commercial College.
EXCELSIOR COMMERCIAL COLLEGE, A. B. Church, principal, Blackford's Building, cor. Washington and Meridian.
Exline George A., grocer, res. 151 N. East.

F

Fagan James, stone cutter, res. S. East.
FAHNESTOCK & CO., dealers in ladies fancy goods, trimmings &c., 18 and 22 S. Illinois.
Fahnestock C. S. R., (F. & Co.,) res. 18 S. Illinois.
FAHNESTOCK JOHN, engraver and printer, 19 W. Washington, bds. 132 E. Market.
Fahnestock Orrin S., printer John Fahnestock, bds. 132 E. Market.
FAHNESTOCK SAMUEL, physician and surgeon, office 19 W. Washington, res. 132 E. Market.
Fahrback Andrew, plasterer, res. 148 S. New Jersey.
Fahrback Phillip, laborer, 148 S. New Jersey.
Failey Thomas, in saw factory, bds. Ray House.
Faly G., painter, res. 143 N. Alabama.
Fancher R. N., carriage trimmer, 44 N. Pennsylvania.
Faries Henry V., res. 66 E. Louisiana.
Farley Thomas, saw manufacturer, bds. Ray House.
Farmers' and Drovers' Hotel, J. Harris proprietor, 212 W. Washington.
FARMERS' HOTEL, H. Buchrig proprietor, 61 S. Illinois.
Farmer James, carpenter, res. 248 Indiana ave.
Farmer J. B., clerk Jeffersonville R. R. freight office, res. 280 Railroad.
Farquhar Geo. W., blacksmith, 36 Kentucky ave., res. 126 New York.
Farral Fergus, porter J. A. Crossland, 176 Illinois.
Farral James, laborer, res. 196 N. Tennessee.
Farral Patrick, retired, bds. E. Knight.
Farrel James, (col.,) white washer, res. 136 N. Delaware.
Farrel John, police officer, res. Wabash, bet. New Jersey and East.
Farrell Miss K., dress maker, 21 S. Delaware, res. same.
Farrell Mrs. C. J., dress maker, 21 S. Delaware.
Faulkner J. B., traveling agent for Sheets & Braden, bds. Pyle House.
Fatoul J. L. & M. R., carpenters and builders, cor. Mississippi and Indiana ave.
Fay Gustavis, carriage painter, res. 143 N. Alabama.
Fay John, tinner, res. 153 N. Liberty.
Fearnley John, bds. 32 E. Ohio.
Fearnley John, carpenter, res. 11 S. Illinois.
FEARY & LOW, carpenters and builders, 18 S. New Jersey.
Feary Jeremiah E., (F. & Low,) res. 154 E. North.
Feary Henry, painter, bds. 154 E. North.
Featherston William E., (Gott & F.,) res. 115 Massachusetts ave.

Felbaum William, engineer, res. N. Mississippi.
Feldpusch John, laborer, res. 83 N. Davidson.
Feling Frederick, teamster, res. 125 South.
Fellbeck John, laborer, res. 273 S. Delaware.
FELLER GEORGE, watches, clocks and jewelry, 17 N.
    Illinois, res. N. Mississippi, bet.Washington and Market.
Fellows James W., daguerreotypist, res. 16 N. New Jersey.
Felt Goodhart, painter, 13 N. New Jersey.
Fenton John, tinner, bds. 19 Circle cor. Market.
Fenton Patrick, laborer, res. 27 N. Railroad.
Fenton Mrs. Rachel, res. 15 S. Georgia.
Ferbanks Andrew, plasterer, res. 149 S. New Jersey.
Ferguson (widow) Andrew, boarding house, 20 N. Pennsyl-
    vania.
FERGUSON C. A. & CO., watchmakers and jewellers,
    7 W. Washington.
Ferguson C. A., (C. A. F. & Co.,) res. Ohio, bet. Meridian
    and Illinois.
Ferguson David, at Bryant's Commercial College, res. 20 N.
    Pennsylvania.
Ferguson Edward H., brickmason, res. 96 N. Meridian.
Ferguson J., res. 96 N. Meridian.
Ferguson James C., pork merchant, res. 28 N. Meridian.
Ferguson Kilby, (Walpole & F.,) res. 207 N. Illinois.
Ferguson Leander, tinner, bds. Little's Hotel.
Ferguson Robert, plasterer, res. N. Meridian.
Ferguson R., cutter Dessar Brothers, res. 134 E. Market.
Ferita Thomas, laborer, res. 3 Noble.
Ferkins Frederick, laborer, res. 253 S. Pennsylvania.
Ferling George, (Leminger & F.,) res. E. Maryland. bet.
    Delaware and Alabama.
Ferry Mrs. Jane, 221 S. Pennsylvania.
Ferry James, driver Adams' Express, res. 48 Indiana ave.
Fershu George W., blacksmith, res. 126 W. New York.
FERTIG FRANK, house and sign painter, 4 E. Washing-
    ton, up stairs.
Fette Charles, machinist Washington Foundry, res. 164 S.
    Alabama.
Fetrow Alexander, carpenter, res. 57 S. New Jersey.
Fetrow Joseph, farmer, res. 57 S. New Jersey.
Ficker George, shoemaker res. 224 N. New Jersey.
Fiebig John, laborer, res. 207 S. Delaware.
Fifeus Thomas W., bricklayer and builder, res. E. side Li-
    berty, 2 doors N. of Massachusetts ave.
Fike Peter, teamster, res. 23 Madison ave.
Filbeck George, bds. 21 N. Meridian.
File F., 74 Bluff road.
Filey John, wagon maker 61 Bluff road.

Finch John, laborer, res. 221 S. Delaware.
Fink John, machinist, cor. Union and McCarty.
Finkbiner Wm., cigar maker, bds. Charles C. Hunt.
Finley Morris, laborer, res. 38 S. Alabama.
Finley William, laborer, res. Blake, bet. Washington and
    New York.
Finn John, cooper, res. 14 Union.
Finn John, laborer, res. 22 S. Delaware.
Finnegan James, laborer, res. 73 S. Noble.
Finney Michael, laborer, res. 263 S. Delaware.
FINNEY ROBERT P., proprietor Capital Mills, cor. Canal
    and Market, res. 128 N. Noble.
Finton Frederick, baker, res. 77 Fort Wayne ave.
Firon George, clerk in Feed store, res. Wyoming.
Fischer Charles, cooper, res. 37 N. Spring.
Fisher Martin, shoemaker, 54 Bluff road.
Fiscus Mrs. Elizabeth, milliner, 174 E. Washington, res.
    same.
Fiscus Wm., grocer, res. 174 E. Washington.
FISHBACK CHARLES, M. D., office 116 Virginia ave, res.
    111 Virginia ave.
FISHBACK JOHN, leather, hides and oil, &c., 30 S. Meri-
    dian, res. 49 S. Meridian.
Fishback Wm. P., (Conner & F.,) res. 50 E. Market.
Fisher A., (F. & Wheatley,) res. 120 N. East.
Fisher Benedict, (F. & Ringle,) res. Illinois, near Union
    depot.
Fisher Charles, shoemaker, res. Bluff road.
FISHER CHARLES, justice of the peace, office 1 N. Meri-
    dian, res. 16 W. North.
Fisher Geo., shoemaker, 224 N. New Jersey, res. same.
FISHER & RINGLE, barbers and hair dressers, Louisiana,
    cor. of Illinois.
Fisher Mrs. M., res. 143 E. Washington.
FISHER & WHEATLEY, agents for sale of patent ma-
    chinery, 6 S. Meridian, opposite Post Office, res. 120 E.
    Massachusetts.
Fisher Wm. J., shoemaker, bds. 53 Massachusetts ave.
Fishner G., res. S. West.
Fitch William H., cabinet maker, res. 91 Indiana ave.
Fitch C. H., machinist, res. 71 Merrill.
Fitchey M. G., carpenter, res. 234 W. Washington.
FITZGIBBON M. & CO, wholesale grocers, 77 S. Meridian.
Fitzgibbon M., (F. & Co.,) bds. Bates House.
Fitzgibbon Thomas, finisher, bds. Indiana House.
Fitzgerald Garret, laborer, bds. 23 S. Georgia.
Fitzgerald James, tailor, bds. Farmers' Hotel.
Fitzgerald John M., tinner, bds. Farmers' Hotel.

Fitzgerald Nicholas, laborer, res. 23 E. Georgia.

Fitzgerald Wm., laborer, res. 198 S. Illinois.

Fitzpatrick John, laborer, bds. 55 S. Illinois.

FLAGG SETH A., proprietor Magnolia Saloon and Restaurant, 9 S. Illinois, res. Georgia, bet. Illinois and Tennessee.

Flagg Wm., 77 Bluff road.

Flaherty John laborer, res. 104 N. Mississippi.

Fleitz Charles, blacksmith, res. 101 Bluff road.

FLETCHER'S BANK, 30 E. Washington.

FLETCHER CALVIN, President Indianapolis Branch Banking Co., res. N. Pennsylvania, bet. First and Second.

Fletcher Calvin, jr., (F., Williams & Loomis,) res. 16 S. Pennsylvania.

FLETCHER REV ELIJAH T., res. 2 Circle.

Fletcher Horace A., (H. A. F. & Co.,) bds. Bates House.

FLETCHER H. A. & CO., dry goods and carpets, 26 and 28 Ray's block, W. Washington.

Fletcher Henry F., express messenger, bds. 57 W. Vermont.

Fletcher John, laborer, 187 S. New Jersey.

Fletcher Milton, laborer, 71 Madison ave.

Fletcher Richard, clerk Post Office, res. 54 N. Pennsylvania.

FLETCHER STOUGHTON A., sen., banker, 30 E. Washington, res. 88 E. Ohio.

Fletcher S. A., jr., clerk Fletcher's Bank, res. 187 Virginia ave.

FLETCHER, WILLIAMS & LOOMIS, nursery 14 S. Pennsylvania.

Fletcher William, boot and shoe maker, res. North, bet. Meridian and Pennsylvania.

Fletcher Z., cabinet maker, 65 W. Vermont.

Flowers A. B. J., carpenter, res. S, New Jersey, near Merrill.

Flowers Samuel, carpenter, res. 166 S. New Jersey.

Fogleman John, res. 149 N. West.

Fold G., painter, res. 13 N. New Jersey.

Foley wid. Jeremiah, res. 196 S. Delaware.

Foley John, telegraph operator I. & C. R. R., bds. Ray House.

Foley Mrs. Julia, 163 S. Tennessee.

Foley Mary, nurse, bds 40 S. Illinois.

Foltz Frederick, retired, 113 N. Alabama.

Fontaine Massena, watchmaker C. G. French, 37 W. Washinton, bds. C. G. French.

Foos Peter, bds. 21 N. Alabama.

Foos Thomas J., baker, 84 N. Mississippi.

Foote Jeremiah, res. 10 E. Michigan.

Forand Christopher, cabinet maker, bds. Pennsylvania House.

Forbes Matthew, engineer Bellefontaine R. R., res. 49 N. Noble.

Ford Miss Gussie, assistant music teacher Indianapolis Female Institute. bds. 34 E. Michigan.

Ford Henry, res. 113 W. Michigan.

Ford John, soap and candle manufacturer, res. 44 Indiana ave.

Forse Matthew, laborer, res. S. Virginia ave.

Forshee G. W., res. 126 W. New York.

Forshee John, conductor L. & I. R. R., bds. Bates House.

Forsythe William, shipping and receiving clerk Bellefontaine R. R., res. 48 S. Meridian.

FORTESCUE W. M., dealer in groceries and provisions, 165 East Washington.

Foster Alfred, boiler maker, res. 57 E. South.

Foster Mrs. Angelina, tailoress, bds. cor. Broadway and Strawberry alley.

Foster Edgar J., clerk L. Street & Co., bds. 136 N. Illinois.

Foster Robert S., clerk A. Wallace, bds. Mrs. Smith.

FOSTER WILLIAM R. & CO., groceries, feed, &c., 21 N. Alabama.

Foudray John E., (Wood & F.,) res. 109 N. New Jersey.

Foudray Mrs. Martha, res. 3 Massachusetts ave.

Foust Daniel, res. 20 N. West.

Fowler Benjamin, fireman on R. R., bds. 70 S. Noble.

Fox John, tailor, Moritz & Bro., bds. Pyle House.

Foy·Owen, engineer B. R. R., res. 24 N. Liberty.

FRAEYSER GEORGE, piano forte manufacturer, corner Washington and Alabama, up stairs.

France Peter, well digger, res. 159 N. Railroad.

Franco Alexander, clothier, res. Hammond's block, West Washington.

FRANCO D., clothing and gents' furnishing goods, 2 Palmer House, res. 106 N Tennessee opp. State House.

Frank Adam, machinist, bds. H. Buchrig.

Frank Andrew, laborer, res. 60 Union.

Frank E., baggageman, Union Depot, res. Union.

Frank Henry, (Spiegle, Thoms & Co.,) res. 162 New York, bet. Noble and East.

Frank James, organist and school teacher, res. 145 S. Delaware.

FRANKEM ISAAC L., tinsmith, 9 Virginia ave., bds. 155 N. Illinois.

Frankem John, res. 155 N. Illinois.

Franklin Anderson, (col.,) res. 130 N. Indiana ave.

Franklin Benjamin, 2d porter Little's Hotel.
Franklin Milton, student N. W. Christian University, bds. 58 W. Vermont.
Franklin William, (col.,) laborer, 119 Indiana ave.
Franryman Adam, clerk, Tousey & Byram, bds. Little's Hotel.
Frasier William, bridge builder, 26 S. Mississippi.
Frauer Emanuel, laborer, res. 32 N. Spring.
Frauer Herman, clerk, bds. 26 Spring.
Frazee S. E., (Edgar & F.,) res. 104 N. Illinois.
Frazier John H , carpenter, res. 121 N. New Jersey.
Freeman John, (col.,) laborer, res, N. Meridian.
Freeman N. B., clerk, Sam'l W. Elliott, res. 41 N. Michigan.
Freher John H., carpenter, bds. 81 N. Illinois.
FRENCH C. G., watchmaker and jeweller, 37 W. Washington, res. one mile out on Washington.
French R. M., laborer, res. 181 S. New Jersey.
Freisey Jacob A., carpenter, res. 15 S. Georgia.
FRENZEL JNO. P., Kansas eating saloon, 85 S. Illinois.
Frerto Frederick, paper maker, res. Blackford.
FRICKE REV. CHARLES, clergyman German Lutheran Church, res. 13 N. East.
Friday Michael, carpenter, res. 211 N. Noble.
Fridley William, clerk, Telegraph office, bds. 6 Meridian.
Fridley Mrs. Susan, agent Kelsey & Co.'s sewing machine, bds. 6 N. Meridian.
Fridley Wm. K., messenger Western Union Telegraph, bds. 6 N. Meridian.
FRINK DR. S. C., dentist, Yohn's block, No. 4 N. Meridian, res. 132 N. Illinois.
Frink Erastus O., dentist with S. C. Frink, bds. 132 N. Illinois.
Frizell Allen, carpenter, res. 172 Blake.
Fromhie Henry, clerk, res. 76 N. Mississippi.
Frommier Henry, packer, Jacob Lindley.
FROST J. M. & CO., patent medicines, 5 N. Meridian.
Frost J. M., (J. M. F. & Co.,) res. 150 N. Pennsylvania.
Frumhold Peter, coppersmith, bds. 14 Illinois.
Fry Nancy, widow, bds. 79 N. Pennsylvania.
Fryberger Francis A., salesman, Coffin & Morton, bds. Little's Hotel.
Fuerchtenicht Ernest, cabinet maker, 297 Virginia ave.
Fullington Chas. D., U. S. Express Messenger, Bellefontaine R. R., bds. Bates House.
Fults Mrs. Eliza, res. 33 and 34 Sentinel building.
Fults John W., clerk, T. D. Bell, bds. Sentinel building.
Fullwiler Charles, woodsawyer, cor. Mississippi and New York.

Funk Mrs. Fannie, res. 131 N. Noble.
FUNKHOUSER DAVID, physician, office 5 S. Meridian,
    bds. Bates House.
Fuqua Andrew W., bridge tender White river bridge, res.
    same.
FURGASON JOHN A., book-keeper Washington foundry,
    res. 37 E. Georgia.
Furguson James, clerk, res. 134 N. Davidson.

G

Gabert Henry, laborer, 39 Union.
Galan Patrick, laborer, res. 17 S. Georgia.
Galehouse John, tanner, John Fishback, res. Wabash, bet.
    New Jersey and East Meridian.
Gallagher A., peddler, res. 135 Liberty.
Gallagher C., peddler, res. 135 N. Liberty.
Gallagher Francis, pedler, res. 42 Massachusetts ave.
Gallagher Mrs. Julia, res. 130 N. Meridian.
Gallagher Michael, laborer, res. 16 S. East.
Gallivan Michael, laborer, res. 16 S. East.
Galligan Mrs., laundress, res. 33 E. Market.
Galloway Mrs. Jane, 69 Indiana ave.
Gallup Edward P., (W. P. & E. P. G.,) bds. Bates House.
GALLUP W. P. & E. P., commission merchants and agents
    Fairbanks' scales, 74 W. Washington.
Gallup William P., (W. P. & E. P. G.,) bds. Bates House.
Gamble James, carpenter and joiner, res. Broadway alley
    near New Jersey.
Gamble John, 1st porter Little's Hotel.
Gamendinger Jacob, blacksmith, res. south side National
    road, out of city limits.
Gammer Conrad, laborer, Kregelo, Blake & Co.
Ganter Cass, confectioner, res. 183 E. Washington.
Gantsberg Frederick, baggageman, Union Depot, res. 318
    Virginia ave.
Gapen Loring W., pressman, Sentinel office, bds. California
    House.
Gardener Wendel, carpenter, res. 183 Indiana ave.
Gardner D. B., printer, Locomotive office, res. 67 N. Ten-
    nessee.
GARDNER FRANK M., printer, Sentinel office, bds. 79½
    E. Washington.
Garmerdeinger Jacob, blacksmith, res. E. Washington.
GARNER HORATIO S., printer, Sentinel office, bds. Pyle
    House.
Garner L. W., watchmaker, Ferguson & Co., bds. Pyle House.
Garrett Cyrus, printer, res. 85 N. East.

GARRATT JOSEPH, brass and bell founder, Union track, near Delaware, res. S. East.

Garver Peter, engineer, bds. S. B. Wilson.

Gass Andrew, butcher, res. 60 E. St. Joseph.

Gass John H., laborer, res. 74 E. St. Joseph.

Gassipor Frederick, bds. 114 S. Noble.

Gaston Edward Y., carrirge maker, H. R. Gaston.

GASTON HIRAM R., carriage manufacturer, 23 N. Illinois, res. 27 Kentucky ave.

GASTON JOHN M., physician, office S. E. cor. New York and New Jersey, res. 77 N. New Jersey.

Gaston Mrs. Ann, res. 19 S. Illinois.

Gates D. S., American Express Messenger, Indianapolis and St. Louis, bds. Bates House.

Gates John, blacksmith, 14 S. New Jersey, res. 85 E. Market.

Gates John, laborer, 73 N. New Jersey.

Gates Uriah, blacksmith, New York near Illinois.

Gates Wesley, blacksmith, bds. 85 E. Market.

Gatlin Geo., moulder, bds. Ray House.

GATLING RICHARD J., real estate dealer and general fire insurance agent, office Blackford buildings, res. 44 S. Meridian.

Gatmey James, laborer, res. 170 East.

Gattenby John, laborer, bds. 73 S. Noble.

Gause Mary L., res. 142 N. Alabama.

Gaver Frederick, laborer, 92 Union.

Gay Alfred, with G. Stevens, res. 69 N. Mississippi.

Gearing Francis, laborer, 43 McCarty.

GEE R. S. & CO., solicitor of patents, Ætna Buildings, N. Pennsylvania.

Gee R. S., (R. S. G. & Co.,) res. 37 N. New Jersey.

Gegar Wm., (Homburgh & Co.,) res. 154 N. Noble.

Gehl Klaudius, clerk F. Blacs, bds. 66 S. Delaware.

Geisel Henry, blacksmith, S. Delaware, res. 188 E. Market.

Geisel George, blacksmith, res. 106 N. Davidson.

Geisel John, blacksmith, res. 121 N. Davidson.

Geisendorff Edward, (G. W. G. & Co., res. 223 W. Washington.

GEISENDORFF G. W. & CO., Hoosier Woolen Factory, 268 W. Washington.

Geisendorff George W., (G. W. G. & Co.,) res. 270 W. Washington.

Geisendorff Jacob C., (G. W. G. & Co..) res. 170 N. New York.

Gelzenleuchter John, laborer, res. 169 N. Railroad.

Gemmer Conrad, laborer, res. 71 N. Noble.

Gentry James, laborer, 77 Bluff Road.

Gentry Thomas J., at Bryant's Commercial College.

Geoeke Adolph, bds. 315 Indiana ave.
Geokeler Christian, hod carrier, res. 75 Fort Wayne ave.
George Austin R., bds. 16 N. Mississippi.
George Isaac, turner, res. 55 McCarty.
George James, grocer and produce dealer, res. 143 W. Washington.
George Mrs. Melvina, res. 76 Kentucky ave.
George Robert, trader, res. 16 N. Mississippi.
Gerard Elias, shoe maker, res. 99 Louisiana.
Ger David, tailor, res. 94 Fort Wayne ave.
German John, laborer, 127 South.
GERMAN MUTUAL INSURANCE CO. OF INDIANA, 95 E. Washington, A. Seidensticker, president; Charles Volmer, secretary.
Gerstner Anthony J., (G. & Rogge,) res. 66 N. East.
GERSTNER & ROGGE, merchant tailors, 164 E. Washington.
Geskink Frederick, blacksmith, res. 42 N. Davidson.
Gess Louis, blacksmith, bds. 44 N. Pennsylvania.
Gettenby wid. John, res. 73 S. Noble.
Gety John, engine cleaner B. R. R. Co., 76 N. New Jersey.
Gherrer John, carpenter, res. Elizabeth.
Gibbons Rodney R., flour miller, res. Strawberry alley, bet. Broadway alley and Market.
Gibbs Reuben, (Shucraft & G.,) res. 154 S. Illinois.
Gibson George, carpenter, bds. 77 N. East.
Gibson John, tinner, W. A. Mars.
Giffin John A., teamster, res. alley, bet. East and Liberty.
Gilbert Mrs. Fannie, res. 99 N. Noble.
Gilbert Harvey A., trader in real estate, bds. Little's Hotel.
Gilkey O. B., carpenter, bds. 154 W. Vermont.
Gill William L., boiler maker, 173 N. Mississippi.
Gillespie Mrs. Jane, res. 44 N. Delaware.
Gillespie William J., bds. 44 N. Delaware.
Gillett Horace, Professor at Indiana Institute for the Education of Deaf and Dumb, res. Oriental, near Michigan Road.
GILLETT JOHN, traveling agent P. C. & C. R. R., 43 N. New Jersey.
GILLIGAN MISS M. A., ladies' fancy store, 5 Bates House, bds. Pennsylvania.
Gilson Frederick A., traveling agent D. Roberts, res. 59 E. Market.
Gimber John, plow maker, bds. E. Michigan, cor. Railroad.
Gimble Martin, carpenter, res. 129 E. Market.
Gimble Michael, clerk J. K. Sharpe, res. 326 S. Delaware.
Girard Elias, laborer, res. 99 S. Louisiana.

7

Gisicking Frederick, blacksmith, res. Davidson.
Githens V., res. 100 S. Noble.
Givan John, M. D., office 25 Ramsey's Block, Illinois.
Givens John, clerk James Hart & Co., bds. 30 Ohio, cor. Illinois.
GLASER & BROTHERS, merchant tailors, 2 Bates House.
Glaser Julius, (G. & Bros.,) res. 15 N. East.
Glaser Max, (G. & Bros.,) res 85 N. Illinois.
Glazier Mrs. Catharine, res. 114 S. New Jersey.
Glazier Charles, (Bradshaw & G.,) res. 100 Virginia ave.
Glazier Daniel, machinist, res. S. New Jersey.
Glazier Francis P., machinist, res. 34 Georgia.
GLENN'S BLOCK, E. Washington, bet. Meridian, and
    Pennsylvania.
GLENN W. & H. & CO., wholesale and retail dry goods,
    Glenn's Block, E. Washington.
GLENN HUGH, (W. & H. G. & Co.,) bds. 73 N. Meridian.
GLENN R. J., (W. & H. G. & Co.,) bds. 73 N. Meridian.
GLENN WILLIAM, (W. & H. G. & Co.,) res. 73 N. Meridian.
Glutz Martin, blacksmith, bds. 135 W. Maryland.
Goddard Samuel, stone cutter, 71 Missouri.
GOEBEL JOHN G., cabinet warerooms, 82 W. Washington, res. 52 South.
GŒPPER FREDERICK, merchant tailor, 15 E. Washington, res. 61 N. Illinois.
Goff Mrs. Eliza, (col.,) res. 127 N. West.
GOGAN JAMES, printer Sentinel Office, res. 64 Merrill.
GOLD ADAM, groceries and provisions, W. Washington,
    opp. Woolen Factory, res. 191 W. Washington.
Gold Samuel, clerk, bds. 191 W. Washington.
Gold William, clerk, bds. 191 W, Washington.
Goldman Jacob, peddler, res. 211 S. Alabama.
GOLDSBERRY LIVINGSTON D., wholesale and retail
    stoves and tinware, 182 E. Washington, res. 43 N. Pennsylvania.
Goldsberry S. S., with W. P. Bingham & Co., bds. 7 E. Ohio.
Goldsmith Myers, clerk Glaser & Bros.
Goodbar A. M., bds. R. B. Duncan.
Goodheart Benjamin F., bds. Wm. Spotts.
Goodman Andrew, tailor, res. 56 E. Market.
GOODWIN REV. ELIJAH, (Christian,) editor Christian
    Record, res. Wisconsin ave.
GOODWIN REV. THOMAS A., editor Indiana American,
    res. 184 E. Ohio.
Goohe Claudius C., bds. 66 S. Delaware.
Gorden James, teamster, res. 69 Indiana ave.

GORDON & BEAL, attorneys at law, 6 Glenn's Block, E. Washington.

GORDON GEORGE E., attorney at law, Odd Fellows' Hall, res. 92 N. Pennsylvania.

Gordon Jonathan W., (G. & Beal,) res. 144 N. Illinois.

Gore James, salesman J. C. Yohn, bds. cor. Delaware and Vermont.

Gorham George L., bricklayer, res. 179 N. Mississippi.

Gorham John M., blacksmith, 76 Indiana ave., res. 109 Michigan.

Gorham Perry S., blacksmith, bds. 109 Michigan.

Gorrell Willis A., clerk H. Babcock, bds. 78 Massachusetts ave.

Gorrell Mrs. Isabella, res 78 Massachusetts ave.

Gosney George R., clerk, bds. Tully House.

Goth Peter, clerk, res. 237 N. New Jersey.

Goth Valentine, cooper, res. 77 N. Spring.

GOTT & FEATHERSTON, auction and commission merchants, 48 E. Washington.

Gott John, tailor, res. 150 N. Liberty.

Gott Thomas, (G. & Featherston,) res. 147 S. Tennessee.

Goughen Thomas, laborer, res. 186 S. Delaware.

Gowan Samuel, spinner, res. cor. West and W. Washington.

Gowins Canada, cooper, west end North.

Grabhorn Henry, varnisher Spiegel, Thoms & Co.

Graffort George, (col.,) barber, res. alley, S. W. Vermont.

Graham A., clerk, bds. 151 N. East.

Graham Samuel, switchman, res. 148 N. Mississippi.

Graham W. A., with McCord & Wheatley, res. 50 Benton.

Graham Rev. William, (Meth. Epis.,) res. 107 N. Tennessee.

Graham Wm. S., driver Adams' Express, res. cor. Pennsylvania and Ohio.

GRAMLING J. & P., merchant tailors and clothiers, 41 E. Washington.

Gramling John, (J. & P. G.,) res. 114 N. Noble.

Gramling Peter, (J. & P. G.,) res. 114 N. Noble.

Graney John, laborer, res. 35 E. Market.

Granrut John L., laborer, res. 139 N. Liberty.

Gray Columbus V., moulder, res. 250 S. Delaware.

Gray John, laborer, res. 192 N. New Jersey.

Gray John W., shoemaker, 5 W. Washington, res. 81 South.

Gray Jonathan, brick mason, 252 S. Delaware.

Gray Major, moulder, res. 250 S. Delaware.

Gray Robert, 64 South.

Gray Samuel R., teamster, 8 S. Mississippi.

Gray Thomas, bds. 64 South.

Gray William, bakery, 64 South, res. same.

Graydon Alexander, township librarian, res. National Road, east of town two miles.

Greab John, stone mason, res. 151 N. Liberty.

Greany Thomas, baggageman I. & C. Railroad.

Greaser Frank, turner, 209 S. Pennsylvania.

GREAT WESTERN DISPATCH, T. A. Lewis, agent, office at A. Wallace's, cor. Virginia ave. and Delaware.

Green Allen T., painter and varnisher, res. 40 E. Louisiana.

Green Geo., tailor, res. cor. Fifth and Mississippi.

GREEN JAMES, secretary and treasurer E. I. & C. Railroad, 3 Post Office Building, res. 93 N. Meridian.

Green John, tailor Dessar Brothers.

Greene N. Scott, clerk Stewart & Bowen, bds. 93 N. Meridian.

Greenert Henry, tailor, 112 E. Washington.

Greenewald Henry, cabinet maker, 79 Davidson, res. same.

Greenfield Daniel C., clerk, bds. 229 W. Washington.

Greenfield Robert, res. 229 W. Washington.

Greenleaf Alvin C., machinist, res. 114 E. Vermont.

Greenleaf C. A., machinist, bds. Tremont House.

Greenleaf Edward, master machinist, res. N. W. cor. Ohio and Mississippi.

Greenstein A., hostler, bds. 67 N. New Jersey.

Greensteinner George, (Herrmon & G.,) res. 114 E. Market.

Greenwood James W., brakeman, bds. 51 E. Georgia.

Greer Mrs. Susan J., bds. 19 N. East.

Greer William H., carpenter, res. 176 S. Mississippi.

Gregg James, wagon maker, 56 Indiana ave.

Greggory David, fur and skin dealer, 65 W. Washington, res. 73 W. South.

Gregoare August, tailor, bds. 67 N. Noble.

GREIN & THALMAN, bakers, 214 E. Washington.

Grein John, (G. & Thalman,) res. 214 E. Washington.

Greiner John, shoemaker, bds. 51 S. Illinois.

Greit John, butcher, res. 184 S. Delaware.

GRESH PROF. BENJAMIN F., musician, 101 W. New York.

Gresham Robert, baggage master Jeffersonville Railroad, bds. 53 N. Pennsylvania.

Greshimer Moritz, clerk M. Dernham, bds. 2 S. Pennsylvania.

Grenzard Louis S., painter, res. E. Washington.

Grieb John G., stone mason, res. 151 N. Liberty.

Griener John, shoemaker, bds. 51 S. Illinois.

Grffin Enos, laborer, res. S. Missouri.

Griffin James, laborer, 300 S. Delaware.

Griffin Michael, res. 67 Bright.

Griffin Patrick, laborer, res. 316 S. Delaware.

Griffin Patrick, laborer, bds. 38 S. Alabama.
Griffin Thomas, laborer, 5 Bates.
Griffin Timothy, cabinet maker, bds. E. Knight.
Griffis Lewis J., currier, bds. Ray House.
Griffith George, plasterer, res. 22 N. New Jersey.
Griffith H., retired, res. 52 N. Illinois.
Griffith I. R., res. 32 S. Mississippi.
GRIFFITH SAMUEL, car builder, res. 263 S. East.
Grim William, laborer, bds. Union Hall.
Grimm Jacob, blacksmith, bds. 106 St. Joseph.
Griswell John N., carpenter, res. Blake.
GROBE CHARLES H., book binder and paper box maker,
    125 E. Washington, res. same.
Grooms A. C., book-keeper Journal office, res. 107 Indiana
    ave.
Grooms Moses, printer Journal office, bds. 44 N. Pennsyl-
    vania.
Grosch John, teamster, res. 113 N. Noble.
Groschel Charles, tailor, res. 135 N. Liberty.
Gross William H., laborer, res. 114 W. Vermont.
Groter Henry, laborer post office, res. 3 N. New Jersey.
GROUT JOSEPH B., boots and shoes, 26 W. Maryland.
Grubbs D. W., clerk Ætna Insurance Co., bds. 87 N. Me-
    ridian.
Gruenert Henry, tailor F. Gœpper, res. Washington ad-
    joining Union Hall.
Guard D. E., clerk Smith & Stevenson, bds. 94 N. West.
Guildersleive Miss Eliza, school teacher, bds. 14 N. Me-
    ridian.
Gukh Edward, machinist, 32 S. Illinois.
GULICK JOHN F., meats, fruits and vegetables, N. Penn-
    sylvania, near Odd Fellows' Hall, res. 26 Massachusetts
    ave.
GULICK SAMUEL W., scenic and frescoe painter, orders
    left at box 167 post office.
Gulliver William, barber cellar Blake's Row, res. 36 Ken-
    tucky ave.
Gummer Albert, machinist, bds. 32 S. Illinois.
Guss Louis, blacksmith, bds. Mrs. Cook.
GUSTIN DR. LEVI, opthalmic physician, office cor.
    Louisiana and Illinois, res. 53 W. South.
GUSTIN E. Q., solicitor for Hall's New Patent Lightning
    Rod, bds. 53 South.
Gutherie Edward, printer, bds. 71 W. Maryland.
Gutig Henry, barber, res. 113 E. Market.
Gutperle Peter, laborer, res. 112 N. Noble.
Guttnecht John, painter, res. 105 Fort Wayne ave.
Gyte Nicholas, turner, bds. Jackson House.

H

Haas George, baker, bds. 150 N. New Jersey.
Hackelburgh Samuel, boot and shoe maker, res. cor. Maryland and Meridian.
Hackett William, laborer, res. 22 S. Liberty.
Hackhiser John C., clerk Boston Store, bds. Mrs. Kinder's.
Hackston Christopher, res. 50 Union.
Hackumber Charley, finisher, res. S. Delaware.
Hadley William, (Taylor, Wright & H.,) res. 151 N. Delaware.
Haerle William, clerk Klotz & Pfafflin, bds. 16 W. Georgia.
HAFNER A. & F., boot and shoe makers, 103 W. Washington.
Hafner August, (A. & F. H.,) boot and shoe maker, res. 103 W. Washington.
Hafner Frank, (A. & F. H.,) res. 185 W. Washington.
Hagar Edward, assistant book-keeper with S. A. Fletcher, bds. 13 Circle.
Hagar Isaac A., book-keeper Fletcher's Bank, bds. 31 Circle.
Hagerhorst Mrs. Mary, res. 156 S. Tennessee.
Hagerhorst William, clerk C. F. Hagerhorst.
HAGERHORST CHRISTIAN F., family grocer, 28 S. Illinois, cor. Maryland.
Haggart William, blacksmith L. & I. Railroad.
Hahan Jacob, baker, bds. 55 Maryland.
Hahan Jacob, tailor, bds. Pennsylvania House.
Hahn Andrew, boarding house, S. East.
Hahn Phillip, musician, res. 68 Fort Wayne ave.
HAHN LOUIS, butcher, 104 W. Washington, res. same.
Hahn Henry, musician, 68 Fort Wayne ave.
HAHN HENRY, proprietor East Street House, near Peru Depot.
Hahn Charles, peddler, res. bet. Market and Ohio.
Haider Julius, carpenter, res. 160 E. Washington, up stairs.
Haightcomb Phillip, driver, res. 7 E. New York.
Hakelburg Samuel, boot and shoe maker with Edgar & Frazee, res. cor. Maryland and Meridian.
Hakell Thurlow, carpenter, 82 W. Maryland.
Hale H. J., machinist, res. 151 N. Illinois.
Haley Jerry, laborer, res. 35 E. Market.
Haley wid. Timothy, res. N. New Jersey.
Hall Charles W., attorney at law, bds. Bates House.
Hall Charlie, res. 94 N. Illinois.
HALL ELI A., merchant tailor, 2 Odd Fellows' Hall, res. 124 N. Pennsylvania.

Hall Harry L., conductor I. & C. Railroad, bds. Bates House.

Hall Jane, seamstress, 95 N. Pennsylvania.

Hall Lewis, tailor, 66 Pennsylvania.

HALL LYTEL, pump maker, E. Vermont, near Massachusetts ave., res. 178 S. Tennessee.

Hall Rev. Perry, (Christian,) res. 172 N. Tennessee.

Hall Richard M., (Spann & Hall,) res. 123 N. New Jersey, cor. Michigan.

HALL REGINALD H., attorney at law, office 24½ E. Washington, res. 47 N. Meridian.

Hall William, machinist, bds. 51 Louisiana.

HALL DR. WILLIAM, agent for Locke & Munson's Patent Lightning Rod, S. W. cor. Washington and Meridian, res. 5 E. New York.

Hallahan Cornelius, res. 33 Elsworth.

Hallahan Jeremiah, laborer, res. Elizabeth, bet. Blake and Dunlop.

Hallahan Louis, shoemaker, bds. 48 Massachusetts ave.

Hallahan Mike, laborer, res. Elizabeth.

Halliday Rev. William A., res. 102 N. Alabama.

Halpin Martin, printer Journal office, bds. Mrs. Kinder's.

Halten William, shoemaker, bds. 51 S. Illinois.

Halter Casper, piano maker, bds. Tremont House.

Hambaugh Charles, waiter Little's Hotel.

Hambaugh Thomas, steward Little's Hotel.

Hamblen Vincent, farmer, res. 65 E. St. Joseph.

Hamer Thomas, moulder, bds. Ray House.

Hamer Thomas, laborer, res. 83 N. Davidson.

HAMILTON JOHN W., attorney at law and notary public, office Court House, res. National Road, two miles from town.

Hamilton William, machinist Bellefontaine shop, res. 44 S. Noble.

Hamilton William H., book binder, bds. Mrs. Bright, Indiana ave.

Hammar John, porter J. Lindley, bds. Farmers' Hotel.

Hammel Andrew, blacksmith, res. 71 N. Davidson.

HAMMOND A. A., Lieutenant Governor of the State of Indiana, bds. Bates House.

Hammond Daniel, city car No. 10, res. Blake.

Hammond Walter P., printer Sentinel office, bds. 138 S. Delaware.

Hanager Michael, machinist, bds. 51 N. Delaware.

Hand Adolphus, brick mason, res. 11 McCarty.

Hand Geo. H., printer Journal office.

Hand Mrs. Mary A., dress maker, 11 Indiana ave., res. same.

Hand Thomas B., res. 11 Indiana ave.
Hanf Andrew, Bellefontaine Railroad shop, res. 151 N. New Jersey.
Hanf Valentine, laborer, res. 123 N. Noble.
Hanley Mrs. Jane, (col.,) wash woman, res. 79 Massachusetts ave.
HANLIN & BARNITT, druggists, 172 E. Washington.
Hanlin William, (H. & Barnitt,) bds. Little's Hotel.
Hanlon Mrs. Maryanne, wash woman, res. 148 E. New York.
Hann A. W., turner, bds. 21 N. Alabama.
Hann Henry, porter American House.
Hanna John, constable, res. 203 E. St. Clair.
Hanna Samuel C., book keeper, bds. Macy House.
Hanna V. C., produce and commission merchant and agent for Queen City Mills, cor. Alabama and Louisiana, res. 89 Virginia ave.
Hannah Samuel, secretary and treasurer of Indiana Central Railroad, res. 26 N. Meridian.
Hanning John G., (Ramsay & H.,) res. 155 Vermont.
Hannaman Douglas, with William Hannaman.
HANNAMAN WILLIAM, drugs and medicines, 40 E. Washington, res. 2½ miles National Road.
Hanranhan Patrick, boarding house, 184 S. Tennessee.
Hansen Charles, grocer, 50 Bluff Road, res. same.
HANWAY SAMUEL, grocer, cor. E. Washington and Virginia ave., res. 75 N. New Jersey.
Happ George, cabinet maker, bds. Kentucky ave.
Harahn John, laborer, res. 210 S. Tennessee.
Harbert Enoch, butcher, res. 150 Blake.
Harbison Alexander, student Bryant's Commercial College, res. 70 W. Vermont.
Harbison Mrs. Sarah, 70 W. Vermont.
Hardesty E. J., engineer Jeffersonville Railroad, bds. Ray House.
Harden Samuel, confectioner, bds. 76 E. Washington.
Hardin E. C., carpenter Bellefontaine shop, res. 173 S. New Jersey.
Harding Thomas W., carriage trimmer, res. 106 N. Pennsylvania.
Harding Wm. H., railroad contractor, res. 126 N. Illinois.
Harding William, laborer, res. 94 Union.
Harkness John, (Elder & H.,) res. 77 N. Pennsylvania.
Harle William, clerk Chas. Mayer, bds. 16 Georgia.
Harlin J. W., clerk N. M. Ross, res. 78 N. Tennessee.
Harlin James W., (Hedges & H.,) bds. 78 N. Tennessee.
Harmon Daniel, bds. 95 S. Tennessee.
Harmon John M., res. 27 S. Liberty.

Harmon Patrick, laborer, res. 108 N. Davidson.
Harness Solomon, laborer, 47 McCarty.
Harper Henry, cooper, 92 Bluff Road.
Harper John A., tinner, res. 169 N. Delaware, bet. North
    and Wood.
Harper John L., civil engineer, office 263 Washington, res.
    115 N. Illinois.
Harrington Dennis, laborer, res. 14 S. East.
Harrington George H., with Dodge & Scott, Glenn's block,
    res. 37 N. New Jersey.
Harrington Patrick, clerk, bds. Ray House.
Harrington Timothy, laborer, res. 149 S. Mississippi.
Harris Charles E., carpenter, res. 114 W. Ohio.
Harris Charles, carpenter, res. 61 S. New Jersey.
Harris E. D., hatter, res. 107 W. Ohio.
Harris E., dyer and scourer, 79 S. Meridian.
Harris Henry, (col.,) bds. 26 North.
Harris Isaac, miller Patterson's Mills, res. 169 W. Vermont.
HARRIS J. W., proprietor Farmers' and Drovers' Hotel,
    212, 214 and 216 W. Washington.
Harris John W., bds. 126 E. Washington.
HARRIS JOSEPH, tailor and scourer, 38 S. Illinois, bds.
    Tremont House.
Harris J., jr., tailor and dyer, 19 S. Meridian, res. same.
Harris Lewis, hackdriver with A. R. Hyde, bds. Little's
    Hotel.
Harris Mandy, (col.,) porter Stewart and Bowen.
Harris M., (col.,) porter D. Roberts.
Harris Silas, teamster, res. 61 S. New Jersey.
Harris Wm. F., clerk Bellefontaine R. R. freight office, bds.
    cor. Washington and Alabama.
Harrison Alfred, (A. & J. C. S. H.,) res. 61 N. Meridian.
HARRISON A. & J. C. S., bankers, 19 E. Washington.
HARRISON'S BANK, Alfred & J. C. S. Harrison, 19 E.
    Washington.
Harrison Benjamin, (Wallace & H.,) res. 127 N. Alabama.
Harrison James H., teller Harrison's Bank, bds. 61 N. Me-
    ridian.
Harrison James, cooper, 14 McCarty.
Harrison Mrs., res. 136 Virginia ave.
Harrison John C. S., (A. & J. C. S. H.,) 63 N. Meridian.
HARRISON W. M., bookkeeper Sentinel office, res. 63 W.
    N. York.
Harrman Jacob, livery stable, res. 112 E. Market.
Harsch Frederick, laborer, bds. 121 Fort Wayne ave.
HART JAMES & CO., grocers and commission merchants,
    wines and liquors, 84 E. Washington.
Hart James, (J. H. & Co.,) res. cor. Ohio and Illinois.

Harter John A., foreman Root, Bennet & Co., E. Washington, res. 139 N. Delaware.

Harting Fred, brewery, res. 9 S. Alabama.

Hartmann Charles, baker in Bates House, res. 63 N. New Jersey.

Hartman Christian, watchman Union depot, res. 15 N. Railroad.

Hartman Christopher, works Bates' City Mills, res. 139 E. Ohio.

Hartman Frederick, wagon maker, bds. 12 Fletcher's ave.

Hartman Matthew, plasterer, res. 108 N. Alabama.

Hartman Oswald, shoemaker, bds. S. Illinois.

Hartman Peter, cigar maker, bds. Union Hall.

Hartwell Capt. Ephraim, bookkeeper Bates House.

Hartewig Henry W., drayman, res. 123 N. Davidson.

Haskell George, carpenter, 82 W. Maryland.

Haskell Wm., carpenter, bds. 82 W. Maryland.

HASKET & KYLE, pump manufacturers, Pearl, rear of Post Office.

Hasket E., (H. & Kyle,) bds. Farmers' Hotel.

Haslup I., superintendent Bellefontaine machine shop, res. S. East.

Haslup J. D., foreman of machine shop of Bellefontaine R. R., res. 221 East.

Hass Frederick, laborer, res. 68 W. Ohio.

Hass Peter, bookkeeper Farmers' Hotel, res. 55 S. Illinois.

HASSELMAN & VINTON, Washington Foundry and machine shop, opp. Union Passenger Depot.

Hasselman L. W., (H. & Vinton,) res. 38 S. Meridian.

Hassey Thomas D., res. cor. West and Maryland.

Hastings Edward, printer, res. 119 E. Market.

Hattcomb Charles, carpenter, res. 260 S. Delaware.

Hattendorf Henry, res. 164 E. Washington.

Haubermie Henry, well digger, res. 103 W. New York.

Haueisen J. F., store keeper Bates House.

Haufler John, laborer, res. 208 N. Alabama.

Haugh Adam, blacksmith, res. 6 N. Meridian.

Haugh Benjamin F., blacksmith, foreman Williamson & Haugh, res. 164 N. Pennsylvania.

Haugh Jacob, laborer, bds. 20 N. Pennsylvania.

Haugh J. R., teller in Fletcher's Bank, bds. 6 N. Meridian.

Haugh Emanuel, (Williamson & H.,) res. 118 E. Vermont.

HAUGHEY THEODORE P., secretary, treasurer and general ticket agent Peru R. R., office at depot, res. 100 N. Pennsylvania.

Hauphart Henry, shoemaker, res. 188 S. Delaware.

HAUSMANN H. & CO., Fancy Bazaar, 6 E. Washington.

Hausmann H., (H. H. & Co.,) bds. Bates House.

Havens Mrs. Susan, 26 Union.
HAWES GEO. W., State gazetteer and directory publisher, office Sentinel building, bds. American House.
Hawes M., (col.,) porter, res. North.
Hawk Jacob, hostler, bds. Mrs. Ferguson.
Hawk William, clerk Colman & Brother, res. 117 S. Alabama.
Hawkins wid. John, res. 56 S. Noble.
HAWTHORNE CHARLES E., china, glass and queensware, 83 E. Washington, res. 177 E. Washington.
Hawthorne William M., salesman H. Babcock, bds. W. H. Lingenfelter.
HAYDEN'S COMMERCIAL COLLEGE, S. W. cor. Washington and Meridian, J. C. Hayden, principal.
Hayden James C., principal Hayden's Commercial College.
Hayes A., cutter, bds. 70 N. Tennessee.
Hayes Patrick, laborer, res. 19 S. Georgia.
Hays Barton S., (Hays & Runnion,) res. 132 N. Alabama.
Hay James, blacksmith, bds. W. Market.
HAYS & RUNNION, photographic artists, 32½ E. Washington.
Hays William, engineer I. C. R. R., bds. Davidson.
Haynes Edward S., baker, res. 40 Philip.
Haynes James, millwright, res. 26 N. Delaware.
HAYNES PHILLIP, wholesale confectioner and dealer in fruits, 40 W. Washington, res. same.
Haynes Wm., printer Journal office, bds. 27 N. Delaware.
Haywood Alfred, carpenter Bellefontaine shop, 52 S. Delaware.
Healy Oliver, engineer, res. 142 Dougherty.
Heart Leon, res. 161 S. Delaware.
Heath wid. Chas., res. 18 S. East.
Heathington Christopher, bds. 255 S. Delaware.
Heaton Wm., conductor Jeff. & I. R. R., bds. American House.
Heck Mrs., res. 164 E. Washington, up stairs.
Heck Joseph, omnibus driver Little's Hotel.
Heckman C., flour and feed store, 266 E. Washington.
HEBBLE JOHN, prop'r of Galt House, Illinois, near Union Depot.
Hedge A., conductor, I. & P. R. R., res. 225 S. Delaware.
Hedge N. H., conductor, B. R. R., res. 225 S. Delaware.
Hedges Alex., (H. & Harlin,) bds. 103 N. Tennessee.
Hedges Elijah, cabinet maker, 70 W. Washington.
HEDGES & HARLIN, city bill posters, office Sentinel buildings.
Hedges Isaac L., book-keeper Stewart & Bowen, res. 103 N. Tennessee.

Hedderich Casper, carver, bds. 64 S. Noble.
Hedderich Peter, machinist, res. 66 N. Noble.
Heely Ann, dressmaker, res. 11 Alabama.
Hees Sebastian, laborer, res. 89 N. Illinois.
Heffren Delos, Deputy Sec'y of State, bds. Palmer House.
HEIDENREICH CHRISTOPHER, saloon and restaurant,
    168 E. Washington, res. 7 New Jersey.
Heider Julius, carpenter, 160 Washington, 3d floor.
HEIDLINGER JOHN A., cigars and tobacco, also dealer
    in choice teas, 10 N. Illinois and 3 Palmer House, res.
    cor. Illinois and Market.
Heimburgh & Co., coopers, alley cor. N. Liberty, bet. Wash-
    ington and Market.
Heimburgh Frederick, (H. & Co.,) res. 25 Centre.
Heimer wid. Jacob, res. 160 S. New Jersey.
Heine Henry, bootmaker, Stephenson, bet. East and Dela-
    ware.
Heine John, clerk Klotz & Pfafflin, bds. 16 W. Georgia.
Heiner Mrs. Ann, res. 160 S. New Jersey.
Heiner Francis, bds. 100 Virginia ave.
Heiner John, bds. 100 Virginia ave.
Heinrichs Charles, grocer, 61, res. 63 Madison ave.
Heinsen Antony, teamster, res. 12 S. West.
Heir Frank, works Central Depot, bds. Cincinnati House.
Heiser Conrad, carpenter, bds. 172 N. Noble.
Heiser John, laborer, res. 172 N. Noble.
Heiser Theodore, teacher, bds. Washington S. E. cor. East.
Heitkam Charles, musician, res. S. Delaware.
Heitkam George, tailor, bds. New York bet. Meridian and
    Pennsylvania.
Heitz Lewis, striker, res. 27 S. Liberty.
Heizer Edward, res. 243 N. New Jersey.
Heizer James, butcher, res. 131 E. Market.
Heizmann Matthias, saw filer, bds C. Rassmann.
Helfe Henry, laborer, res. 150 S. New Jersey.
Helfmann Jacob, baker, bds. 165 S. Delaware.
Helm Adam, carpenter, res. 62 N. Noble.
Helm Henry, stone mason, res. Washington east of Noble.
Helwig Charles, carpenter, res. 113 E. Ohio.
Hembaugh Joseph, laborer, res. 44 S. East.
Hembry Joseph, blacksmith, bds. A. Hines.
Hemmerling John, packer Jacob Lindley, bds. Farmer's
    Hotel.
Hemner Charles, weaver, res. California.
Hemp Henry, res. 150 S. New Jersey.
Henchen William, carpenter, bds. 68 Merrill.
Henderson Andrew, engineer, res. 330 S. Delaware.
Henderson Duncan, agent sewing machine, res. 52 Bates.

Henderson J., laborer, res. 25 S. Alabama.
HENDERSON WILLIAM, attorney at law and agent of
Ætna Insurance Co., office 14 N. Pennsylvania, res. 163
N. Illinois.
Henderson William W., plasterer, res. 165 E. New York.
HENDRICKS & CO., wholesale boots and shoes, 76 W.
Washington.
Hendricks Isaac, res. 110 Blake.
Hendricks James, teamster, 81 Bluff road.
Hendricks Victor K., (H. & Co.,) bds. Bates House.
Hennesse Daniel, res. 56 Bright.
HENNING & STELZELL, prop'rs Bates House shaving
saloon, N. Illinois.
Henning F. A., (H. & Stelzell,) bds. Bates House.
HENNINGER CHARLES & CO., manufacturers and
dealers in tobacco and cigars, 42 E. Washington.
Henninger Charles, (C. H. & Co.,) bds. 69 N. Delaware.
Henninger G., (C. H. & Co.,) bds. 69 N. Delaware.
HENNINGER RICHARD, publisher Indiana Free Press,
office 83 E. Washington, res. 69 N. Delaware.
Henry E., bds. Harris.
Henry George, porter Farmer's Hotel.
Henry George, woodsawyer, res. 226 N. New Jersey.
Henry John, laborer, res. 61 E. St. Joseph.
Henry Joseph, carpenter, res. S. Georgia.
Henry Lawrence, laborer, res. 182 East.
HERALD & ERA, Williamson & Lee, editors and pub-
lishers, 66½ E. Washington.
Hereth George, res. 9 Vermont.
Hereth Henry, carpenter, res. 131 N. Noble.
Hereth John C., (Hinesley & H.,) res. 29 N. Noble.
Hereth Louis, laborer, res. 181 E. Vermont.
Hereth Peter, carpenter, res. 72 S. East.
Herman wid. George, res. 332 S. Delaware.
Herman Jacob, carpenter, bds. E. Washington.
Hermann John, cabinet maker, bds. Union Hall.
Herrmann John, bar tender Tremont saloon, bds. Tremont
House.
HERRMON & GREENSTEINNER, undertakers, 114 E.
Market.
Herrmon J., (H. & Greensteinner,) res. 114 E. Market.
Herrington Patrick, clerk, bds. Ray house.
Hervey James, res. Louisiana.
Hertzman Martin, saw filer, Delaware S. of Washington.
Hesling B., tailor, res. 160 E. Washington.
Hesse Henry, painter and varnisher, bds. cor. Merrill and
Alabama.
Hetherington Benjamin F., machinist, res. 91 Bridge.

Hetherington Christopher, machinist, bds. 255 S. Delaware.
Hetselgesser Samuel, miller, res. 148 S. Illinois.
Heyser Henry, plasterer, res. 177 N. Railroad.
Henel Francis, bootmaker, bds. 188 S. Delaware.
Hiatt John R., house painter, res. 32 E. Market.
Hiatt John, cabinet maker, 28 Forest ave., Fletcher's add.
HICKOK & STARR, hats, caps and furs, 30 W. Washington.
HIELSCHER THEODORE, editor Indiana Free Press, res. cor. Washington & Alabama.
High Rev. B. D., bds. 51 N. Tennessee.
Highet James, stone cutter, res. S. Alabama.
Higgins Andrew F., chair maker, bds. Penn House.
Higgins S. Ross, American Express messenger Bellefontaine R. R., bds. Bates house.
Higgins William B., silver plater, res. 136 N. Alabama.
Hightcomb John, cabinet maker, res. N. Winston.
Higley Wm., blacksmith, bds. 44 N. Pennsylvania.
Hildebrand Jacob S., clerk J. H. Vagen, res. 111 N. Illinois.
Hildebrand Henrich, carpenter, res. 97 Fort Wayne ave.
Hildemeyer Harmon, boot and shoe maker, bds. 54 N. Noble.
Hilgenburg Christopher H., butcher, res. 127 N. Delaware.
Hill Mrs. Fanny L. C., bds. 55 S. Illinois.
Hill Frank, laborer, 186 N. Tennessee.
HILL GEORGE W., saw and planing mill, cor. East and Georgia, res. 68 S. East.
Hill, George W., (col.,) cook Pyle house, res. 105 W. North.
Hill George W., auctioneer, res. 55 S. Illinois.
Hill James, res. 38 N. Alabama.
HILL J OSCAR, plaining mill, bds. 68 S. East.
HILL REV. JOHN, (Meth. Epis.,) bds. 143 N. Pennsylvania.
Hill John F., nurseryman, res. 38 N. Alabama.
Hill William O., clerk A. B. Willard & Co., res. 26 N. Pennsylvania.
Hillis D., room, 140 N. Delaware.
Hillman Frederick H., laborer, P. & I. R. R., res Fletcher's addition.
Hillman William, blacksmith, 306 and 310 Virginia ave.
Hilt Charles W., salesman Edgar and Frazee, bds. Palmer House.
Hilt Frank L., carriage blacksmith, bds. 72 W. Maryland.
Himbough Joseph, laborer, res. 44 N. East.
Hinckley D. J., clerk B. R. R., office, bds. Bates house.
Hinde Edward, clerk Miss M. E. Hinde, 155 E. Washington.
HINDE MISS M. E., groceries and provisions, under Littles Hotel.
Hinde P. J., groceries and provisions, res. Massachusetts ave. cor. Delaware.

Hinds F., res. 74 N. East.
Hinds Jesse, brickmason, res. 74 N. East.
Hinds Soloman, brickmason, res. 38 N. East.
Hine Charles, laborer, res. N. Davidson.
Hiner Jacob, laborer, Kregelo, Blake & Co.
HINES EDWARD, professor of music and dancing, bds. 18 N. East.
HINES C. C., attorney, office Johnston's Building, E. Washington, res. 152 N. Pennsylvania.
Hinesley Andrew J., (H. & Hereth,) res. 119 Massachusetts ave.
HINESLEY & HERETH, saddles, harness and saddlery hardware, 34 W. Washington.
Hinesley John, butcher, bds. National Hotel.
Hinesley William, (Allen & H.,) res. 56 S. Illinois,
Hinesley William, butcher, bds. National Hotel.
Hininger George, laborer, res. 51 E. St. Joseph.
Hinton James, carpenter, res. 155 E. Massachusetts ave.
Hirsching Theodore, architect, bds. 61 N. Illinois.
Hiser Charles, blacksmith, bds. cor. North and Noble.
Hiss Frederick, shoemaker, bds. 89 N. Illinois.
Hitchcock Alex., secret police, res. 119 N. Alabama.
Hitcomb Phillip, laborer, res. New York bet. Pennsylvania and Meridian.
Hobbs Abner, res. 10 N. Mississippi.
Hobbs Rev. A. J., (Christian,) res. 159 N. New Jersey.
Hobson John, machinist, I. & C. R. R., bds. 51 S. Louisiana.
Hobt Robert, res. 209 N. Alabama.
Hockersmith Thomas M., baggagemaster I. & C. R. R., bds. Tremont house.
Hodgson Isaac, architect, room 5 Glenn's block, res. N. Meridian.
Hoefgean Samuel B., law student, bds. N. 44 Pennsylvania.
Hoehn Rev. Matthias, (G. E. Association,) alley, bet. New Jersey and East.
Hoereth George J., carpenter, res. 137 N. East.
Hoffman Casper, blacksmith, res. 224 N. Alabama.
Hoffman Henry, tannery, bet. Washington and Maryland, res. 197 E. Washington.
Hoffman Jacob, paper box maker, res. cor. Alabama and Washington.
Hoffman John, brewer, bds. 135 W. Maryland.
Hoffman Michael, blacksmith, res. 63 Bluff road.
Hoffman Valentine, laborer, res. 68 S. Noble.
Hoffman W., laborer, res. 64 S. Noble.
Hofmeister Christian, grocer, bds. 82 N. Noble.
Hofmeister Joseph, shoemaker, res. 70 N. Noble.
Hofmeister Nicholas, grocer, 82 N. Noble, res. same.

Hogan M., bds. California House.
Hogan Mrs. Julia, seamstress, res. 168 E. Ohio.
Hohl Christopher, clerk, res. 160 E. Washington.
HOHL CHRISTIAN, grocery, 77 E. Washington, res. same.
Hoiley Morris, laborer, bds. 55 S. Illinois.
Holbrook Asa, shoemaker, bds. W. Washington.
Holbrook Henry C., Bryant's Commercial College, res. 77 N. Alabama.
Holbrook Thomas E., book-keeper, res. 77 N. Alabama.
Holland Charles E., clerk J. W. Holland, res. 58 N. Pennsylvania.
Holland Charles W., res. 140 W. Market.
Holland Dennis, laborer, res. N. Winston.
Holland Dorey, clerk J. W. Holland, bds. 126 E. Washington.
Holland G. B., agent with M. Seybold & Co., bds. 21 Ohio.
HOLLAND JOHN W., wholesale grocer and commission merchant, 72 E. Washington, res. 58 N. Pennsylvania.
Holland John, laborer, res. 177 East.
Holland John, carpenter, res. 219 S. Delaware.
Holland T. F., book-keeper J. W. Holland, bds. cor. Alabama and Washington.
Holler Geo., stone mason, res. 154 N. New Jersey.
Holler John, laborer, res. 177 S. East.
Holler Phillip, laborer, res. 117 N, Noble.
Holley Theodore, shoemaker, res. 9 Liberty, cor. Market.
HOLLIDAY ADAM, local agent Bellefontaine Railroad, res. 59 N. Meridian.
Holliday Elias, school teacher, bds. 17 W. Georgia.
HOLLIDAY ELIAS G., attorney at law and notary public, res. 17 W. Georgia.
HOLLIDAY REV. F. C., presiding elder M. E. Church, 117 E. Ohio.
Holliday Gideon, agent patent medicine, res. 106 N. Meridian.
Holliday John H., res. 102 N. Alabama.
Holliday Samuel, conductor L. & I. Railroad, bds. American House.
Holliday Samuel, laborer, res. 118 N. Meridian.
Holliday Wm. J., (Murphy & H.,) res. 85 N. Meridian.
Holliday W. F., clerk Tousey & Byram, bds. 117 E. Ohio.
HOLLOWAY C. B., exchange dealer, notary public and collecting agent, 6½ W. Washington, up stairs, res. 9 E. North.
Holman Isaac W., salesman Merrill & Co.
Holman Geo. G., res. 60 N. Pennsylvania.

8

Holman Milton C., teacher in Indiana Institute for the Education of the Blind.
Holman James B., clerk Holman & Bro., bds. 60 N. Pennsylvania.
Holman Joseph W., (H. & Bro.,) bds. Palmer House.
Holmes Henry, plasterer, res. California.
HOLMES WM. H., general western agent Pennsylvania Railroad, res. S. W. cor. Illinois and Ohio.
HOLMES & NEIL, wholesale egg and packing establishment, 184 E. Washington.
Holmes Samuel, (H. & Neil,) res. N. New Jersey.
Holt wid. Franklin, res. 87 N. East.
Holton Thomas, U. S. express messenger Bellefontaine Railroad, bds. Bates House.
Holter Wm., shoemaker, bds. 51 S. Illinois.
Holtzlaw Marshal, student Bryant's Commercial College, res. 44 N. Pennsylvania.
Holzer John, baker, bds. 55 Maryland.
Homan Jeremiah, laborer, res. 30 N. Davidson.
HOMBURG KONRADIN, M. D., office 24½ E. Washington, res. 161 N. Illinois.
Hook John, clerk Jefferson House.
Hooker E. M. B., printer Sentinel office, res. Buchanan, bet. Virginia ave and East.
Hooker Henry, clerk T. H. & R. Railroad office, res. 145 South.
Hopkins I. H., traveling agent for New York Central Railroad, res. 60 S. Illinois.
Hoppe George, saloon and res. 81 S. Meridian.
Hora Anthony, laborer, res. 96 W. New York.
Horn Henry J., dry goods merchant, res. 42 N. Mississippi.
Hornaday Anson D., carpenter, res. 118 N. East.
Hornaday John E., carpenter, res. 144 E. Walnut.
Horst Hermann, tailor, res. 275 S. Delaware.
Hort William, Washington Hall Saloon.
Hortmann O., shoemaker, bds. 34 N. Illinois.
HOSBROOK DANIEL B., surveyor, res. 108 N. Mississippi.
HOSHOUR SAMUEL K., A. M., president N. W. C. University, res. 84 Massachusetts ave.
Hoskins Josiah, engineer T. H. Engine House, res. 207 S. Alabama.
Hoskins Robert S., teamster, res. 160 E. Ohio.
Hoss George W., professor of mathematics, res. N. Wisconsin ave.
Hossfeld Charles, clerk, res. 212 E. Washington.
Hotz & Co., merchant tailors, Illinois, bet. Georgia and Louisiana.

Hotz George, (H. & Co.,) bds. Farmers' Hotel.

Houlton John, driver American Express wagon, bds. American House.

Houper Isaac, railroad employee, res. 35 S. Liberty.

Houpt Robert, dry goods, 209 Alabama, res. same.

Housum Martin, printer Atlas office, bds. 22 S. Meridian.

Houzlot Peter, stone mason, res. 137 N. Railroad.

Hoverbet William, res. 71 Bright.

Howard Alexander C., publisher, Shelbyville State Road, S. of city.

HOWARD & CONWELL, physicians and surgeons, 52 S. Illinois.

Howard C. O., watch maker, bds. Bates House.

Howard C. L., sawyer at Gay & Stephen's, res. 73 Merrill.

Howard Dr. F., (H. & Conwell,) res. 52 S. Illinois.

Howard Henry, carpenter, res. 194 E. St. Clair.

Howard Samuel W., plasterer, res. 53 N. East.

Howard wid. John, res. 45 S. East.

Howarth John, printer Herald and Era, bds. Mrs. Hoyt.

Howes Henry, carpenter, res. 79 Massachusetts ave.

Howland J. D., (Barbour & H.,) res. Tennessee, N. E. cor. Vermont.

Hoyt Daniel W., bds. 52 S. Delaware.

Hoyt Mrs. Harriet, millinery and dress making, 52 S. Delaware, res. same.

Hubbard Samuel N., last turner, res. 149 S. Tennessee.

Hubbard William, manufacturer of pressed brick, res. Circle.

Hudley Patrick, 75 Bright.

Hudson Mrs. Josephine, dress maker, res. 71 E. Market.

Huestis Zeph, conductor I. & C. Railroad, bds. Palmer House.

Huey Miss Sinesia, milliner and dress maker, bds. 18 N. Illinois.

Huff John E., confectioner, 76 E. Washington, res. same.

Huffer James M., saddle maker, bds. Pyle House.

Hug Matthew, watch maker, bds. 103 E. Washington.

HUG MARTIN, proprietor Capital Saloon, 14 E. Washington, res. 45 N. New Jersey.

Hug Joseph, waiter Capital Saloon, res. Washington, E. of Noble.

Huggins William, brickmoulder, 312 S. Delaware.

Hughes Nixon, res. 229 S. Pennsylvania.

Hughey William, res. 86 S. Louisiana.

Hugo Charles D., plasterer, res. 33 N. Noble.

HULINGS JOHN P., painter and glazier, 12½ S. Pennsylvania, res. E. Washington, near Bates' City Mills.

Hume James M., (H. A. Fletcher & Co.,) bds. cor. Pennsylvania and Market.

Hume Newton, clerk H. A. Fletcher & Co., bds. Pyle House.

Humphrey James W., res. 148 E. New York.

Hunt Aaron L., auctioneer with Gott & Featherston, res. 15 Lockerbie.

Hunt C., 15 Lockerbie, bet. East and Liberty.

Hunt C., teacher Fifth Ward, bds. 94 N. Illinois.

HUNT CHARLES C., cigars and tobacco, 61½ E. Washington, res. same.

HUNT DAVID B., general business agent, bds. 78 Massachusetts ave.

Hunt Jacob, cigar maker G. F. Meyer, bds. Farmers' Hotel.

Hunt John C., res. 94 N. Illinois.

Hunt Jesse C., clerk, res. 164 S. Alabama.

Hunt Mrs. Julia, res. 5 Circle.

Hunt Louisa A., bds. 78 Massachusetts ave.

Hunt Mrs. Mary A. H., bds. 78 Massachusetts ave.

HUNT P. G. C., dentist, 7 W. Maryland, res. same.

Hunter Belle, music teacher, bds. 125 E. New York.

Hunter Ralph, machinist, res. 188 E. Ohio.

Hurd Eugene T., bookbinder, bds. 26 N. West.

Hurd D. D., res. 26 N. West.

Hurrle Ignatius, tailor, res. 7 N. Railroad.

Husband Linza, (col.,) bds. 156 Canal.

Hushkop William, carpenter, 295 S. Delaware.

Huston Cephas B., clerk Root, Bennett & Co., E. Washington, res. 129 Massachusetts ave.

Huston William H., forger, bds. Michigan Road.

Hustus John, fireman T. H. & R. R. R., bds. 141 W. Market.

Hutchins Henry H., book-keeper J. K. Sharpe, res. 148 Virginia ave.

HUTCHINSON CHARLES P., foreman job room Sentinel Office, bds. 27 Indiana ave.

Hutchinson William, machinist, res. 72 N. East.

Hyatt J. A., stone cutter, 159 S. Alabama.

HYDE ABNER R., proprietor Little's Hotel, cor. Washington and New Jersey.

HYDE REV. N. A., pastor Congregational Church, study in Congregational Church.

Hyland James, brick mason, res. 148 N. East.

Hyland Michael, res. N. Illinois.

Hypher William, porkpacker, res. 153 E. Market.

I

IGOE MARTIN, attorney, notary public and insurance agent, 70 E. Washington, res. 16 Lockerbie.

Iler Margaret Mrs., res. 101 N. Railroad.
Iliff Charles E., clerk Moses Myer.
Iliff Richard W., res. 37 N. Alabama.
IMBERY AUGUSTUS, prop'r St. Charles saloon and billiards, 86 E. Washington, res. 13 N. New Jersey.
Imes Mrs. Mary A., res. 109 N. Meridian.
Ince Joseph, shoemaker, res. 176 Massachusetts ave.
INDIANA CENTRAL FREIGHT DEPOT, Delaware, bet. Georgia and Louisiana.
INDIANA CENTRAL R. R. CO., office junction Virginia ave. and Maryland.
INDIANA FARMER, (weekly,) J. N. Ray, editor and publisher, office over Post Office.
INDIANA FEMALE COLLEGE, (Methodist,) No. 16 N. Meridian.
INDIANA FREE PRESS, (German,) R. Henninger, prop'r, Theodore Hielscher, editor, 83 E. Washington.
Indiana House, E. Market.
INDIANA STATE SENTINEL, Daily and Weekly, Bingham & Doughty, prop'rs, 16, 18 and 20 E. Washington.
Indiana State Arsenal, Delaware, bet. Washington and Market.
INDIANA VOLKSBLATT, (German,) Julius Bœtticher, proprietor, 13 E. Washington.
INDIANAPOLIS BRANCH BANKING CO., S. W. cor. Washington and Pennsylvania, Calvin Fletcher, Pres., Thomas H. Sharpe, Cashier.
INDIANAPOLIS & CINCINNATI R. R. OFFICE, cor. Delaware and Louisiana.
INDIANAPOLIS CAR WORKS, Bellefontaine Road, head of Massachusetts ave.
INDIANAPOLIS DAILY & WEEKLY JOURNAL, published by Indianapolis Journal Co., 8 S. Pennsylvania, new building Circle, cor. Meridian.
INDIANAPOLIS GAS LIGHT & COKE CO., cor. Pennsylvania and Louisiana, office S. W. cor. Meridian and Washington.
INDIANAPOLIS FEMALE INSTITUTE, 34 E. Michigan.
INDIANAPOLIS INSURANCE CO., T. A. Morris, Pres't, S. F. Covington, Sec'y, office 14 and 16 S. Meridian.
INDIANAPOLIS LIFE INSURANCE CO., office 14 S. Meridian.
INDIANAPOLIS ROLLING MILL CO., J. M. Lord, Pres't and Sup't, C. B. Parkman, Sec'y, cor. Merrill and Mississippi.
Indicut Rev. John W., (Methodist Epis.,) res. 86 alley, bet. Missouri and West.
Ingersoll B. F., engineer, bds. 233 S. Delaware.

Ingersoll Henry W., (Sloan, & I.,) res. 152 S. New Jersey.
Ingersoll Miss S. J., music teacher, Indianapolis Female
    Institute.
Inlow A., laborer, res. 63 N. Spring.
Iredall William, at Osgood, Smith & Co.'s, res. 103 S. Ten-
    nessee.
Irick Adam, laborer, res. 9 alley, bet. East and Liberty.
Irick William C., bricklayer, res. 174 N. New Jersey.
Irick William H., brickmason, 156 N. New Jersey.
Irvin Benjamin, bds. 245 W. Washington.
Irwin Mrs. Ann, 165 S. Tennessee.
Irwin wid. John, res. 217 S. Alabama.
Irwin Mrs. M., res. 139 N. New Jersey.
Irwin Robbins, with Wm. Brown, 150 New Jersey.
Irwin Mrs. Sophia, res. 137 E. Washington.
Ittenbach Geo. & Co., groceries and provisions, 180 S. Dela-
    ware.

J

Jackson wid. Charles, 70 S. Noble.
Jackson John, waiter Tremont House.
JACKSON WILLIAM N., ticket agent, Union Depot, bds.
    53 S. Meridian.
Jackson William, roofer, res. 126 E. Market.
Jacksonian Abraham, laborer, S. of Madison R. R.
Jacobs Valentine, marble cutter, 26 S. Meridian, res. 105 N.
    Noble.
JACQUET ADOLPH, French wine dealer and brewer,
    278 E. Washington.
Jaenke Edward, clerk C. Volmer, bds. Union Hall.
Jakin John, grocer, Indiana ave., cor. North.
James J. W., laborer, res. City Hospital.
JAMES SETH C., marble works, 104 S. Illinois, res. 14 E.
    Ohio.
James Wilson W., draftsman, bds. Macy House.
Jameson Alexander C., clerk City Treasurer's office, res. 97
    W. South.
JAMESON & FUNKHOUSER, physicians and surgeons,
    5 S. Meridian.
JAMESON JAMES M., City Treasurer, office Odd Fellows
    Hall, res. 74 N. Illinois.
JAMESON REV. L. H., (Christian,) res. 97 W. South.
Jameson P. H., (J. & Funkhouser,) res. 51 N. Alabama.
Jasper Frederick, laborer, res. 116 S. Noble.
Jay Albert, teamster, bds. 42 N. Alabama.
Jay wid. Stacy, plain sewer, 42 N. Alabama.

Jeager & Schmidt, brewers, Wyoming, bet. Alabama and New Jersey.

Jean Nicholas, carpenter, res. 38 N. Spring.

Jefferson Robert, carpenter, res. 37 McAllister.

Jeffersonville R. R. freight office, 43 E. South.

Jeffrey Mrs. Mary B., boarding house, res. 150 W. Washington.

Jeffrey Cyrus, bds. 150 W. Washington.

Jempel Michael, 326 S. Delaware.

Jenison Alexander F., clerk No. 9 W. Ohio.

Jenison G. M., jeweler, W. H. Talbott & Co., res. 9 W. Ohio.

Jenison Mrs. Harriett, 9 W. Ohio.

Jenkins A. W., clerk, res. 70 N. Alabama.

Jenkins Ebenezer, house painter, rear of Bates House.

Jenkins Mrs. Elizabeth, res. 52 N. Spring.

Jenkins John, foundryman, res. 227 S. Alabama.

Jenkins John R., house painter, res. 114 N. Missouri.

Jennings J. W., American Express messenger, bds. 19 Circle, cor. Market.

Jennings Patrick, teacher, res. 182 S. Pennsylvania.

Jennings William T., tinner, res. 87 N. East.

Joachime Augustus, chandler, res. cor. Mississippi and Maryland.

Jock John, showman, bds. 212 W. Washington.

JOHN CHARLES, market master, res. 199 E. Washington.

Johns Samuel E., bookbinder Sheets & Braden.

Johnson Aaron, trader, res. 151 W. Washington.

JOHNSON BENJAMIN F., saloon, basement of Palmer House.

Johnson Edward, carpenter, bds. W. H. Lingenfelter.

Johnson Edwin, bds. 81 S. East.

Johnson George, (col.,) works at Wm. Johnson.

Johnson George H., clerk A. D. Wood, 71 E. Washington, res. 70 S. East.

Johnson Hubbard G., salesman Tousey & Byram, E. Washington, bds. 121 E. Ohio.

Johnson James, clerk, bds. S. Illinois.

Johnson Miss Maria, milliner, 3 N. Meridian.

Johnson Mrs. Mary A., res. 237 Indiana ave.

Johnson Marquis L., cabinet maker, res. 184 S. Pennsylvania.

Johnson Peter, laborer Patterson's mills, res. Blake, bet. Washington and Market.

Johnson Phillip A., carpenter, res. 155 N. East.

Johnson Robert, res. W. North.

Johnson Samuel Law, printer Sentinel office, bds. 79 E. Washington.

Johnson William J., salesman Wm. N. Spinney, bds. Macy House.

Johnson William, res. 160 Blake.

Johnson William, res. 110 Blake.

Johnson William, grocer, res. 167 S. Tennessee.

Johnson William W., printer, Sentinel office, res. 112 E. Vermont.

Johnston Fidella, res. 184 N. East.

JOHNSTON DR. JOHN F., dentist, 11 W. Maryland, res. same.

Johnston John G., blacksmith, res. 74 E. Louisiana.

JOHNSTON OLIVER, livery and sale stable, Pearl, res. South.

Johnston Samuel A., clerk Boston store, res. 86 E. Vermont.

Johnston Mrs. Sophia, res. 24 S. Maryland.

Johnston Wm. J., (Munson & J.,) res. 86 E. Vermont.

Jolly Miss Jessie, 4 S. Meridian.

Jolly John, laborer, res. 11 E. Lord.

Jolley Joseph A., blacksmith, res. 154 N. Delaware.

Jolly William, fireman, bds. 11 E. Lord.

Jones Aquilla, (Vinnedge & Jones,) res. 79 N. Pennsylvania.

JONES BARTON D., local editor Indianapolis Journal, bds. American House.

Jones Brown, mason, res. 137 N. Alabama.

Jones Edward B., smith Bellefontaine R. R., bds. S. Delaware.

Jones Isaiah, (col.,) driver Bates House.

Jones Jesse, res. 106 N. Illinois.

Jones John, clerk Vinnedge & Jones, bds. 79 N. Pennsylva.

Jones J. W., butcher, bds. National Hotel.

Jones John W., checkman T. H. & R. R. R.

Jones Lewis H., harness maker, res. 106 W. Vermont.

Jones Mrs. Mary, res. 154 W. Vermont.

JONES NED R., conductor T. H. & R. R. R., res. Georgia bet. Illinois and Tennessee.

Jones Samuel, (col.,) barber Bates House shaving saloon, bds. Pyle House.

Jones Spicer, bridge builder, res. 206 N. Illinois.

JONES & VAN BLARICUM, wagon manufacturers, 6, 8, 10 and 12 E. Maryland.

Jones W. H., (J. & Van Blaricum,) res. 115 W. Maryland.

Jones William B., switchman Union Track, bds. Ray House.

JONES WILSON & CO., wholesale and retail grocers, N. E. cor. Meridian and Maryland.

Jones Wilson, (W. Jones & Co.,) res. 205 N. Illinois.

Jordan Mrs. Elizabeth, res. 67 S. Pennsylvania.

Jordan Gilmore, clerk Auditor's office, res. 18 S. West.

Jordan Joseph, teamster, 33 Union.

Jordan Miles, laborer, res. 189 N. New Jersey.
Jordan Phineas, apprentice Herald & Era office, bds. 67 S.
    Pennsylvania.
Jordan Samuel I., tailor, 157 cor. Mississippi and Garden.
JORDAN THOMAS, wholesale and retail grocer, 9 W.
    Washington, res. 12 N. East.
JORDON J. & J., feed store, 50 South.
Jordon James, (J. & J. Jordon,) res. 50 South.
Jordon John, (J. & J. Jordon,) res. 50 South.
Jose Albert, clerk N. Jones.
Jose Nicholai, cabinet maker and furniture dealer, 21 S.
    Meridian.
Joseph J. G., clerk, bds. 100 Illinois.
Joseph Sarah, bds. A. Franco, W. Washington.
Judd Ozias E., res. 161 N. Noble.
Judd Harvey, railroader, bds. 91 S. Illinois.
Judge John, 15 Willard.
Judge James, laborer, 127 South.
Judson Charles, clerk Bates House.
JUDSON WILLIAM, prop'r Bates House, cor. Illinois and
    Washington.
Jakes Israel, 15 Willard.
Justus James, clerk H. K. Eastman.
Kœffeld Frederick, barkeeper State House saloon, res. 95
    W. Washington.
Kael Conrad, pump maker, res. 59 New Jersey.
Kahn Casper, cabinet maker, res. 172 E. Michigan.
Kahn Earnest, tailor, bds. Ohio bet. Liberty and Noble.
Kahn Jacob, salesman with D. Franco.
Kaiser Adam, boot and shoemaker, bds. 138 W. Washington.
Kalb Henry, laborer, res. 98 St. Joseph.
Kalb Phillip, laborer, res. 65 E. St. Marys.
Kale David, mail agent I. & C. R. R., res. 135 N. East.
Kaling Andrew, shoemaker with Vinnedge & Jones, res. 91
    St. Joseph.
KALISCH B., dyeing and scouring, 11 N. Illinois.
KALOR JOHN, hackman, car No. 16, res. 66 W. Vermont.
Kamm Mrs. Nancy, res. 70 N. Spring.
KAMM GOTTLIEB, groceries and provisions, 322 Virginia
    ave
Kampman M., laborer, res. 58 Massachusetts ave.
Kappel John, school teacher, res. 144 E. Ohio.
Karcher John, res. Union.
Karle Christian, boot and shoe dealer, 79 E. Washington, res.
    72 Delaware.
Karle Joseph, boot and shoemaker, 64 E. Washington, res.
    35 South.
Kares Joseph, carpenter, res. 58 N. Davidson.

Kassick John, grocer, res. 43 S. West.
Kathe William, watchman, res. 69 N. Davidson.
Kaufman Adam, laborer, res. 14 Garden.
Kaufman Adam, collar maker, res. 128 N. Tennessee.
Kautt George F., shoemaker, res. S. Delaware.
Keating Jeffery, laborer, res. 328 S. Delaware.
Keefe James, laborer, res. 199 Ohio.
Keehn H. W., clerk J. & G. Bradshaw, bds. Pyle House.
Keeler George W.. res. 210 N. Alabama.
Keeler William, laborer, res. 44 N. Spring.
Keely Daniel, sr., brick mason, res. 124 E. Ohio.
Keely Daniel, jr., brick mason, bds. E. Ohio.
Keely H. St. Clair, printer Sentinel Office, bds. 159 E. Ohio.
     cor. Liberty.
KEELY ISAAC I., physician, bds. 62 E. Michigan.
Keely John, brick mason, res. 48 N. East.
Keely Oliver, brick mason, res. 159 E. Ohio.
Keely Samuel, brick mason, res. E. North.
Keely William, carpenter, res. 62 E. Michigan.
Keely William H., grocer, 19 N. Noble, res. 163 E. Ohio.
Keese William N., carpenter, 144 North, cor. Blake.
Keeshan Mrs Mary, res. alley, bet. Ohio and New York.
Kehlhans John, currier with John Fishback, res. Market,
     bet. New Jersey and Alabama.
Kehling Andrew, shoemaker, res. 91 St. Joseph.
Keil Conrad, pump maker, res. 69 N. New Jersey.
Keil John, cook Farmers' Hotel.
Kein Ernest, bds. Ohio, cor. Noble.
Keistner Henry, bds. 60 South.
Kekar wid. William, res 186 N. New Jersey.
Keller Frederick, editor Free Press, E. Washington, res.
     alley, bet. New York and Vermont.
Kellermeyer C., laborer, bds. 155 S. Alabama.
Kellermeyer Henry, shoemaker, res. 155 S. Alabama.
Keleyhan Michael, laborer, res. 27 Ellsworth.
Kellinger John, carpenter, res. 146 E. Market.
KELLY MRS. ANN, millinery and fancy goods, 3 N. Meri-
     dian, res. N. Meridian.
Kelly & Fetrow, flour and feed store, Virginia ave.
Kelly H., res. 174 E. Washington.
Kelly James, trader, 66 Bluff Road,
Kelly James, (col.,) boarding house, 145 W. Washington.
Kelly James, res. W. end North,
Kelly wid. Mary, res. Washington, S. E. cor. East.
Kelly Patrick, laborer, res. 168 E. Ohio.
Kelly Thomas, laborer, bds. 55 S. Illinois.
Kelly Thomas, currier Mooneys & Co., res. 98 S. Illinois.
Kelly William, butcher, bds. 22 Indiana ave.

Kellogg Henry S., jr., salesman City hardware store, 12 W. Washington.

Kellogg Justen A., bds. 87 N. Meridian.

KELLOGG NEWTON, edge tool manufacturer, W. Washington, near River.

Kemper Charles, groceries and provisions, res. 12 McCarty.

Kemper Henry, carpenter, bds. 114 S. New Jersey.

Kemper John M., pattern maker, res. 122 S. New Jersey.

Kendrick James, student Bryant's College, bds. Dr. Kendrick.

Kendrick Oscar H., dentist, res. 132 N. Davidson.

KENDRICK WM. H., physician, 33 N. East, res. 35 N. East.

Kennedy James, res. 21 Benton.

Kennedy James H., carpenter, res. 75 N. Mississippi.

Kennedy L., laborer, res. 320 S. Delaware.

Kennedy Thomas, house and sign painter, S. Meridian.

Kennedy Thomas, laborer, res. Virginia ave.

Kennet William, baker, res. 112 E. Washington.

Kennington Robert, blacksmith Bellefontaine R. R. shop, res. 35 S. Georgia.

Kentzel Edward L., boot maker, bds. Mrs. Ferguson.

Kentzel John, shoemaker, bds. Mrs. Ferguson.

Kentzel Joseph S., bookkeeper Herald and Era, bds. 36 N. East.

Kentzel Wm. G., bds. 36 N. East.

Kenzelmeyer Wm., Farmers' Hotel.

Keohlin John, hack driver, res. 56 W. Vermont.

Keran Mrs. Mary, laundress. res, 79 E. Market.

Kerber John M., telegraph operator, bds. American House.

Kerby Jacob, res. 153 W. Michigan.

Kerle Christ. boot and shoe maker, 79 East Washington, res. 72 Delaware.

Kern Casper, cabinet maker, res. 172 E. Washington.

Kern Jacob, with W. Dagget, 172 cor. Michigan and Railroad.

Kern John, tailor, 38 Bluff road.

Kerns John, laborer, res. 9 N. Railroad.

Kern Lewis, porter H. A. Fletcher & Co., res. 72 E. Michigan.

Kern Patrick. steward Little's Hotel.

Kerper John M., operator L. & I. R. R. telegraph office, res. 28 Indiana ave.

KETCHAM & COFFIN, attorneys at law, Blackford's building, Washington.

Ketcham John L., (K. & Coffin,) res. 97 E. Merrill.

Kettenbach Edward, tinner, bds. 214 N. Noble.

KETTENBACH HENRY, grocer, 207 Massachusetts ave., res. 214 N. Noble.

Kevill Robert L., copper, tin and sheet iron worker, res. 70 E. Louisiana.

KEYS WM. A., marble dealer, 26 S. Meridian, res. Georgia, W. of Canal.

Kichdson Wm., stone cutter, res. 60 N. Noble.

Kiemer James H., (col.,) blacksmith, res. 82 alley N. West.

KIGER HARRY, attorney at law, S. E. cor. Washington and Meridian.

Kihn Ernst, tailor, bds. 173 E. Ohio.

KILE, CLEVELAND & CO., book agents, opposite Union Depot.

Kile G. W., book agent, res. 112 N. New Jersey.

Kiley John, porter with S. S. Avery, bds. 144 Pennsylvania.

Killehar Mike, laborer, bds. Kilkeny Hotel.

Killinger John, carpenter, res. 146 E. Market.

Kimmell George, conductor T. & R. R. R., bds. Tremont House.

Kimley William, works at Central depot, bds. Cincinnati House.

Kinder Charles, gunsmith, bds. 49 S. Illinois.

Kinder Mrs. M. W., boarding house, 79½ E. Washington.

Kindler Charles, locksmith, bds. Illinois, S. of Washington.

Kindy Leary, laborer, res. 320 S. Delaware.

King Cornelius, (Walker & K.,) res. 141 N. Ohio.

King David, carpenter, res. 157 N. Mississippi.

King E., res. 97 N. Meridian.

KING FRANCIS, secretary Masonic Grand Lodge, office under Masonic Hall, res. 72 N. Tennessee.

King H., bds. 71 Indiana ave.

King H. L., express messenger Adams Express Co., bds. Palmer House.

King John B., gas fitter, bds. 41 Mississippi.

King Peter, moulder, res. 270 S. Delaware.

King Robert H., res. 71 Indiana ave.

King W. H., clerk B. R. R. office, bds. Mrs. Kinder.

KINGSLEY A. S., proprietor Macy House, cor. Illinois and Market.

King W. L., express messenger Adams & Co., Ind. & Cin. R. R., bds. Bates House.

Kingman Nelson, tinner and salesman W. A. Mars, res. 127 Massachusetts ave.

Kingsbury John R., grocer, res. 181 Massachusetts ave.

Kinnan Augustus, marble polisher, bds. 151 Ohio.

Kinner Theodore, land agent, res. 133 N. West.

Kinney H. P., tailor, res. 34 S. West.

Kinning Thomas, laborer, 61 S. Noble.

Kinsel George, laborer, res. 139 E Washington.
Kinsey Mrs. Elizabeth, bds. 145 cor. Michigan and West.
Kinsler Patrick, division master Ind. & Laf. R. R., res. 204 N. Mississippi.
Kirby James, res. 109 E. South.
Kirby Thomas, cooper, res. 57 South.
Kirby Thomas, res. 109 E. South.
Kirby Zachariah, cooper, res. South.
Kirk Mrs. E., milliner, bds. 39 N. Pennsylvania.
Kirk N., res. 39 N. Pennsylvania.
KIRKLAND P., commission merchant, 73 S. Meridian, bds. Bates House.
Kirkwood George, workman I. & C. machine shop, res. S. side National road.
Kirkwood John, fireman, res. 12 Bates.
KIRLIN JAMES, dry goods and groceries, 36 W. Washington, res. N. Illinois, near city limits.
Kirstner Frederick, clerk with John Fishback, res. 56½ Market.
Kissel Benjamin, American Express messenger I. & St. L. R. R., bds. Bates House.
Kissel Frederick, house and sign painter, 55 N. Liberty, res. same.
Kissel Jacob W., huckster, res. 175 Massachusetts ave.
Kisten Wm., carrier, res. 20 Pennsylvania.
Kister Rev. C., pastor Presbyterian Church, res. 241 S. Delaware.
KISTNER ADAM, proprietor California House, 136 S. Illinois, near Union Depot.
Kistner Henry, shoemaker, res. South.
Kistner John G., boot and shoe dealer, 51 S. Illinois, res. same.
KITCHEN J. M., physician and surgeon, office S. W. cor. Washington and Meridian, res. 67 N. Pennsylvania.
Kittel N. W., American Express messenger Peru Railroad.
Kizer John, carpenter, res. 72 E. St. Clair.
Klaiber John L., confectionery, 81 E. Washington, res. same.
Klause Frederick, carpenter, 63 Union.
Klausman Louis, res. 63 E. St. Mary's.
Klein Emel, physician, res. 100 E. New York.
Kleitz George T., salesman New York Store.
Klerrin Henry, res. 173 S. Delaware.
KLINE HENRY, brokers office, 77 S. Illinois, res. 55 South.
Kline Nicholas, shoemaker, res. N. Spring.
Klingensmith wid ——, 173 S. Delaware.

Klingensmith Isreal, professor in Bryant's Commercial College.

Klotz Emil, (K. & Pfafflin,) res. 61 Illinois, bet. New York and Ohio.

KLOTZ & PFAFFLIN, wholesale and retail dealers in fancy articles, 29 W. Washington.

Knauff Adam, baker, 248 W. Washington, res. same.

Knapton James, stone cutter, res. 56 N. Noble.

Knaus Charles, clerk National Saloon, bds. same.

KNAUS S., baker N. side E. Washington, res. same·

Knause William J., miller, bds. California House.

Kneipe John, carpenter, res. 160 N. Liberty.

Knefler Frederick, deputy county clerk, res. 11 E. Michigan.

Knepper James S., shoemaker and brick mason, res. 67 Spring.

KNIGHT ELIJAH, boarding house, 17 and 21 Kentucky ave, res. same.

Knight John, (Cottrell & K.,) bds. Ray House.

Knight James, laborer, res. S. Missouri.

Knight Newton, painter, res. 81 W. Maryland.

KNODLE A. & SON, manufacturers and dealers in boots and shoes, 32 E. Washington.

Knodle Adam, (A. K. & Son,) 8 Indiana ave.

Knodle George, (A. Knodle & Son,) bds. 8 Indiana ave.

KNOTTS NIM K., sign and ornamental painter, office 35½ E. Washington, res. 51 N. New Jersey.

Knopper James S., shoemaker, res. 67 N. Spring.

Kobb John A., grocer, 69 S. Illinois.

Koch George, boot and shoe maker, bds. 174 E. Washington.

Koch H. H., boot and shoe maker, 53 E. South, res. N. Noble.

Koch Henry, laborer, res. 185 N. East.

Kock wid. John, res. 20 Chatham.

Kock Thomas, laborer Kregelo, Blake & Co.

Koehne Charles J., salesman J. S. Wilson, res. 178 Ohio

Koeniger George, groceries and provisions, 60 South, res. same.

Koestle Jacob, City Bakery, 201 E. Washington, res. same.

Kohlback John, blacksmith, bds. 168 S. Delaware.

Kolb Dewit, turner, res. E. Georgia.

Kolb J. A., grocer, S. Illinois, bet. Georgia and Union Depot, res. same.

KOLB LOUIS, wood turner, Georgia, near Pennsylvania.

Kolb William, boarding, 30 Kentucky ave.

KOLLER & COOK, dry goods and groceries, 189 E. Washington.

Koller E. A., (K. & Cook,) res. E. Washington.
KOLLMEYER JOHN C., Eagle Saloon, 138 E. Washington, res. same.
Kolthoff Hendrich, laborer, res. 141 N. Liberty.
Koontz Peter, tailor, bds. 229 N. Tennessee.
Kowen William, teamster, res. 155 E. New York.
Kragle Joseph, cistern builder, res. Market.
Kramer Henry, butcher, res. 71 E. St. Mary.
Kramer Henry, book binder, res. Delaware, near Maryland.
Krapton James, stone carver, res. 56 N. Noble.
Kraus Phillip, laborer, res. 66 E. St. Mary's
KREGELO, BLAKE & CO., planing, sash, doors, &c., cor. Canal and New York.
Kregelo David, (K., Blake & Co.,) 132 N. West.
Kregelo Jacob, sash maker, res. 40 E. St. Clair.
Kreger Christ, carpenter, bds. 45 E. Ohio.
Kreger Mrs. Christina, bds. 258 E. Washington.
Kreger Henry, currier Jno. Fishback, res. Market, bet. Tennessee and Mississippi.
Kretsch Matthew, cook Crystal Palace Saloon, 44 W. Washington.
Kretch Peter, (Speckman & K.,) res. Illinois.
Kropp Henry, gardener, res. S. side National road.
Krote Henry, currier with John Fishback, res. New Jersey, bet. Washington and Market.
Krozier George, salesman, New York Store.
KRUG G., grocery and provisions, 24 E. Georgia, res. same.
Kruse Christian, carpenter, 9 E. McCarty.
Kuehne Louis, musician, res. 67 N. New Jersey.
Kuester Edward, with Lichtenhein & Son, 85 E. Washington.
Kuester Wm. res. 85 E. Washington.
Kugelman William, cigar maker G. L. Meyer, 66 Indiana ave.
KUHLMANN E. H. L., groceries and provisions, 187 W. Washington.
Kuhn Charles, butcher, res. 107 Michigan.
Kuhn Henry, employee Bellefontaine R. R.
Kuhn William, baker, 181 E. Washington, res. same.
Kune Mrs. Caroline, res. 60 S. Meridian.
Kunkelman Rev. John A., pastor of 1st Lutheran Church, res. 136 N. Pennsylvania.
Kunklemann J., employee Madison R. R.
Kuntmann ——, well digger, res. Massachusetts ave.
Kuntz George, clerk Hanlin & Barnett, bds. B. H. Beck.
Kushhover Casper, stone mason, res. 146 S. New Jersey.
Kustee Charles E., cigar maker, bds. 241 S. Delaware.
Kustner Frederick, res. 56½ E. Market.

Kutnecht Randolph, shoemaker, res. 269 N. Illinois.
Kyer David, tailor, 94 Fort Wayne ave.
Kyle C., (Hasket & K.,) res. New Jersey cor. Ohio.
Kyle James, laborer, res. 89 S. Tennessee.

L

Lachenae Charley, bootmaker, alley, bet. Delaware and
    Pennsylvania.
Lafever Samuel, bricklayer, res. 84 Indiana ave.
Lagg George, showman, bds. 212 W. Washington.
Lahmann Charles, carpenter, bds. F. H. Lahmann, out side
    city limits.
Lahmann Frederick H., boot and shoe maker, E. Washing-
    ton, south side, E. of Michigan.
Lahr Henry, carpenter, res. 74 N. Noble.
Lahr Philip, carpenter, res. 72 N. Noble.
LAIMAN CHARLES, groceries and provisions, 317 Vir-
    ginia ave.
Laing Samuel, with R. L. & A. W. McOuat, res. 9 Missis-
    sippi.
Laird H., tinner, bds. 54 N. East.
Laird John, porter, bds. 139 N. Alabama.
Laird Robert, clothier, res. 54 N. East.
Laird Wm. H., bowling alley, Georgia, bet. Illinois and Me-
    ridian, res. 54 N. East.
Lake Joseph, carpenter, bds. 87 N. Indiana ave.
Lamaire H., school teacher, bds. among patrons.
Lamb Yancy, res. 166 S. New Jersey.
Lamb L. R., at Bryant's Commercial College.
Lambert James, (Ray & L.,) res. Ray House.
Lambley George W., sexton Robert's Chapel, res. 123 N.
    East.
Lamley Moses, salesman with A. Rosenthal.
Lancaster George, tinner, bds. 11 Noble.
LANCASTER WASHINGTON, manufacturer and dealer
    in boots and shoes, 12 S. Illinois, res. same.
Landaur Frederick M., porter, bds. W. Kolb.
LANDES JACOB, livery stable, 18 E. Maryland, bds. Pyle
    House.
Landes Thomas, res. 198 S. Delaware.
Landes Austin M., livery stable, 18 E. Maryland.
Landis M. M., freight agent T. H. & R. Railroad, res. 88 W.
    Maryland.
Landis Milton, (col.,) fireman, 170 North.
Lane Charles, conductor Bellefontaine Railroad, bds. Bates
    House.

Lane Uriah, laborer, res. 89 N. Noble.
Laner Peter, shoemaker, bds. 164 W. Washington.
LANG DAVID, deputy U. S. Marshal, res. 49 W. South.
Lang John H., cooper and brewer, bds. S. East.
LANG LEWIS, eating saloon, 17 E. Washington, res. same.
Lang William W., book binder, bds. David Lang.
Langbein Joseph, fancy goods and groceries, 160 E. Washington, res. same.
LANGENBERG HENRY H., wholesale and retail grocery and provisions, 134, cor. W. Washington and Mississippi.
Langsworth Mrs., res. 210 N. Alabama.
Lanum W. W., brakeman M. & I. Railroad, bds. Ray House.
LaRue William C., plasterer, bds. Pyle House.
Latz Henry, 59 Alabama.
Latheur William, teacher Indiana Institute for the Education of the Deaf and Dumb.
Laudeu Thomas, laborer, res. 198 S. Delaware.
Lauer Charles, bar keeper Empire Saloon, res. 54 Indiana ave.
Laux Mrs. Josephine, res. 270 E. Washington.
LAW GEORGE, carriage and wagon manufacturer and dealer, res. 113 N. Pennsylvania.
Lawler William, engineer Bates House, res. 184 S. East.
Lawrence Arthur W., grocer, 161 E. Ohio, res. 164 E. Ohio.
Lawrence Henry, res. East.
Laws Thomas, laborer, res. Elizabeth.
Lawson George W., res. 73 N. Missouri.
Lawson Joseph, Shakspearian reader, room rear of Sentinel Building.
Lawton Orin, laborer, 78 Madison ave.
Lawton Mrs. Susan A., private boarding, res. 71 W. Maryland.
Lawton Mrs. Sarah, res. 59 E. St. Mary's.
Lawton William E., bds. 71 W. Maryland.
Lax Mrs. Elizabeth, res. 178 E. Vermont.
Leach David J., laborer, 91 S. Tennessee.
Leam William, res. 144 East.
Leathers Wallace, 150 New Jersey.
Lebhene Charles, boot and shoe maker, opposite Madison Railroad Depot.
LEDLIE JOHN, proprietor Pearl Saloon Little's Hotel, res. 155 Virginia ave.
Lee B. J., clerk New York Store.
LEE MANDEVILLE G., editor and proprietor Herald and Era, res. 36 N. East.

9

Lehr F. A., carpenter, res. 98 N. East.
Leidy John, laborer, res. S. New Jersey.
LEIER ANTON, wholesale wines and liquors, 140 E. Washington, res. up stairs.
LEIMINGER & FERLING, barbers, cuppers and bleeders, Blackford's Building, E. Washington.
Leitus William, stone cutter, res. 79 Vermont.
Lemons William, brick layer, bds. 159 E. Ohio. .
Lendorme Emile, moulder, res. 168 E. Michigan.
Lennert Ferdinand G., stamping and embroidery, res. 16 S. Illinois, up stairs.
LENNERT SARAH E., embroidery stamper, 16 S. Illinois, up stairs, res. same.
Lentz Christian, laborer, res. 115 Fort Wayne ave.
Lenz Amel, turner, bds. East, S. of Union Railroad.
Leoine Louis, painter, res. 160 N. Noble.
Leonard Mrs. Abigail, nurse, 60 N. Delaware.
Leonard Michael, laborer, res. near Madison Depot.
Leplyeu John, photographer, res. 21 Michigan.
Lesges Nicholas, tailor, 3 W. Washington, res. Louisiana.
Lesman August, stone mason, res. 332 Virginia ave.
Levi Joseph, tinner, res. 191 W. Washington.
Levi Mrs. Mary, res. 74 W. Vermont.
Levering Amos, salesman New York Store.
Lewis Hiram T., teamster, res. 281 East.
Lewis John, at Rolling Mill, bds. 13 Willard.
LEWIS T. A., agent Great Western Dispatch, cor. Virginia ave. and Maryland, res. 14 W. North.
Lewis William, teamster, bds. 94 New Jersey,
Lex Jacob, pressman Sentinel office.
Lex Louis, pressman Indianapolis Journal, res. Vermont, near Noble.
LICHTENHEIN & SON, wholesale cigar manufacturers, 85 E. Washington.
Lichtenhein Zacherias, (Lichtenhein & Son.) res. 18 N. Delaware.
LIEBER HERMAN, gilt frames, mouldings and books, Ætna Building, res. 39 N. East.
Liebhart Joseph, dyer Ohio Woolen Factory, bds. Washing-House.
Liebrich Louis, porter Robert Browning, res. 111 W. Michigan.
Lilly Benjamin, machinist, bds. 42 Bates.
Lilly Jeremiah, (col.,) bds. Elizabeth.
LILLY J. O. D., superintendent L. & I. Railroad, 22 Louisiana, res. 28 Indiana ave.
Limar Frederick, res. 62 South.

Lindley Henry J., notary public and book-keeper, res. 23 Indiana ave.

Lindley Hiram, boarding, 45 N. Pennsylvania.

LINDLEY JACOB, importer of china, glass and queensware, Britania goods, &c., 16 W. Washington, res. 35 N. Meridian.

Lindley John M., clerk Jacob Lindley, bds. J. Lindley.

Lindeman Frank, clerk Wm. Shoppenhorst, bds. 101 E. Washington.

Lindorme William, laborer, res. 91 N. Railroad.

Line Isaac N., brick layer, res. 160 E. New York.

Lingenfelter William L., (Coburn & L.,) res. 83 N. Alabama.

Lingenfelter W. H., boarding, 19 Circle, cor. Market.

Lingins John, laborer, res. 330 S. Delaware.

Linn Adam, teamster, res. 246 S. Alabama.

Lippert Henry, laborer, res. 97 N. Railroad.

Lintner Amos, saloon, bds. 48 cor. St. Clair and West.

LINTNER C. H. & CO., groceries and provisions, Indiana ave., cor. Illinois.

Lintner Christian H., (C. H. L. & Co.,) bds. 48, cor. St. Clair and West.

Lintner Isaac, clerk C. H. Lintner & Co., bds. 48, cor. St. Clair and West.

Lintner John, (C. H. L. & Co.,) res. 48 N. West.

Lintner John C., res. 277 N. East.

Lintner Reuben, grocer, Crane's addition, bds. 48, cor. St. Clair and West.

Lisgas N., tailor, res. W. South.

Lister M., cor. Illinois and Vermont.

Lithgow Phillip M., machinist, res. 84 S. East.

Little Washington K., painter, res. 20 S. East.

LITTLE'S HOTEL, Abner R. Hyde, proprietor, cor. Washington and New Jersey.

Little Mrs. Mary E., res. 130 N. Alabama.

LITTLE MATTHEW, commission dealer, res. 167 E. Market.

Little wid. Joseph, res. 130 N. Alabama.

Little Wilber Franklin, printer, Herald and Era, bds. 130 N. Alabama.

Lock Henry, engineer, res. 30 W. North.

Locke Elam, checkman L. & I. Railroad, res. 163 N. Pennsylvania.

LOCKE ERIE, freight agent Indianapolis & Lafayette Railroad, office at Depot, res. 40 California.

LOCKE & BROTHER, insurance agents, 1 Blackford's Building, cor. Washington and Meridian.

Locke Josiah, (L. & Bro.,) res. 163 N. Pennsylvania.

LOCKE & MUNSON, lightning rod manufacturers and
    dealers, 1 Blackford's Building.
Lockhart Jacob, flour dealer, 5 S. Delaware.
Lockhart Warren T., deputy auditor. bds. Pyle House.
Lockwood C. F., student N. W. C. University, bds. 175 N.
    Alabama.
Lockwood Isaac, cooper, res. 35 N. East.
LOCOMOTIVE, (weekly,) Elder & Harkness, proprietors,
    2 S. Meridian, up stairs.
Logan Burnett, res. 155 South.
Logan John, moulder, bds. 258 S. Delaware.
Logan John, laborer, res. 217 S. Delaware.
Logan Leonard, feed store, near Madison Depot, res. 127
    South.
Logan Michael, laborer, res. 189 S. New Jersey.
Logan Patrick, laborer, res. 179 S. New Jersey.
Lohman Anthony, teamster, res. 120 E. Market.
Londeregger Fidel, porter, res. 64 St. Joseph.
Lonergan John, bds, 66 South.
Long Christ, res. 248 W. Washington.
Long D. D., house and sign painter, 28 S. Meridian, res.
    same.
Long E. C., grainer and marbler, res. 173 N. New Jersey.
Long Rev. E. D., res. 104 Virginia ave.
Long Rev. George, (Presbyterian,) res. 33 N. New Jersey.
Long H. C., carrier at Sentinel office, res. 33 N. New
    Jersey.
Long Joseph, shoemaker, res. 147 N. Pennsylvania.
LONG MATTHEW, undertaker, 28 S. Meridian, res. same.
Longenback William, drayman, res. 169 S. Alabama.
Looker I. A., brick mason, res. 164 N. Tennessee.
Loomis Wm. H., (Fletcher, Williams & L.,) res. 153 East.
LOOMIS A. O., bds. Little's Hotel.
Lord E. N., (H. A. Fletcher & Co.,) res. 91 E. Ohio.
Lord Frank B., conductor I. & C. R. R., bds. Bates House.
Lord Julian F., teacher of piano forte, 89 E. Ohio.
Lord H. C., director Union Railway Co., office Union Depot.
LORD J. M., President and Superintendent Indianapolis
    Rolling Mill Company, office 1 Blake's Commercial Row.
    res. 141 N. Illinois.
LOUCKS CORNELIUS, grocer, 165 Virginia ave, res. 46
    Benton.
Loucks C. R., painter, res. 125 N. Alabama.
Loucks David W., constable, bds. 23 Madison ave.
Loucks George, clerk with C. Loucks, bds. 46 Benton.
Loucks James, carpenter, res. 194 N. New Jersey.
Loucks William, carpenter, res. 123 N. Alabama.
Louden Andrew A., carpenter, res. 57 N, Illinois.

Louer Charles, at Bryant's Commercial College.
LOUNEY DENNIS, agent Indiana Central R. R., res. 110 Georgia.
Louterback Joseph, with W. Daggett, bds. Farmers' Hotel.
Love Isaiah, res. 111 Blake.
Love Capt. John, res. 49 N. Tennessee.
Love Samuel, watchman I. & C., Depot, res. 93 S. Alabama.
Low Charles G., carpenter, bds 148 E. North.
Low N. H., (Feary & L.,) res. 148 E. North.
LOWDEN JAMES, coal and lime dealer, opp. Madison Railroad, or at J. H. Vajen's hardware store, 21 W. Washington, res. 140 Virginia ave.
LOWE GEORGE, carriage maker, 40 N. Pennsylvania. res. 113 N. Pennsylvania.
Lowes John, carpenter, res. 152 N. Delaware.
Lower Charles, bar keeper Empire Saloon. res. 54 Indiana ave.
Lowman Mrs. Nancy, dress and shirt maker, res. 58 E. St. Clair.
Lowery wid. George, res. 247 W. Washington.
Lowery George D., physician and surgeon, res. 164 N. Noble.
Lowery John, miller, res. 237 W. Washington.
LOWERY WILEY M., druggist, 49 Massachusetts ave., res. 53 Massachusetts ave.
Lucus James, (col.,) painter and white-washer res. 149 N. Alabama.
Luce Douglass, salesman with William Hannaman, bds. 3 Circle.
LUDDEN BENJAMIN M., physician and surgeon, 14 N. Illinois, res. Meridian, cor. Circle.
LUDDEN & CO., drugs and medicines, also teas, 14 N. Illinois.
Ludlow Silas, vinegar manufacturer, res. 191 S. Delaware.
Ludlum Joseph E., painter, res. 230 N. Illinois.
Ludmy William, laborer, res. 54 Union.
Luebking Charles H., boot and shoe maker, and dealer, 194 E. Washingtion, res. 58 N. Noble.
Lueders Camelia, school teacher, res. 16 S. Illinois, 3d floor.
LUEDERS ELIZA, teacher and maker of embroidery, 16 S. Illinois, 3d floor.
Luken Harm, printer, bds. 132 E. Washington.
Lupton Thomas, res. N. Pennsylvania, cor. First.
Lurenkemp Henry, cooper, bds. 91 Union.
Luse Gottfried, boot and shoemaker, res. 148 New Jersey.
Lusk James, brakeman T. H. & R. R. R., res. 141 W. Market.
Lutz George, shoemaker, res. 39 E. New York.
Lynch J. J., salesman New York Store, res. 131 Mississippi.

Lynch John, laborer, res. 98 E. Maryland.
LYNCH MICHAEL, M. D., Virginia ave., near Washington.
Lynn David H., collar maker, bds. Temperance House.
Lyons George W., laborer, res. 286 S. Madison R. R.
Lyons John, express driver, res. 83 N. New Jersey.

M

McAdams Hugh H., painter, bds. 17 Harris.
McANULTY P. A., passenger conductor T. H. & R. R. R.,
   bds. Palmer House.
McBaker Thomas, tailor, res. 68 E. Michigan.
McBride Michael, peddler, res. 142 N. Liberty.
McCabe Matthew, machinist, res. S. Forest ave.
McCallian John, Bellefontaine shop, res. 284 S. Madison.
McCann John, engineer, res. 297 Virginia ave.
McCann Patrick, laborer, res. 182 S. Delaware.
McCann Samuel D., physician, res. 29 N. East.
McCardy John, conductor freight train T. H. R. R., bds.
   Union House.
McCarthy Simon, cor. Mississippi and Washington.
McCarty Eugene, moulder, bds. National Hotel.
McCarty Jeremiah, marble cutter, bds. cor. East and Market.
McCarty Mrs. Margaret, res. 22 S. Liberty.
McCarty Michael, laborer, bds. 38 S. Alabama.
McCARTY NICHOLAS, attorney at law, 70 E. Washington, res. 10 Madison ave.
McCarty Timothy, laborer, res. S. Missouri.
McChesney Jacob B., clerk Sinking Fund office, res. cor.
   Virginia ave. and Pennsylvania.
McChesney William L., assistant book-keeper of the Branch
   of the Bank of the State of Indiana. bds. J. McChesney.
McChesney Jeremiah, res. 61 N. Pennsylvania.
McClamrock Thomas, res. Indiana ave.
McClintock Otis, baggage master T. H. & R. R. R., bds.
   Palmer House.
McClure Theopholus, printer Journal Office, bds. 133 N.
   Mississippi.
McCoffry John, coal carter, res. 157 W. Maryland.
McCOLLIN PHILLIP G., hosiery and trimmings, 7 N.
   Meridian, res. 37 St. Clair.
McCool, hub mortiser, res. 239 S. Delaware.
McCord Benjamin R., (McC. & Wheatley,) res. 110 N. Meridian.
McCord Mrs. Hannah, res. 159 N. Alabama.

McCORD & WHEATLEY, lumber dealers, 119 S. Delaware.
McCORMICK HENRY, printer Sentinel Office, bds. Pyle House.
McCoy Thomas S., (col.,) barber, 4 N. Pennsylvania.
McCoy Rev. James, res. 69 Merrill.
McCoy Theodore, baggageman I. C. R. R., res. 12 Bates.
McCoy Wm., baggageman T. H. & R. R. R.
McCullough William, stone cutter, res. 18 E. Market.
McCune Thomas J., carpenter, res. E. Lord.
McCulloch Gertrude, teacher Indiana Institute for the Education of the Blind.
McCurdy, (E. Wallingford & Co.,) bds. 15 E. Lockerbie.
McCurdy George W., student, bds. 15 E. Lochibie.
McCutcheon H. C., checkman Central depot, bds. W. Washington.
McDaniel Mrs. Sarah, res. Blake.
McDONALD C. E., inventor, patent right, and model builder, Sentinel buildings, bds. 85 N. Pennsylvania.
McDonald David, (McD. & Walker,) res. 85 N. Pennsylvania.
McDonald Joseph E., (McD. & Roache,) res. 93 N. Pennsylvania.
McDONALD & ROACHE, attorneys at law, McOuat's block.
McDONALD & WALKER, attorneys at law, Yohn's block, cor. Meridian and Washington.
McDonald Mrs. A., res. Douglas.
McDonough D. B., carpenter, Vermont, near Massachusetts ave., res. 103 Indiana ave.
McDougal William, night watchman Bellefontaine R. R., res. 50 S. East.
McDougal Mrs. Louisa, bds. N. B. Palmer.
McDougal John, engineer Bellefontaine R. R., res. 50 S. East.
McELVAINE J. V., general freight agent Madison R. R., res. 57 N. Meridian.
McElwee John, carpenter, res. 154 N. Mississippi.
McEntire Charles, laborer, res. 133 N. Tennessee.
McEntire Elizabeth, res. N. Mississippi.
McEntire J. W., clerk, bds. 13 N. Mississippi.
McEntire L., bds. 13 Willard.
McEVOY HENRY N., (SUTHERLAND & McEVOY,) bds. Little's Hotel.
McEwen R., conductor T. & R. R. R., bds. Bates House.
McEwen Thomas, laborer, res. N. Wisconsin ave.
McFarland Miss Charlotte, teacher, res. 14 E. St. Clair.
McFarland Miss Laura W., teacher, res. 14 E. St. Clair.
McGarvey Richard, laborer, bds. 38 S. Alabama.

McGinn Charles, moulder, 255 S. Pennsylvania.
McGiffin Samuel, broom maker, bds. 130 N. Pennsylvania.
McGinnis George F., hatter, res. N. Meridian, N. of Second.
McGINNIS OWEN, clothier, 39 E. Washington, res. 26 Virginia ave.
McGinnis S., salesman Owen McGinnis, bds. 26 Virginia ave.
McGinnis Steward, student Bryant's Commercial College, bds. 26 Virginia ave.
McGinnis Nicholas, tailor O. McGinnis.
McGinnis Patrick, tailor O. McGinnis.
McGinnis Peter, tailor O. McGinnis.
McGlenn Michael, laborer, cor. North and Powell.
McGraw Patrick, laborer, res. 19 E. Georgia.
McGrew John, clerk L. S. Avery.
McIntosh Aeneas, bds. 119 Indiana ave.
McIntosh Rev. Stephen S., pastor M. E. (col.) Church, bds. 119 Indiana ave.
McIVER JOHN C., agent for Braman & Co.'s sewing machines, 6½ W. Washington, up stairs, bds. 23 Indiana ave.
McKenna James, clerk, res. 69 S. New Jersey.
McKenna John, machinist Bellefontaine R. R. shop, res. 69 S. New Jersey.
McKenna Wm. B., machinist Bellefontaine R. R. shop, bds. 69 S. New Jersey.
McKENZIE WM. A., attorney at law, 30½ W. Washington, bds. Macy House.
McKERNAN & PIERCE, real estate agents, 39½ W. Washington.
McKernan James H., (McK. & Pierce,) res. Circle.
McKinley Alexander, expressman, res. 100 Fort Wayne ave.
McKinley Hugh, carriage painter, bds. 100 Fort Wayne ave.
McKinnie L. P., tinner, bds. Tremont House.
McKinney M., bds. 81 Bluff road.
McKinney Wm., (col.,) res. 141 W. Washington.
McKnightly Wm., laborer, res. S. Delaware.
McLane Albert, painter, res. 8 W. North.
McLane Wm., hack driver, res. 278 S. Madison.
McLEAN C. G., principal McLean's Female Seminary, 27 N. Meridian.
McLEAN J. W., model builder and inventors' assistant, 6 S. Meridian, opp. Post Office, up stairs, res. 13 S. Minnesota.
McLene Jeremiah, jeweler, 1 Bates House, bds. Bates House.

McLaughlin C. W., bds. 149 S. Delaware.
McLAUGHLIN JOHN A., gunsmith, 254 E. Washington, res. 232 S. Alabama.
McLaughlin Rodger, laborer, 70 Bluff road.
McMahan Patrick, laborer, bds. Elizabeth, W. of Canal.
McMammon Michael, breakman M. & I. R. R., bds. Ray House.
McMillin Samuel, (Eldridge, McM. & Biddle,) res. 38 E. Vermont.
McMullen George S., engineer, res. 213 N. Noble.
McNairy Wm., machinist, bds. Ray House.
McNamara Michael, brakeman Indianapolis and Cincinnati R. R., res. 95 S. Alabama.
McNarley F., Fletcher's addition.
McNAUGHT PETER, at 9 W. Washington, bds. Meridian.
McNaughton Thomas J., butcher, bds. Bender House.
McNeal George H., laborer, res. 191 E. St. Clair.
McOuat Andrew, plasterer, res. cor. Patterson and Elizabeth.
McOuat Andrew W., (R. L. & A. W. McO.,) res. 67 N. East.
McOUAT'S BLOCK, Kentucky ave., S. W. of Illinois.
McOuat Geo., U. S. Register, office McOuat's Block.
McOuat Mrs. Janet S., res. 67 N. East.
McOUAT R. L. & A. W., stoves and tinware, 69 W. Washington.
McOuat R. L., (R. L. & A. W. McO.,) res. cor. New York and Illinois.
McPhaw John H., laborer, res. McCarty.
McPhillips H. P., salesman New York Store.
McPhillips Michael, clerk New York Store, res. 9 Elsworth.
McQuality William, tinner, bds. Lindsey's.
McQuithey Howard J. B., clerk Ind. Central Railway.
McQuithey Monroe T., clerk I. C. Railroad, bds. Pyle House.
McRae John H., bds. 44 S. Meridian.
McReady James, clerk post office, res. 146 N. Illinois.
McTAGGART & DOUGHERTY, meat dealers, Bates House, 15 N. Illinois.
McTAGGART ISRAEL, pork packer, office 23 N. Illinois, res. 83 N. Illinois.
McTaggart John W., bds. 83 N. Illinois.
McVay Barney, laborer, bds. 38 S. Alabama.
McVay James, laborer, bds. 38 S. Alabama.
McVey David, res. W. Market.
McVey James, blacksmith, res. W. Market.
McWilliams Mrs., 74 W. Michigan.
McWORKMAN & BRO., grocers, cor. Pennsylvania and North.

McWorkman Daniel, (McW. & Bro.,) res. 17 E. North.
McWorkman Henry, (McW. & Bro.,) res. 17 E. North.
McWORKMAN JAMES, superintendent Indiana Institute for the Education of the Blind.
Maby Oscar H., printer John Fahnestock, bds. Massachusetts ave.
Macauley D., book binder Sentinel office.
Machett R. M., carpenter, res. 95 St. Joseph.
MAC INTIRE THOMAS, A. M., superintendent Indiana Institute for the Education of the Deaf and Dumb.
Mack James, baggageman I. & C. Railroad, bds. Tremont House.
MACY DAVID, attorney at law and superintendent of Peru & Indianapolis Railroad, 10½ E. Washington, up stairs, res. 78 N. Delaware.
MACY HOUSE, A. S. Kingsley, proprietor, cor. Market and Illinois.
Maginta Martin, laborer, res. North.
MADISON & INDIANAPOLIS RAILROAD, office South, bet Pennsylvania and Delaware.
Maguire H. N., bds. 38 W. Market.
Maguire H. B., bds. 38 W. Market.
Maguire Douglass, res. 38 W. Market.
MAHONEY JAMES, gas fitter, 36 N. Illinois, res. cor. Alabama and Maryland.
Mahoney William, carpenter, bds. E. Knight.
Mains Leroy M., apprentice with Dr. Frink, bds. 132 N. Illinois.
Mains Samuel, accommodation hack, res. 59 N. Pennsylvania.
MAJOR STEPHEN, attorney at law, res. west of city.
Maker George W., painter, S. W. cor. Washington and Meridian, res. 139 Massachusetts ave.
Maker Job D., painter, bds. 139 Massachusetts ave.
Maker Seth, laborer, res. 139 Massachusetts ave.
Maker Thomas J., painter, res. 137 N. East.
Malone Abner, res. 145 Virginia ave.
MALONE B. F., carpenter, bds. Macy House.
Malone Patrick, laborer, res. Wyoming.
Manea Charles, carpenter, res. 137 N. Railroad.
MALONEY JOHN, boot and shoe maker, 11 S. Meridian, res. 169 Mississippi.
Malott V. T., teller Branch Bank, bds. J. F. Ramsay.
Maney Samuel, laborer, res. Indiana ave.
Manker John, cabinet maker, res. S. Delaware.
Manley John, (col.,) wood sawyer, res. 130 Indiana ave.
Mann Austin W., tinner, bds. cor. Market and Alabama.
Mann Daniel, carpenter, res. 139 N. Alabama.

Mann James B., teamster, res. 142 E. New York.
Mann Samuel R., teamster, res. 71 N. Spring.
Manning Patrick, laborer, res. 210 S. Delaware.
Manning Thomas S., res. 38 W. Ohio.
Manny John, moulder, bds. National Hotel.
Mansfield Geo., tailor, bds. 16 W. Georgia.
Mansfield Julius, tailor, bds. 40 W. Georgia.
Mansfield Thomas, blacksmith, bds. E. Knight.
MANSUR FRANK, bds. 8 E. Vermont.
Mansur Isaiah, (W. & I. M.,) bds. 4 East Vermont.
Mansur Jeremiah, pork merchant, res. 8 E. Vermont.
Mansur W. & I., pork packers, 14 S. Meridian.
Mansur William, (W. & I. M.,) res. 9 Ohio.
Mapes Caleb, res. 74 Missouri.
MARCHANT ISAAC, superintendent of Little's Hotel.
Marchant Isaac, jr., book-keeper, res. cor. Indiana ave. and
    Tennessee.
Mark Martin, fireman, bds. E. Washington.
MARKHAM THOMAS, blacksmith, cor. Pennsylvania and
    Maryland, res. 124 N. East.
Markley Matthew, butcher, bds. National Hotel.
Marquis Joseph O., city express man, res. 113 McCarty.
Mars W. A., stoves and tinware, 188 E. Washington.
MARSEE J. & CO., lumber merchants, office 146 E. Wash-
    ington.
Marsee John L., (J. Marsee & Co.,) bds. 147 E. South.
Marsee Joseph, (J. Marsee & Co.,) res. 47 E. South.
Marsh John, laborer, res. 163 N. Noble.
Marshall Charles M., tobacconist, res. 75 W. Maryland.
Marshall George S., assistant clerk Supreme Court, bds. 55
    W. Michigan.
Marshall Levi, carpenter Bellefontaine shop, res. 80 S. East.
Martin Mrs. G., 38 Bluff road.
Martin John, carpenter, res. 38 Bluff road.
Martin John, (col.,) res. 111 W. North.
Martin John, bricklayer, res. Oriental.
MARTIN L. R., at Wiley's real estate agency, 10½ E.
    Washington, bds. Bates House.
Martin Patrick, tailor Moritz & Bro., bds. S. Illinois.
Martin Philan, currier Mooneys & Co., res. 20 Pennsylvania.
Martin William, tailor, 3 W. Washington, res. Wiley's ad-
    dition.
Martindale Henry S., printer Atlas office, bds. 52 S. Dela-
    ware.
Martindale Mrs. Julia A., seamstress, res. 65 N. Noble.
Martz Isaac, farmer, res. N. University ave.
Martz Mrs. Sarah, dressmaker, res. 39 N. Alabama.
Marvell George, plasterer, res. 156 N. West.

Maryland Francis, carpenter, res. 41 St. Clair.

Massena Fontaine, apprentice C. G. French, bds. E. end Washington.

Mason Hamilton, res. 47 W. Georgia.

Mason Madison, (col.,) laborer, res. 47 W. Georgia.

MASONIC HALL, cor. Washington and Tennessee.

Mather John, engineer, res. 93 E. Bates.

Mathias David, jr., at Rolling Mill, bds. 192 S. Tennessee.

Mathwig John, boot and shoemaker, res. 20 N. Illinois.

Matthews William, clerk, bds. 124 E. Market.

Matthews Mrs. Margaret, dress maker, res. 124 E. Market.

MATTLER JOHN, proprietor Washington House, 83 S. Meridian.

Mattler Stephen, Union House, cor. Illinois and South, res. same.

Mattox Eli, baggage master I. & C. R. R., bds. 51 Louisiana.

Mauzy James H., student, bds. R. B. Duncan.

Maxfield George W., (Donaldson, M. & Prine,) res. New Jersey, bet. Market and Ohio.

MAXWELL SAMUEL D., Mayor, office Odd Fellows' Hall, res. 156 E. Ohio.

Maxwell William D., bds. 156 E. Ohio.

MAY ANDREW, commission and produce merchant, 85 E. Washington, res. 81 S. East.

May Andrew, cooper, res. 58 S. East.

MAY EDWIN, architect, and inventor of May's patent jail, 18 E. Market, res. 75 N. Pennsylvania.

May John, drayman, res. 119 McCarty.

May R. K., res. 61 West.

MAYER JOHN F., manufacturer and dealer in umbrellas and parasols, 60 E. Washington, res. 161 N. Illinois.

Mayer W. C., carpenter, bds. C. Nutmeyer.

MAYHEW E. C. & CO., wholesale boots and shoes, 8 W. Louisiana, opp. Union Depot, also at retail, 5. W. Washington.

Mayhew Enoch C., (E. C. M. & Co.,) res. 138 N. Pennsylvania.

MAYHEW J. N., model builder, Blake's Row, bds. 91 Maryland.

Mayhew Oscar F., clerk R. J. Gatling, res. 20 Circle.

Mead James, groceries and provisions, 106 S. Illinois, res. Virginia ave.

Mearhoff Henry, laborer, res. 158 S. Alabama.

Mears George W., physician, 14 Circle.

Mears L. R., student Bryant's Commercial College, bds. Dr. Mears.

Meary Phillip, plummer, bds. 12 Willard.

Meconi Dionisio, laborer, res. alley, bet. Ohio and New York.

Meek E. S., salesman D. C. Middlemas, res. cor. First and Howard.
Meek Robert, superintendent of motive power I. & C. R. R., res. 103 S. Alabama.
Megrew John P., clerk, bds. Pyle House.
Megrew Willis H., miller, bds. 47 N. Noble.
Meikel Mrs. Catharine, res. 174 E. Ohio.
Meikel C. P., res. 65 N. Mississippi.
Meikel Mrs. Catharine, 65 N. Mississippi.
Meikel George W., clerk Perkins & Coon, res. 65 N. Mississippi.
Meikel Henry, brewer, bds. 135 W. Maryland.
Meikel John P., brewer, res. 135 W. Maryland.
Meikel M. I., jeweler, bds. 65 N. Mississippi.
Meller Edward, laborer, res. 135 E. Ohio.
MELVILLE ROBERT B., cutter Glaser & Bros., 112 N. Mississippi.
Mena John, carpenter, res. 67 N. Noble.
Menghlet Abraham, tailor, res. 81 S. Illinois.
Mengis Frank, cigar maker, res. 107 E. Washington.
Mercer Isaiah, machinist, bds. National Hotel.
Meredith William, compositor Journal Office, res. bet. Michigan and North.
Meredith S. C., express messenger Adams express, res. 52 Blackford.
Merick Martin, engineer, bds. Knaus' bakery, E. Washington.
Merick Henry C., apprentice Sentinel news room, bds. 22 N. Pennsylvania.
MERRILL & CO., books and stationery, 19 E. Washington.
Merrill Samuel, (M. & Co.,) res. 83 Merrill.
Merrill Dr. John F., 134 W. New York.
Merrillas John, salesman New York store.
Merriman John M., paint manufacturer, E. Washington, res. 71 N. East.
MERRITT & COUGHLEN, proprietors Ohio Premium Woolen Factory, S. side, W. Washington, near River.
Merritt George, (M. & Coughlen,) res. 102 N. West.
Merritt Joseph S., carpenter, res. 114 W. Georgia.
METROPOLITAN HALL, V. Butsch, proprietor, cor. Tennessee and Washington.
METZGER A. & J., bakers and confectionery, 11 N. Pennsylvania.
Metzger Alexander, (A. &. J. M.,) res. 55 W. Maryland.
Metzger Jacob, (A. & J. M.,) bds. 55 W. Maryland.
MEYER GEORGE F., cigars and tobacco, 35 W. Washington, res. 56 W. Vermont.
Meyer John, tinner, 69 Madison ave.

Meyer Ludwig, drayman, res. 49 N. Davidson.
Meyer William, drayman, res. 90 Union.
Meyers Charles, retired merchant, res. 175 N. Illinois.
Meyers E. F., upholsterer, bds. Tremont House.
Meyers Joseph, harness maker James Sulgrove.
Meyers Phillip, shoemaker, res. cor. Tennessee and Indiana
    ave.
Meyers Peter, res. 69 Madison ave.
Midall John, res. Blake.
MIDDLEMUS DAVID C. & CO., groceries, stoneware and
    liquors, 107 W. Washington.
Middlemus David C., (D. C. M. & Co.,) res. 89 W. Mar-
    ket.
Millar Henry, carpenter, res. 228 N. Alabama.
Miller A., carpenter, res. 169 S. Alabama, in rear.
Miller Anthony F. W., carpenter, res. 109 E. Vermont.
Miller Anthony, drayman, res. 162 S. Tennessee.
Miller Augustus, watch maker, cor. South and East, res.
    same.
Miller Charles, brick layer, res. 242 E. Washington.
Miller Charles T., lager beer saloon and bowling alley, S.
    side National road.
Miller Charles H., carpenter, res. 99 E. Maryland.
Miller Christian, carpenter, res. 125 N. Davidson.
Miller Mrs. Elizabeth, res. 86 N. Mississippi.
Miller Mrs. Emily, res. 155 N. Mississippi.
Miller Frederick W., carpenter, bds. 109 E. Vermont.
MILLER REV. GEORGE F., pastor German M. E. Church,
    res. 122 E. Ohio.
Miller George W., machinist, res. St. Clair, W. of Canal.
Miller's Garden, S. side National road.
Miller Henry, grocer, res. 165 N. Noble.
Miller Henry, helper, res. 118 cor. Vermont and Canal.
Miller Henry, brick layer, res. 103 N. Railroad.
Miller Henry ?., carriage trimmer, bds. Pyle House.
Miller Henry W., carpenter, res. 135 N. Noble.
MILLER REV. HUGH B., pastor Baptist Church, res. 11
    Madison ave.
Miller Jacob R., clerk Elias Werden & Co.
Miller John, drayman, res. 185 N. East.
Miller Joseph F., carpenter, res. 86 E. Michigan.
Miller L., law student, bds. Macy House.
Miller Mrs. Mary, res. 195 Indiana ave.
Miller R., barber, cor. South and East, res. same.
Miller Mrs. Sarah, boarding, 12 Kentucky ave.
Miller Wm., laborer. res. in rear 169 S. Alabama.
MILLS, ALFORD & CO., wholesale and retail grocers, 36
    E. Washington.

Mills Howard W., (M., Alford & Co.,) res. 71 N. Pennsylvania.
Mills W. H., (M., Alford & Co.,) res. 115 E. Ohio.
MILNER J., attorney at law and notary public, 84 E. Washington, bds. 44 N. Pennsylvania.
Milner Davis, student N. W. C. University, bds. Mrs. Smith.
Milton H. T., carpenter, res. 237 Indiana ave.
Minahan Andrew, res. 221 S. Delaware.
Mineek Harvey, steamboat pilot, bds. 229 S. Delaware.
Minehart Phillip, laborer, res. 29 N. Spring.
Minger Charles, telegraph operator, bds. California House.
Mink William, boot and shoe maker, bds. S. East, over Union Railway.
Minnely Henry, shoemaker, bds. Little's Hotel.
Mitchel Jacob, salesman Glaser & Brother, bds. Palmer House.
Mitchell Marl, blacksmith, bds. National Hotel.
Mittay John C., saddler, res. 159 E. New York.
Mittay John C., barkeeper Eagle Saloon, res. 138 E. Washington, up stairs.
Mittay William M., barkeeper Nebraska Saloon, res. 11 E. Georgia.
Mittiffer Henry, Bluff road.
Mitten George, engineer I. & C. R. R., bds. Bates House.
Mock Martin, tailor, res. 178 E. Ohio.
Moesch T. H., at Apollo Garden, res. cor. Kentucky ave. and Tennessee.
Moda Michael, shoemaker, res. 51 S. Illinois.
Moffitt E. R., law student with McDonald & Walker.
Moffitt John, machinist, res. 69 W. South.
MOFFITT JOHN, dentist, Sentinel building, res. cor. First and N. Illinois.
Moffitt John, jr., compositor Locomotive, bds. cor. South and Tennessee.
Moffitt Oliver, printer, bds. cor. South and Tennessee.
Moffitt William, (Beck & M.,) bds. 21 S. Delaware.
Móltare Gottlieb, 50 Union.
Molton Charles, engineer R. R., res. 20 N. West.
Molton John, driver American and United States Express, bds. American House.
MONNINGER DANIEL & CONRAD, Court House Saloon and billiards, 121 E. Washington, res. same.
Monroe John, carpenter, 107 E. Ohio.
Monroe William M., messenger Adams Express Madison & Indianapolis R. R.
Montague William, wagon maker, 12 N. Delaware, res. 59 S. New Jersey.
Monteeth James, brick moulder, bds. 59 S. New Jersey.

Monteeth John, carpenter, res. 81 E. South.
Montgomery Andrew, shoemaker, res. 112 N. Meridian.
MONTGOMERY CHAUNCY, proprietor Washington Hall Billiard Saloon, W. Washington, res. 75 Maryland.
MONTGOMERY JAMES, hack driver, res. Louisiana, bet. Illinois and Tennessee.
Mooklar William B., clerk J. P. Pope, 33 W. Washington, bds. 111 East.
MOONEYS & CO., dealers in leather, hides and oil, 75 S. Meridian.
Mooney James E., (M. & Co.,) res. Edinburgh, Ind.
Mooney Wm. W., (M. & Co., res. Edinburgh, Ind.
Moore Mrs. Catharina E., res. 68 E. St. Joseph.
Moore Chauncey G., bds. 100 N. Pennsylvania.
Moore Charles P., foreman Kregelo, Blake & Co., res. 123 N. Meridian.
Moore Charles W., (Merrill & Co.,) res. Merrill, bet. New Jersey and Alabama.
Moore Deborah D., res. 9 E. Michigan.
Moore George W., 283 Virginia ave.
Moore Mrs. Hattie, school teacher, res. 41 W. Walnut.
Moore Henry, fireman I. & C. R. R., res. 161 S. Delaware.
Moore Isaac P., fireman B. R. R., res. 81 N. East.
Moore John, laborer, bds 76 E. Market.
Moorhead Phineas B., foreman Bellefontaine R. R., bds. Little's Hotel.
Moran Patrick, laborer, res. 192 S. East.
Morgan David, heater Rolling Mill, res. 16 Willard.
Morgan Dennis, clerk, bds. N. Mississippi, bet. New York and Vermont.
Morgan Dennis, cor. Ohio and Tennessee.
Morgan E. R., machinist Bellefontaine shop, bds. S. Delaware.
Morgan Edward, machinist, bds. Ray House.
Morgan Mrs. Elizabeth, 99 Louisiana.
Morgan Mrs. H., boarding house, 51 E. Louisiana.
Morgan James, clerk, bds. Ray House.
Morgan Samuel, (Smith & M.,) res. 57 E. New York.
Morgan William, student Bryant's Commercial College, bds. 101 E. Louisiana.
Morgan William D., res. W. Market.
Morgenweek V., laborer, res. 9 Chatham.
Moriarty Daniel, laborer, res. 174 S. Delaware.
Mority Patrick, laborer, res. 11 Railroad.
MORITZ & BRO., clothiers and merchant tailors, 3 E. Washington and 19 W. Washington.
Moritz Solomon, (M. & Bro.,) bds. Bates House.

Morley A. J., bookbinder Sheets & Braden, bds. Palmer House.

Morley Thomas, laborer, res. 159 W. Maryland.

Morley Walter, laborer, res. 159 W. Maryland.

MORNINGSTAR PETER, meat market, N. Pennsylvania, near Odd Fellows' Hall.

Morrell William S., school teacher, res. 59 N. Mississippi.

Morris Mrs. A. W., res. 53 S. Meridian.

Morris Charles G., bds. 50 S. Meridian.

Morris George W., bds. E. Maryland, bet. Meridian and Virginia.

Morris James W., bds. 50 S. Meridian.

Morris John D., freight agent I. & C. R. R., res. 50 S. Meridian.

Morris John, shoemaker, res. 65 N. Noble.

Morris Mrs. Catharine, res. 155 N. Railroad.

Morris John, bds. cor. Tennessee and Indiana ave.

Morris L. T., res. 53 S. Meridian.

Morris N. N., student N. W. C. University, res. 53 S. Meridian.

Morris Sanford V., clerk Danforth & Simpson, res. 113 W. South.

MORRIS SAMUEL, attorney at law and notary public, 24½ E. Washington, res. foot of Madison ave.

MORRIS THOMAS A., president Indianapolis Insurance Co., 14 and 16 S. Meridian, res. Fort Wayne ave.

Morrison A. F., clerk Mills, Alford & Co., bds. Fort Wayne road, N. E. part of city.

Morrison Mrs. Ann F., res 32 N. Pennsylvania.

Morrison Charles J., clerk W. H. Talbott & Co., bds. cor. Pennsylvania and Market.

Morrison James, (M. & Ray,) res. cor. St. Mary and Fort Wayne road.

Morrison John T., clerk, res. 12 E. Michigan.

Morrison Michael, teamster, res. 19 Union.

MORRISON & RAY, attorneys at law, 26 E. Washington, up stairs.

Morrison Wm. H., sen., (Mills, Alford & Co.,) res. Pennsylvania, N. of city limits.

Morrison Wm. H., jr., book-keeper Mills, Alford & Co., bds. N. E. part of city, Fort Wayne road.

Morrow B. B., (Wiggim & M.,) American House.

Morrow Thomas, laborer, res. north of Carlisle's old mill.

Morrow. Walter L., bds. 34 E. Market.

Morton John, watchman Rolling Mill, bds. 13 Willard.

Morton William S. T., (Coffin & M.,) res. Centreville.

10

ELIJAH HASKET. CONRAD KEIL.

E. HASKET & CO.,

STAR PUMP MAKERS,

No. 26 Kentucky Avenue, below State Offices,

AND PEARL ST., OPP. CAMERON'S JOBBING OFFICE,

INDIANAPOLIS, INDIANA.

PUMPS MADE TO ORDER

AND READY MADE ALWAYS ON HAND.

All Work promptly executed at Moderate Terms. Call and give us a Trial.

MOSES LUCIUS W., optician, 20 E. Washington, res. 13 E. Market.

Mosher Theodore, machinist, bds. L. B. Wilson.

Mosher Tracy D., clerk Eldridge, McMillin & Biddle.

Moss Lewis, machinist, at Rolling mill, res. 136 E. Washington.

Moss Mrs. Lydia, (col.,) res. W. North.

Moss Nathan, (col.,) barber, bds. W. North.

Mot Jacob, showman, bds. 212 W. Washington.

Mothershead John L., bds. 54 S. Meridian.

Mottis Henry, stone mason, res. 270 Fletcher's addition.

Mount A. S., (Mooneys & Co.,) res. 50 S. Illinois.

Mount Humphrey, carpenter, res. 144 E. North.

Mowry C. R., harness maker, James Sulgrove, bds. Temperance House.

MUELLER JOHN, importer of wines, liquors and cigars, 212 E. Washington, res. same, up stairs.

Muir James, tea dealer, 33 W. Market, res. same.

Muirson Alexander, stone dealer, 143 Virginia ave.

Mull Jacob, carriage maker, res. 233 N. Illinois.

Mullen John, laborer, res. 144 E. New York.

Mullen Roger, brick maker, res. 189 S. New Jersey.

Mulleney Patrick, with C. A. Elliott & Co., bds. 32 Kentucky ave.

Mulleney D., clerk, bds. 32 Kentucky ave.

Muller Fred, cook Capital Saloon, bds. 14 E. Washington.

Muller John A. D., carpenter, res. 196 N. East.

Munsell Ezra, wagon maker, bds. 175 E. Ohio.

MUNSELL HENRY, wagon maker, Wabash alley, bet. Liberty and Noble, res. 175 E. Ohio.

Munson C. H., (M. & Johnson,) res. 119 E. Ohio.

Munson David, (Locke & M.,) res. Market, bet. East and New Jersey.

MUNSON & JOHNSON, stoves and tinware, 62 E. Washington.

Murlaugh John, carpenter, res. 137 W. New York.

MURPHY & HOLLIDAY, iron, steel and springs, 34 E. Washington.

Murphy James, laborer, res. Elizabeth, near Blake.

Murphy John W., (M. & Holliday,) res. 33 E. Ohio.

Murphy John, brakeman, res. 153 S. Minnesota.

Murphy Jonathan, res. 93 E. Louisiana.

Murphy Mrs. Kate L., res. 64 Bright.

Murphy Mike, res. Blackford.

Murphy Timothy, boot and shoe maker, 4 W. Market. res. same.

Musgrove Dr. Philip B., bds. N. Tennessee.

Musgrove Moses, spinner, res. California.

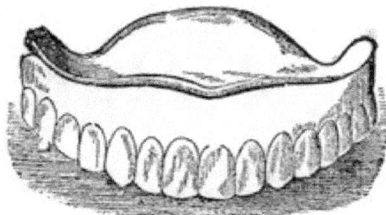

Muth Matthew, baker, bds. 55 Maryland.
Myer Christian F., carpenter, res. 41 N. East.
Myer Martin, umbrella maker, res. 171 E. Washington.
Myer Moses, clothier and dealer in furnishing goods, N. W.
cor. Washington and Meridian, res. 116 Ohio.
Myer William, blacksmith, res. 47 E. Georgia.
Myers C. J., (M. & Witthoft,) bds. Pattison House.
Myers Henry, carpenter, res. 69 Davidson.
Myers Henry, res. 65 Merrill.
Myers John, carpenter, res. 124 N. Davidson.
Myers John M., tinner, res. 69 S. Pennsylvania.
Myers Joseph, harness maker, bds. 59 Maryland.
Myers Leonard, confectioner, res. 149 E. Ohio.
Myers Philip, boot and shoe maker, res. 2d door cor. Ten-
nessee and Indiana ave.
MYERS & WITTHOFT, wholesale and retail manufac-
turers of furniture, 171 E. Washington.

N

Nagel Daniel, laborer, res. 23 E. Harrison.
Naltner A., Nebraska Saloon, res. 117 S. Tennessee.
Naltner Martin, bar tender, Magnolia Saloon.
Nassoy Henry, laborer, res. 161 N. Noble.
Neall Jonathan R., produce dealer, 134 E. Washington, res.
89 N. New Jersey.
Nealy Hugh, clerk, res. E. Vine.
Neas Louis, carpenter, res. 82 E. St. Joseph.
Neffing Nicholas, cabinet maker, 246 old Madison road.
Neffle Frederick, watchman Kregelo, Blake & Co., res. S.
West.
Nehling Frederick C., teamster, res. 125 cor. South and
New Jersey.
Neil Jonathan, (Holms & N.,) bds. N. New Jersey.
Neiman Christian, carpenter, res. 122 N. Davidson.
Neiman Jacob, township trustee, office Court House, res. 4
miles N. W. of town, on Lafayette Railroad.
NEIMEYER JOHN H., portrait painter, over A. B.
Willard & Co.
Neimeyer William, laborer, res. 66 S. Noble.
Neis Adam, blacksmith, res. 139 E. Washington.
Nelson Henry H., sheriff Supreme Court, res. 73 N. Missis-
sippi.
Nelson John, machinist, res. E. Hosbrook.
Nelson Sandy, (col.,) washerwoman, res. 78 N. Missouri.
Nevitt William, res. 59 E. Ohio.
NEW JOHN C., clerk Circuit and Common Pleas Courts,
office at Court House, res. 102 N. Pennsylvania.

New Rev. John B., pastor Christian Church, res. 56 N. Illinois.

Newcomb Horatio C., (N. & Tarkington,) 58 N. Alabama.

NEWCOMB & TARKINGTON, attorneys at law, 24 E. Washington, up stairs.

NEWCOMER CHRISTIAN, saloon, 13 W. Washington, res. same.

Newcomer F. S., physician and surgeon, office 14, res. 15, Circle.

Newell L. S., retired, res. 24 N. Mississippi.

Newland John T., clerk Wm. Worland, bds. 37 Virginia ave.

NEWMAN JOHN S., president Indiana Central Railroad Co., office cor. Virginia ave. and Delaware, res. Centreville.

Newman Peter, laborer, res. 149 S. Mississippi.

Newman Walter, clerk Ind. Central R. R. office.

NEW YORK DRY GOODS STORE, W. & H. Glenn & Co., proprietors, Glenns' Block, E. Washington.

NICHOLAS SEBASTIAN C., printer Sentinel office, bds. Little's Hotel.

Nicholas Miss Georgiana, school teacher Indianapolis Female Institute, bds. 34 E. Michigan.

Nicholas Joseph W., law student, bds. 93 N. Pennsylvania.

NICHOLS T. M., surgeon dentist, 24 S. Meridian.

Nichols Willard, foreman Atlas office, res. 93 Massachusetts ave.

Nicholson David, stone cutter, res. 120 E. Michigan.

Nicholson William, stone mason, res. 60 N. Noble.

Nichol Robert, carpenter, res. 238 S. Alabama.

NICOLAI CHARLES, harness maker and saddler, 268 E. Washington, res. same.

Nicolai Julius, retired, 89 W. Washington.

Nicolai L., meat store, 39 E. New York, bds. 48 E. New York.

Nieman William, carpenter, bds. 157 E. Ohio.

Niles Thomas N., Bryant's Commercial College, bds. Pyle House.

Nobbe Henry, printer Sentinel Office, res. 112 N. Noble.

NOBLE WILLIAM H. L., general ticket agent I. & C. R. R., res. 30 N. Delaware.

Noble Winston P., res. E. Market.

Nofsinger W. R., East of City limits.

Noltary Charles, baker Cincinnati bakery, bds. 91 E. Washington.

Nolting Charles, laborer, res. 197 N. Alabama.

Nolting John, laborer, res. 199 N. Alabama.

Nooe wid. A., res. 73 S. New Jersey.

Norris Amos, res. 243 S. Pennsylvania.
Norris Stephen, res. 20 N. Delaware.
NORTH CAPT. MYRON, livery and sale stables, 24 S. Pennsylvania, res. 19 W. Maryland.
North Oliver M., bds. 19 W. Maryland.
North S. P., clerk, bds. Farmers' Hotel.
NORTH-WESTERN CHRISTIAN UNIVERSITY, N. E. of City limits.
Northway George, plasterer, res. 94 N. New Jersey.
Northway John, plasterer, res. 146 E. North.
Norton John, Farmers' Hotel, res. 61 Illinois,
Norwood Elbert F., tinner, res. 26 N. Illinois.
Norwood George, bds. 95 N. Illinois.
Norwood Mrs. Margaret, res. 72 W. Maryland.
Norwood Richard, res. 26 N. Illinois.
Nulting Charles, with F. Ballman, bds. 91 E. Washington.
Nurman Christ, shoemaker, bds. 176 E. Washington.
Nuttmeyer Charles H., carpenter, res. 181 E. Ohio.
Nuttmeyer Christian, carpenter, res. 151 E. Ohio.

O

Ober David J., clerk, res. 101 Tennessee.
O'Brian Jeremiah, tin smith, res. 1 N. New Jersey.
O'Brien Timothy K., clerk Ind. Cen. R. R., bds. American House.
O'Brien Thomas, hostler, res. W. Maryland.
O'Connor Patrick, bds. 245 W. Washington.
O'Connor Edmund, laborer, bds. 29 N. Davidson.
ODD FELLOWS' HALL, N. E. cor. Pennsylvania and Washington.
O'Donell Thomas, laborer, bds. 204 S· Delaware.
Ohler A., watch maker, res. Washington, bet. Tennessee and Mississippi.
Oelschlager Benjamin, clerk Perkins & Coon, res 111 Fort Wayne ave.
Off Christian, sawyer, bds. 189 N. Davidson.
Off Gottlieb, bar tender St. Charles saloon.
Oglesby John H., res. Alvord's Block, 3d door, S. of Maryland.
OGLESBY WILLIAM F., clerk and telegraph operator, bds. Alvord's Block, S. Pennsylvania.
O'Hara Mrs. Sarah, res. 79 E. Market.
Oehelar David, shoemaker, res. 38 Bluff Road.
Ohr Aaron D., ticket agent Union Depot, res. 80 E. Market.
Ohr Henry, grand scribe of G. D. S. of T., 28 W. Washington, res. 48 N. Delaware.

MUSIC STORE,

INDIANA PIANO FORTE WAREROOM,

WILLARD & STOWELL.

NO. 4 BATES HOUSE,

INDIANAPOLIS, IND.

OHR JOHN H.,(agent Adams Express Co.,) res. 92 N. New Jersey.

Ohr M. L., messenger Adams Express Co T. H. R. R. R.

Okey Edward H., mason, res. 167 N. New Jersey.

Okey James, res. 183 N. New Jersey.

Okey Joseph B , solicitor of patents, res. 144 N. East.

Okey Phillip, carpenter, res. 124 E. Michigan.

Oldmans Harmon, clerk, bds. cor. Washington and Mississippi.

Ollom Jacob, teamster, res. Elizabeth, bet. Blake and Dunlap.

O'Neal Hugh, attorney at law, Ætna Building, N. Pennsylvania.

O'Neal Patrick, laborer, res. 14 E. Georgia.

O'Neal Richard, real estate agent, 12 S. Pennsylvania, res. 99 Virginia ave.

O'Neal Timothy, laborer, res. 9 N. Railroad.

O'NEAL ROBERT E., business agent Atlas, bds. Palmer House.

O'Rafferty A., boot and shoemaker, res. 169 Mississippi.

O'Reilly Douglass, plasterer, res. S. East.

ORIENTAL HOUSE, F. Costigan, proprietor, S. Illinois, bet. Maryland and Georgia.

Orlopp Richard, American Express messenger I. & St. L. E. R., bds. Bates House.

Orr G. B., brick mason, res. Indiana ave.

Osbourne Samuel, secretary Gov. Willard, bds. 53 W. Michigan.

OSGOOD J. B., house and sign painter, 24 Kentucky ave., res. 34 N. Mississippi.

Osgood J. B., jr., bds. with J. B. Osgood.

OSGOOD SMITH & CO., last, peg, hub, spoke and felloe manufacturers, 180 S. Illinois.

Osgood J. R., (O., Smith & Co.,) res. 17 W. Georgia.

Ostermeyer Christian, drayman, res. 137 E. Ohio.

OSTERMEYER FREDERICK, dry goods, groceries and provisions, 258 E. Washington, res. same.

Ostermeyer Louis, sr., laborer, res. 145 N. Liberty.

Ostermeyer Louis, marble polisher, res 147 N. Liberty.

Oswald Godfried, laborer, res. 165 N. Railroad.

OTT JOHN & CO., wholesale and retail dealers and manufacturers of furniture, 117 W. Washington.

Ott John (J. O. & Co.,) res. 117 W. Washington.

Ott Michael, res. 102 cMCarty.

Otte William, carpenter, res. 155 E. Ohio.

Otten Deitrich, chair maker, res. 41 N. Spring.

Otten Deitrich, cigar manufacturer, 159 E. Washington, res. Spring.

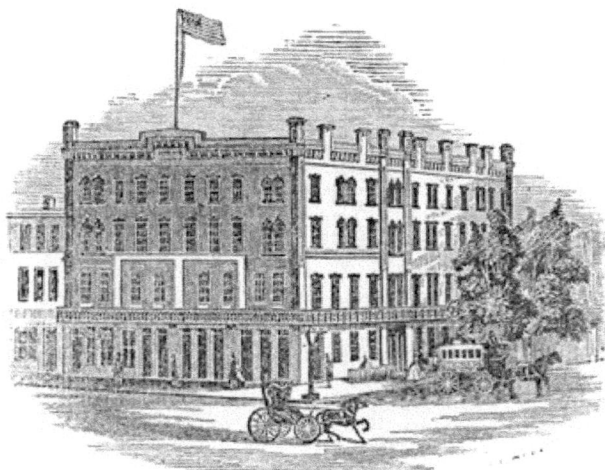

Otis W. H. auditor B. R. R. Line, bds. Maryland.
Otto B., printer Volksblatt Office, 130 E. Washington, res. same.
Otto Phillip, laborer, 139 N. Alabama.
Over D. J., clerk, res. 101 N. Tennessee.
Owen John, clerk 13 S. Meridian, res. same.
Owens Nathaniel, plasterer, res 87 E. South.
Owens wid. William, res. 161 Liberty.
Oyler William, varnisher Sloan & Ingersoll, res. 101 S. Alabama.

P

Palmer Charles, C., retired, bds. 37 W. Maryland,
Palmer Edward S., (Douglass &. P.,) res. 40 S. Illinois.
PALMER HOUSE, Jesse D. Carmichael, cor. Washington and Illinois.
Palmer John, blacksmith, bds. Michigan Road.
Palmer Nathan B., retired, res. 37 W. Maryland.
PALMER & TALBOTT, dry goods wholesale and retail, 37 E. Washington.
Palmer T. G., deputy auditor of State, 7 McOuat's Block.
Palmer T. G., (P. & Talbott,) res. 90 N. Illinois.
PARISETTE JAMES, pharmaceutic confectioner, 15 N. Illinois, res. same.
PARK THERON, agricultural implement dealer, 86 W. Washington, res. cor. Tennessee and Washington.
Parks James, pattern maker, res, 12 N. New Jersey.
Parks John, (col.,) chief cook Little's Hotel.
Parker Benjamin, Bryant's Commercial College, bds. Macy House.
Parker Columbus, bds. S. Illinois.
Parker Mrs. Catharine, 134 E. Washington.
PARKER EDGAR, dealer in guns, pistols and fancy goods, 17 S. Illinois.
Parker Scott W., law student with Smith & Smith.
Parker Wilson, brick mason, 103 S. Tennessee.
PARKMAM CHARLES B., secretary Rolling Mill Co., res. cor. Mississippi and Maryland.
Parmerlee James C., (Yandes & Co.,) res. Brown county.
Parmelee W. H., clerk Ind. & Laf. R. R.
Parrish H., attends to his own business, office 24 E. Washington, bds. Palmer House.
Parrish John, finisher, bds. 258 S. Delaware.
Parrish Solomon, with I. Davis & Co., res. 104 S. New Jersey.
PARROT HORACE, general ticket agent Ind. Central R. R., res. 141 N. Delaware.

PARRY & WRIGHT, physicians and surgeons, office 12 E. Market.

Parry Charles, M. D., (P. & Wright,) res. 23 N. Meridian.

Parsley Ashbury, teamster, res. 161 N. Alabama.

Parsons Charles A., conductor P. & I. R. R., bds. American House.

PARSONS JOHN J., superintendent Sentinel Bindery, Sentinel Building, res. 61 W. New York.

Partridge Joseph, express messenger Adams & Co., T. H. & R. Railroad & Evansville Railroad, bds. Palmer House.

PARVIN THEOPHILUS, M. D., res. 69 N. Alabama.

Pascoe James, boiler maker, Bellefontaine R. R. shop, res. 75 S. New Jersey.

Pasquire John B., carpenter, res. 176 E. Michigan.

Patterson Edward W., stock dealer, res. 32 N. Delaware.

PATTERSON J. M., livery stable, 34 E. Maryland, res. 104 Massachusetts ave.

Patterson John, carpenter, res. 156 N. Delaware.

Patterson John P., traveling agent J. W. Holland, res. 85 N. New Jersey.

Patterson T. T. N., speculator and tanner, res. 71 N. Alabama.

Patterson R. H., book-keeper, bds. W. end North.

PATTERSON S. J., flouring and saw mill, W. Washington, near river bank, res. W. end North.

PATTERSON WILLIAM, attorney at law and notary public, 30 W. Washington, up stairs, res. 152 E. Ohio.

Pattison Aug. E., at N. W. C. U., res. 71 N. Alabama.

Pattison wid. Jehu, (col.,) res. 139 N. East.

Pattison W. T., 17 N. Alabama.

Paxton Mrs. Elizabeth, res. 3 Circle.

Paul Henry, shoemaker, res. 173 S. Delaware.

Payne Alice, tailoress, res. Kentucky.

Paynter Edward W., printer Sentinel office, bds. Tennessee, bet. Ohio and New York.

Payton William, (col.,) currier Jno. Fishback, res. 139 N. West.

Peacock Wm. H., engineer I. & C. R. R., res. S. side National road.

Pearson Joseph, stone cutter, res. 18 E. Market.

Pearson Leonard, American Express messenger T. H. & R. Railroad, bds. Palmer House.

Pearson L., brick mason, res. 114 N. Alabama.

Peasley Abraham, res. 126 N. West.

PECK E. J., president and superintendent T. H. & R. Railroad, office at depot, res. Maryland, bet. Illinois and Tennessee.

Peck George W., cabinet maker, res. 156 N. Delaware.

Indiana Central
RAILWAY.

INDIANAPOLIS, DAYTON AND COLUMBUS
SHORT LINE.
Three Daily Trains from Indianapolis to Columbus

The Indiana Central Railway, with its connections, forms the

Great Central National Route,
FROM INDIANAPOLIS TO THE EAST.

This being one of the old established Routes, the road beds and machinery are kept in the very best condition.

On the above line travelers will find all the modern improvements which can add to their comfort.

TIME ALWAYS AS QUICK AND FARE AS LOW
AS BY ANY COMPETING LINE.

To all Eastern Points
CINCINNATI, VIA RICHMOND AND HAMILTON.

Cars Run Through without Change.
ASK FOR TICKETS VIA INDIANA CENTRAL.

H. PARROTT, Gen'l Ticket Agt.   **H. L. POPE, Supt.**

Peek Thomas, pattern maker, bds. 154 N. Delaware.
Pedicord R. M., railroad bridge builder, res. 179 E. Market.
Pedlow James C., blacksmith, res. S. E. Michigan ave.
Pee Geo. W., salesman J. Crossland, res. 72 N. Alabama.
Pells Isaac T., salesman New York Store.
Pence Nicholas, laborer, bds. N. Noble.
Pender Thomas, res. 56 E. Market.
Penn S. W., 24 Mississippi.
PENNSYLVANIA HOUSE, 208 E. Washington, cor. East.
Penticost M., retired, res. 173 N. Alabama.
Penticost S. F., cor. St. Clair and Alabama.
Perdue H., daguerrean artist, 39½ W. Washington, res· same.
Perdue Milton W., brakeman B. R. R., res. N. 67 Noble.
PERINE & MAYHEW, model builders, 1 3d floor Blake's Building, cor. Washington and Kentucky ave.
Perine Alfred T., (P. & Mayhew,) bds. 91 Maryland.
PERRINE CHARLES O., news stand Union Depot, res. 26 Maryland, cor. Illinois.
PERRINE JAMES, res. New Jersey, bet. Market and Ohio.
Perkins Barzelia, machinist, res. E. Louisiana.
PERKINS & COON, drugs and medicines, 14 W. Washington.
Perkins C. G., (P. & Coon,) res. 40 N. Mississippi.
Perkins William I., (col.,) laborer, 139 N. West.
PERKINS SAMUEL E., Judge of Supreme Court, res. N. side New York, bet. California and West.
PERRIN GEORGE K., attorney at law and notary public, College Hall Buildings, E. Washington, bds. Pyle House.
PERROTT SAMUEL & SON, grocers, 200 W. Washington.
Perrott William W., (S. P. & Son,) 200 W. Washington.
Perry John, turner, res. 11 Elsworth.
Pearsall Peter R., professor of music, 26 S. Tennessee.
PERU & INDIANAPOLIS RAILROAD, Depot S. New Jersey.
Pesser Charles, stone cutter, res. S. Delaware.
Peters Harrison, wagon maker, bds. Farmers' and Drovers' Hotel.
Peters Henry, breakman T. H. & R. Railroad, bds. Union House.
Peterson John D., carpenter, res. 92½ N. New Jersey.
Petty James E., res. Drake & Mayhew's addition.

11

Petrie John, saloon and boarding, 222 E. Washington, res. same.

Pfaff William I., clerk, bds. 35 E. Michigan.

Pfafflin Theodore, (Klotz & P.,) res. 68 N. Mississippi.

Pfeiffer George, laborer, res. 86 St. Joseph.

Pfeiffer John, scissor grinder, res. 89 Fort Wayne ave.

Pflegar George, laborer, res. 27 N. Noble.

Phelan Martin, currier Mooneys & Co., bds. Mrs. Ferguson.

PHELPS O., editor School Journal, res. N. Ash.

Phelps Simon B., engineer, res. 100 E. Louisiana.

Phillips John, res. 8 Willard.

Phillips William, 27 McCarty.

Phipps H. C., clerk Samuel Rosengarten.

PHIPPS ISAAC N., real estate agent, office 28 E. Market, res. 26 E. Market.

Phipps John M., carriage maker, res. 179 E. Vermont.

Pick Henry, baker Cincinnati Bakery, bds. 91 E. Washington.

Pickering C. H., pattern maker, 261 W. Washington.

PICKERILL O. F., daguerrean operator, bds. Mrs. Kinder.

Pickett Henry, (col.,) driver Bates House.

Pickett John A., laborer, res. 178 N. East.

Piele Henry, bar keeper Capital Saloon, bds. 14 E. Washington.

PIEL WILLIAM F., general store, 240 E. Washington, res. same.

Pierce Winslow S., (McKernan & P.,) res. New York, cor. West.

Pierson Levi, brick layer, res. 114 N. Alabama.

Pierson S. D., salesman and cutter Owen McGinnis, res. 109 E. Ohio.

Pigg James, carpenter, res. 104 McCarty.

Pigg Francis, painter, res. Harris.

Pigg John, pump maker, res. 42 E. Louisiana.

Pike Charles R., engineer, res. 55 S. Bennett.

Piland Anderson, carpenter, bds. 188 Indiana ave.

PINNEY SIDNEY A., produce dealer, 192 E. Washington, res. 70 N. East.

PINNEY WILLIAM H. H., produce dealer, 192 E. Washinton, res. 70 N. East.

PITTS GEORGE W., ice merchant, res. 78 Indiana ave.

Plasnick Christian, cabinet maker, res. 145 N. Alabama.

Plasnick Henry, blacksmith, bds. 145 N. Alabama.

PLEASANTS JOHN, physician and surgeon, office 30 E. Market, res. 90 E. Market.

Ploch John, bar keeper Union Hall, bds. same.

Plogstarth Victor D., stone mason, res. 164 N. Liberty.

Plumb Charles, bakery, S. Meridian, bds. 4 S. Meridian.

Plummer Miss Amanda M., bds. 164 N. Noble.
Plummer wid. Hiram, 82 E. Market.
Pohler Louis, switchman I. P. & C. R. R., res. 142 E. Market.
Pohler William, laborer, res. 114 Virginia ave.
Polster Frederick, laborer, res. 116 E. Market.
Pond Frederick S., turner, res. 208 McCarty.
Poole Adoniram J., engineer Bellefontaine Railroad, res. 123 E. Market.
Poorman D. S., plasterer, res. 44 Pennsylvania.
Pope Christian, laborer, res. 33 Harrison.
Pope Henry, paper maker, res. 117 N. West.
POPE HENRY L., sup't Ind. Cen. R. R., office cor. Delaware and Virginia aves., res. Cambridge City.
POPE J. P., wholesale and retail druggist, 33 W. Washington, res. 111 East.
Pope William S., clerk Vinnedge & Jones, res. 117 cor. Washington and Vermont.
Pope William, (Hotz & Co.,) bds. Farmers' Hotel.
Poppensicker C., employee B. R. R., res. 108 S. Noble.
Poppensicker Gottlob, res. 108 S. Noble.
PORTER ALBERT G., attorney at law, res. 109 N. Delaware.
Porter Theodore R.. tailor, res. 81 N. Meridian.
POST OFFICE, John M. Talbott, P. M., 1 and 3 S. Meridian.
Pottage Charles E., clerk, bds. 12 W. Market.
POTTAGE BENJAMIN, dealer in hardware and iron, 76 W. Washington, res. 12 W. Market.
Potter James B., butcher, res. 30 N. Spring.
Potts Chas., sen., moulder, res. 216 S. Alabama.
Potts Chas., jr., moulder, bds. 216 S. Alabama.
POURDER & BORST, meat market, cor. E. Washington and Pennsylvania.
Pourder Milton, (P. & Borst,) res. 15 Indiana ave.
Powle Henry, carpenter, res. 88 N. Noble.
Powle John, carpenter, res. 107 N. Noble.
POWELL WILLIAM M., agent I. & C. R. R., res. 45 S. Meridian.
Powers Martin, porter Bates House.
Powers Patrick, laborer. res. 209 S. Pennsylvania.
Prange Charles, clerk A. & H. Schnull, bds. Alabama, bet. Market and Ohio.
Prassa Henry, boot and shoe maker, 174 E. Washington.
Pratt Mrs. L. A., milliner, Dunlop's Row, N. Meridian.
PRATT WILLIAM B., local agent P. & I. R. R., office at depot, res. E. Market, bet. Noble and Railroad.
Preis John, shoemaker, 218 E. Washington, res. same.

BACON'S
Mercantile College,
NORTH-WEST CORNER SIXTH AND WALNUT STREETS,
CINCINNATI, OHIO.

" A knowledge of the Science of Business, as well as its art, is necessary to the complete education of the Merchant. A knowledge of the theory of the profession gives stability to character. It gives wisdom in practice, and traces out consequences by the light of experience. * * * * A counting-house education will be of advantage to every man, whatever his future occupation may be. To farmers it will teach business habits and attention to accounts, which will give them increased interest and success in their business; to the mechanic it will teach order, system, management, the practical value of Book-Keeping, and remedy many of their deficiencies; to the professional man it will afford a clearer insight into the practical operation of business affairs, and giving them facilities in obtaining practice."—FREEDLEY.

OPINIONS OF THE PRESS.

BACON'S MERCANTILE COLLEGE.—The attention of young men who design devoting themselves to Mercantile pursuits, is directed to the advertisement of Bacon's Mercantile College. This is one of the best institutions of the kind in the country. A scientific knowledge of Book-Keeping and Commercial Law is indispensable to a first class business man. In addition to the thorough course of instruction embraced in the catalogue, we understand that Mr. J. H. Doty, one of the leading professors connected with the College, will shortly introduce, as a branch of Mercantile Education, Thompson's Celebrated Method for Detecting Counterfeit Money.— *Lafayette Daily Courier, Ind., December 19th,* 1859.

This whole Institution is undoubtedly the most elegant and finished establishment, for its purpose, in the world.— *Cincinnati Enquirer.*

Mr. Bacon, and the Institution which bears his name, have grown up with our city, and it is a source of gratification to observe that liberal enterprise and well directed energy have met their reward, in the prosperity and renown which his College has attained.— *Cincinnati Daily Gazette.*

Mr. Bacon is so well and favorably known to the commercial community of this city, and the entire West, as a competent and successful teacher of Book-Keeping, and every other branch requisite to a finished Mercantile Education, that it would be supererogatory in us to set forth his high claims to public favor. We will say, however, he is eminently worthy of the patronage of those who wish to enter a counting room.— *Daily Cincinnati Commercial.*

Mr. Bacon is unrivalled as a teacher, a diploma from his College in Cincinnati, is required as a *sine qua non* in obtaining a situation in the best Mercantile Houses in large cities.— *Chillicothe Ancient Metropolis.*

(FOR COURSE OF INSTRUCTION SEE PAGE 168.)

Presley John T., engineer Bellefontaine Railroad, res. 75 S. East.

Pressel Augustus, carpenter, res. N. Cherry.

PRESSEL & STOELTING, grocers, cor. North and West.

Pressel Charles, (P. & Stoelting,) res. 131 W. Vermont.

Pressel Mrs. Mary, res. 72 N. Mississippi.

Pressel Phillip, carpenter, res. N. University ave.

Pressel William H., carpenter, res. N. Cherry.

Price Joseph R., book binder, bds. Pyle House.

Prine Thomas, (Donaldson, Maxfield & P.,) bds. Bates House.

Pringer William, cooper, res. 163 N. New Jersey.

Prinz John D., porter Mills, Alford & Co., bds. Mrs. Ferguson.

Probus Mrs. Anne, res. 41 S. West.

Prosser Capt. Henry, cutter Moritz & Bro., res. 70 S. Delaware.

Prosser John, tailor Moritz & Bro., bds. Mrs. Hoyt.

Protzman Ferdinand, salesman Hickok & Starr.

Protzman John H., sexton Baptist Church, res. 20 S. Illinois.

Pronger Frederick, watchman Peru Depot, res. 195 E. St. Clair.

Prufield A. S., nurseryman, bds. 153 N. East.

PURCELL C. W., daguerrean artist, 8 Ray's Block, W. Washington, res. 21 W. Michigan.

Purcell W. C., clerk A. B. Willard & Co., bds. 20 N. Pennsylvania.

Pursel Jonathan, boot and shoemaker, res. 78 Pennsylvania.

Purviance J. H., American Express messenger Ind. Cen. R. R., bds. Bates House.

Pusey F. J., painter A. Brown, cor. Illinois and Washington. res. 173 E. Ohio.

PYLE JOHN, proprietor Pyle House, cor. Maryland and Illinois, res. same.

Pynefeld Henry, Union.

Q

Quante Frederick W., cigar maker, bds. Jefferson House.

Queisser Julius, harness maker, res. 275 Virginia ave.

Quickly Patrick, shoemaker, res. 204 S. Delaware.

Quinn James, res. Merrill.

Quinn John, laborer, res. 98 E. Maryland.

Quinn William, steward Farmers' Hotel.

Quinn William, res. 159 S. Delaware.

Quintel Jacob, harness maker, bds. S. East, over Union Railway.

COURSE OF INSTRUCTION.

The College Rooms have been refitted in magnificent style, and the Course of Instruction greatly improved by the introduction of all the latest and most approved methods of Keeping Books, making the Course here given more thorough, comprehensive, and practical than in any similar Institution in the United States, embracing all branches requisite for fitting young men for the active duties of the Counting House.

DOUBLE ENTRY BOOK-KEEPING

Is thoroughly taught in its practical application to every department of business. And in addition to the usual course of studies is included

BACON'S NEW METHOD OF
KEEPING BOOKS BY DOUBLE ENTRY,

Which will save half the usual amount of labor, and is accurate and readily comprehended. All interested in the Science of Accounts are invited to call and examine this new method, and judge for themselves.

PENMANSHIP

Is carefully observed. Mercantile Forms are thoroughly explained, and full and familiar instruction is given in

MERCANTILE MATHEMATICS,

Included in which is a beautiful and reliable mode of computing Interest, introduced by Mr. J. H. Doty. It has the merit of being *unsurpassed in brevity*, and is certainly withal, the *easiest* method known.

Besides Lectures on the Political Economy of Trade, Banking and Currency, there is a full, regular, systematic and practical course of instruction in

COMMERCIAL LAW.

By an intelligent and diligent student the course may be completed in from eight to twelve weeks, and on graduation a beautiful diploma is awarded.

Terms for the Full Course, - - - - - $40.00,
PAYABLE IN ADVANCE.

HOURS OF INSTRUCTION,—From 9 to 12 o'clock, A. M., from 2 to 4½, and from 7 to 9 o'clock, P. M.

For further particulars address or apply to

R. S. BACON, Principal.
Or J. H. DOTY, First Assistant.

R

Rabb Samuel, laborer, res. 192 N. New Jersey.
Radcliff William, laborer, res. 65 E. South.
Raeger William, carpenter, res. 40 N. Davidson.
Raesner William, laborer, 37 Union.
Rafert Charles (H. R. & Bro.,) res. 119 N. Meridian.
Rafert Charles, laborer, res. 79 Merrill.
Rafert Frederick, carpenter, res. E. First.
Rafert Henry, jr., (H. R. & Bro.,) res. 193 N. Illinois.
RAFERT H. & BROTHER, carpenters, 195 N. Illinois.
Rafert Harvey. sr., res. 193 N. Illinois.
Raferty A., with John Maloney, bds. 169 S. Mississippi.
Rager Edward, laborer, res. 168 S. Tennessee.
Raible Charles P., carpenter, res. E. Washington.
Raine Edward, wagon maker, res. 51 S. New Jersey.
Raine Thomas, laborer, res. 25 N. Railroad.
RAMSAY'S BLOCK, cor. Illinois and Maryland.
RAMSAY JOHN F., furniture ware-room 21 S. Illinios, res.
    21 W. Maryland.
Ramsey B., (col.,) res. 129 N. West.
Ramsey Mrs. Elizabeth, (col.,) res. 147 N. Alabama.
RAMSEY & HANNING steam and gas fitters, 85 W. Wash-
    ington.
Ramsey Thomas H., teamster, res. 41 E. St. Clair.
Ramsey Walter L., (R. & Hanning,) res. 155 Vermont.
RAND FREDERICK, attorney at law, 26½ E. Washington,
    res. 162 N. Illinois.
Randall Benjamin F., railroader, res. 168 N. Tennessee.
Randall John H., printer, res. 56 N. Delaware.
Randall Nelson A., printer Journal Office, res. Wabash, bet.
    New Jersey and East.
Randolph Lot, res 247 Indiana ave.
Rann Mrs. Eva, (col.,) res. Douglass.
Ranner Christian, blacksmith, 61 Bluff Road.
Rapp Frederick, plow maker, 144 E. Washington, res. 125
    N. Railroad.
RASCHIG CHARLES M., cigars and tobacco, 15 E. Wash-
    ington, res. 111 E. Vermont.
Raschig Edward, carriage painter, bds. Pyle House, cor.
    Maryland and Illinois.
Raskop George, manufacturer of fireworks, res. N. Winston.
Rasner William. checkman P. & I. R. R., res, 144 S. Illinois.
Rassmann Charles, saloon and boarding, 119 E Washington.
Ratti Francis, peddler, res. 128 E. St. Clair.
Ratti Francis, pressman Sentinel Office.
Ratti Joseph, printer, res. St Clair, bet. East and Liberty.

THE

Indiana American,

T. A. GOODWIN, EDITOR & PROPRIETOR.

Issued Wednesday and Saturday of each Week.

Having been in successful operation since 1832, the *American* is not only among the oldest papers in Indiana, but has by far the largest circulation of any other paper published in the State, except it may be one or two religious papers. While it battles manfully against moral, political and social wrongs, and always stands up for the right, its claims as a good family paper, and also a good newspaper, renders it a favorite in most of families.

Apart from its miscellany it devotes a large portion to

AGRICULTURE,

Under the editorial supervision of one of the best practical farmers in the State. Publishing no Daily, it has a city and suburban circulation greater than the combined daily and weekly circulation of any paper published in Indianapolis. It furnishes, therefore, a superior medium of advertising, at most reasonable rates.

TERMS OF THE AMERICAN.

Single Subscribers, paid at the end of the year......... $3 00
Single Subscribers, paid within the year.................... 2 00
Two Subscribers, to one office, within the year......... 3 00
Ten Subscribers, and one to the getter-up of the club 15 00
All additional Subscribers, to one office................... 1 50

Subscribers are understood to engage to continue, unless notice to the contrary is given before the expiration of the time paid for, and to continue at the above rates.

Rauth Henry, clerk, bds. Mrs. Kinder.

Ray Andrew, carpenter Bellefontaine R. R. Shop, res. 82 East.

RAY CHARLES A., (Morrison & R.,) res. 80 N. Illinois

Ray David, grocer, res. 133 N. Pennsylvania.

RAY HOUSE, Ray & Lambert proprietors, cor. South and Delaware.

RAY JAMES M., cashier of Bank of the State of Indiana, res. 19 N. Meridian.

RAY JAMES N., editor Indiana Farmer, office over Post-office, res. 31 N. East.

Ray M. M., (R. & Lambert,) Ray House.

Ray & Lambert, proprietors Ray House, cor. South and Delaware.

Ray wid. William, res. 11 Alabama.

Rea John H., clerk U. S. District Court, office Masonic Hall, bds. Bates House.

Readamon Henry, laborer, res. 15 St. Clair.

Reasarner William, railroader. res. S. Illinois.

Rebentisch Charles, shoemaker, 79 E. Washington.

Rech M. dealer in clocks and watches, 80 W. Washington.

Rechter Frederick, res. 309 Virginia ave.

Recker G., clerk H. Lieber, bds. Washington, cor. New Jersey.

Recker Hubert, carpenter, res. 110 E. Ohio.

Redfield Alexander, clerk G. W. Hawes, bds. Little's Hotel.

Redfield David A., compiler G. W. Hawes, bds. Little's Hotel.

Reding Alexander D., plasterer, res. 13 E. Lockerbie.

Redman Dennis, policeman, res. 123 South.

Redmond John, foundryman, res. 262 S. Delaware.

Redmond Mrs., res. 260 S. Delaware.

REDSTONE ALBERT E., inventors' agent for sale of patent territory, S. Meridian, opp. post office, res. 35 N. Alabama.

Redstone John H., (Ellsworth, Colley & R.,) res. 35 N. Alabama.

REED BENJAMIN F., hats, caps, furs and straw goods, 22 E. Washington. res. 156 N. Pennsylvania.

Reed E. R., engraver with W. H. Talbott & Co., res. Maryland bet. Pennsylvania and Delaware.

Reed Mrs. Elizabeth, bds. 15 N. Mississippi.

REED FISHE P., artist, 6 Ray's Building, res. 127 Mississippi.

Reed George, teamster, bds. 245 W. Washington.

Reed James A., shoemaker, bds. cor. Maryland and Delaware.

Reed John, blacksmith. 98 W. New. York.

Reed John F., clerk Hausmann & Co., bds. 54 N. East.
REED JOHN W., traveling agent with Sutherland & Mc-
Evoy, res. St. Louis.
Reed wid J. W., res. 54 N. East.
Reed Mrs. Rebecca B., bds. 93 Massachusetts ave.
Reed Thaddeus, clerk B. F. Reed, bds. 156 N. Pennsylvania.
Reese Charles, cabinet maker, res. 81 N. Davidson.
Reese Charles, laborer, res. N. Cherry.
REESE HENRY, grocer, 91 and 93 W. Washington, res.
same.
Reeves Louis B., bds. 12 St. Clair.
Reeves W. M., res. 12 St. Clair.
REGENAUER WM., saloon. 25 S. Meridian, res. same.
Rehling Charles, boot and shoemaker, 176 E. Washington,
res. same.
Rehling Wm., shoemaker, res. 189 S. Delaware.
Reid Mrs. Julia, res. 153 Virginia ave.
Reid J. B. E., foreman City shoe store, bds. Pyle House.
Reimansnyder Herman, shoemaker, res. 47 N. New Jersey.
Reinechar Jacob, laborer, res. 158 N. New Jersey.
Reinert Frederick, currier J. Fishback, bds. George.
Reines Victor, nurseryman, res. 88 Fort Wayne ave.
REINHARDT JOSEPH, locksmith and bellhanger, Illi-
nois, S. of Washington, res. same.
Reinhardt Ludwig, boot and shoe maker, res. 48 Massachu-
setts ave.
Reinhardt Valentine, cabinet maker, 59 Madison ave.
Reinkin Henry, cigars and tobacco, res. 93 Fort Wayne ave.
Reisee Conrad, stone mason, res. E. Washington, W. of
Cady.
Reisner Mrs. Ellen, res. 160 S. Tennessee.
Reissel ——, carpenter, res. 55 N. Liberty.
Reissner Albert, currier, North, near Michigan road.
Reistner Henry, shoemaker, res. 311 Virginia ave.
Reistner H., shoemaker, bds. 36 South.
Reitz F. A., bar tender Crystal Palace Saloon, bds. 44 W.
Washington.
Renard John, stone cutter, res. 151 E. New York.
Renard E., beer saloon, 278 E. Washington, res. 91 Rail-
road.
Rencham James, porter Bates House.
Rencham Joseph, laborer, res. 136 N. Mississippi.
Renner John, bar keeper, res. 91 N. Railroad.
Reno Wilkinson, res. 218 Indiana ave.
Rentsch Edward, groceries and provisions, 126 S. Illinois,
res. same.
Rentsch Harmon, Railroad Bakery, 134 S. Illinois, res.
same.

Reppert John, brick mason, bds. rear 169 S. Alabama.
Resener Christian F., boot and shoe maker, E. Washington, E. end.
Resner H., employee peg factory, res. 155 S. Mississippi.
Resner William, checkman P. & I. R. R., res. 144 S. Illinois.
Rester Henry, machinist, res. 213 S. Alabama.
REVELS THOS. W., (col.,) barber, N. of Tremont House, res. cor. West and Vermont.
REXFORD & SMITH, dealers in stoves and tinware, 11 S. Illinois.
Rexford Eugene, M., (R. & Smith,) res. 66 N. Mississippi.
Reynolds Chesly, laborer, res. 16 N. Mississippi.
Reynolds Frank, yard master, res. 98 N. Mississippi.
Reynolds John, book-keeper James Sulgrove, res. 87 N. Pennsylvania.
Reynolds John, carpenter, res. 50 Benton.
Reynolds John, res. 24 Virginia ave.
Reynolds Levi S., patentee, res. 16 Lochibie.
Reynolds Mrs. Mary, res. 124 N. East.
Reynolds Mrs. Sarah, res. 69 N. Noble.
Reynolds William, bds. 16 N. Mississippi.
Reynolds William, checkman T. H. & R. Railroad, bds. 98 W. Mississippi.
Rhiling William, shoemaker, res. S. Delaware.
Rhoads Charles W., carpenter, res. 129 W. New York.
RHOADS JOHN W., physician and surgeon, office 25 Ramsay's Block, res. 145 cor. Michigan and West.
RHODIUS GEORGE, proprietor National Saloon, 27 S. Meridian, res. same.
Riber Frederick, stone cutter, res. 190 S. Delaware.
Rice James, res. 61 West.
Rice John, res. 61 West.
Rice Oliver, pump maker, Pearl, rear post office.
Richards Richard, stone cutter, 108 W. Vermont.
RICHARDS & GODDARD, stone cutters, cor. Market and Tennessee.
Richards Thomas, carpenter, res. 128 E. Market.
Richardson I. I., 65 N. Tennessee.
RICHARDSON WARREN private secretary with Sutherland & McEvoy, bds. Little's Hotel.
Richey Julius, tinner, bds. 67 N. Noble.
Richey John, teamster, res. 74 N. Missouri.
RICHMANN & BUCHANAN, wagon makers, 211 E. Washington.
Richmond Mrs. Elizabeth S., school teacher, res. 83 E. New York.
Richmond John, laborer, res. 87 S. Illinois.

RICHTER ADOLPHUS I., boot and shoe maker, 161 E. Washington, res. same.

Richter Augustus, res. 315 Virginia ave.

Richter Florence, bar keeper Bates House Saloon, res. 9 Mississippi.

Richter Henry, saw mill, res. 213 S. Alabama.

Richwine John, laborer, res. 98 N. Davidson.

Richard Edward, baker, bds. 55 Maryland.

RICKARDS THOMAS, carpenter and builder, cor. Delaware and Maryland.

Ricketts George, baker, res. 102 E. New York.

Ricketts William H., book binder Campbell & Bro., bds. Magnolia Saloon.

Rider Henry, (col.,) barber, 81½ E. Washington, res. 127 Michigan.

Rieggar Arnold, res. bet. Illinois and Meridian.

Riemenschneider Hermon, boot and shoe maker, 179 E. Washington, res. New Jersey, bet. Ohio and Market.

Riggs John, (Davids & R.,) res. 82 W. South.

Riggs Simpson, butcher, res. 83 W. South.

Rihl Charles, res. 128 N. West.

Riley Benj. F., Bryant's Commercial College, res. California.

RILEY GEORGE W. H., printer Sentinel office, bds. Little's Hotel.

Riley James T., salesman New York Store.

Riley James, waiter Bates House.

Ringer wid. Daniel, res. 121 N. East.

Ringer J. Q. A., carpenter and builder P. & I. Depot, res. 92 St. Joseph.

Ringer Mrs Susanna, 108 St. Joseph.

Ringle David, (Fisher & R.,) res. Illinois, near Union Depot.

Rinkle Jacob, proprietor of Tremont House, cor. Illinois and Louisiana.

Rinkle Jacob, clerk Tremont House, res. same.

Rinn Edmond, res. 51 S. New Jersey.

Riple David, wood sawyer, res. 128 W. Maryland.

Rippit John, brick mason, bds. 169 S. Alabama.

RISING SUN INSURANCE CO., agency 14 and 16 S. Meridian.

Ritter Augustus, laborer, res. S. Delaware.

Ritter Peter, marble cutter W. A. Keys, res. 161 N. New Jersey.

Ritzinger Frederick, pork packer, res. 35 N. New Jersey.

Ritzinger J. B., clerk Fletcher's Bank, bds. 37 N. New Jersey.

12

River Frederick, res. 190 S. Delaware.

Roache Addison L., (McDonald & R.,) res. 97 N. Pennsylvania.

Roache Charles, breakman I. & C. R. R., bds. 51 Louisiana.

Roache Mrs. Mary Ann, res. 167 E. Market.

Roache R. S., 97 N. Pennsylvania.

Roback Eli book binder, bds. 139 N. Pennsylvania.

Roback Henry, moulder, res. 139 N. Pennsylvania.

Roback Mrs. Sarah, res. 139 N. Pennsylvania.

Roberts Mrs. A. W., bds. 160 N. Tennessee.

Roberts Mrs. Catherine, res. Alabama.

Roberts Dwight, dealer in patent medicines, 6 Louisiana, res. 160 N. Tennessee.

Roberts John W., machinist Bellefontaine shop, bds. 114 S. New Jersey.

Roberts Thomas L., machinist Bellefontaine R. R. shop, res. 261 Virginia ave.

Roberts Rev. Turner, (col.,) M. E. Church, res. 54 Blackford.

Roberts W. G., book-keeper Union Foundry, res. 297 S. Delaware.

ROBINSON CHARLES B., superintendent Peru & Ind. R. R., office at depot, res. 249 S. Alabama.

Robinson C. S., carpenter, res. N. Tennessee, bet. First and Second.

Robinson Francis, bds. 132 N. Illinois.

Robinson Frank, boot and shoe maker, res. cor. Michigan and Tennessee.

Robinson Geo., engineer I. & C. R. R., bds. 70 S. Noble.

Robinson Goodell, marble cutter, bds. 96 E. Market.

Robinson Joseph, flour miller, res. 64 N. Pennsylvania.

Robinson Martin S., pattern maker, res. 27 N. East.

Robinson Robert W., carpenter, res. 68 N. Missouri.

Robinson S., marble engraver, bds. N. W. cor. East and Market.

Robinson William J. H., deputy sheriff, office Court House, res. 49 N. Alabama.

Robison James, plasterer, res. 225 S. Alabama.

ROBINIUS & MYERS, boot and shoe makers, 51 Blake's Row, Washington.

Robson Mrs. Charlotte, res. 87 N. Pennsylvania.

Robson George W., foundryman, res. 140 N. Illinois.

Rockey H. S., clerk, res. 24 N. West.

Rockey J. L. D., bookbinder, bds. 24 S. W. cor. Market and West.

ROCKWELL ADOLPHUS F., secretary White River Valley Insurance Co., Ray's Block.

SHORTEST ROUTE BY 30 MILES.

CINCINNATI,

Southern Ohio and North-Eastern Kentucky.

INDIANAPOLIS & CINCINNATI

SHORT LINE

RAIL ROAD.

NO CHANGE OF CARS TO CINCINNATI.

Three Trains leave Indianapolis daily, Sundays excepted
THROUGH TO CINCINNATI IN ADVANCE OF ALL OTHER ROUTES.

Connecting at Cincinnati with all the Great Eastern and Southern Railroad Lines, and with Steamers on the Ohio River.

Patent Sleeping and Smoking Cars on this Route.

FARE THE SAME AS BY ANY OTHER ROUTE.

Call for your Tickets via the Indianapolis & Cincinnati R. R.

Baggage Checked Through.

Through Tickets for Sale at all Ticket Offices in the North-West.

SPECIAL NOTICE.

Be sure you get in the right Train at Indianapolis. THE ONLY CINCINNATI TRAIN stands on the Fifth Track, being the farthest Track South in the Union Depot, at Indianapolis.

H. C. LORD,
    President.

W. H. L. NOBLE,
    Gen'l Ticket Agent.

ROCKWELL R. E., agent Forest City Sewing Machine, 2
Ray's Building, bds. Palmer House.
Rockwood W. O., treasurer Indianapolis Rolling Mill, res.
30 S. Tennessee.
Roda Anthony, laborer, res. 148 N. Noble.
Rodes Jos., (col.,) auction-bell ringer, res. 129 W. Georgia.
RODEWALD HENRY, groceries and liquors, res. 288 In-
diana ave.
Roe Mrs. Mary E., res. 132 N. East.
ROESCH CHARLES, drugs and medicines, 185 E. Wash-
ington, res. E. Washington, bet. New Jersey and East.
Rogan George, at Rolling Mill, bds. 184 S. Tennessee.
Rogers B., laborer, res. E. Wabash, bet. Noble and Liberty.
Rogers Charles A., bar tender Farmers' and Drovers' Hotel.
Rogers George, conductor, bds. American House.
Rogers James, 50 W. Vermont.
Rogga Rudolph, tailor. res. 169 S. Alabama.
Rohlfing Christopher, laborer, res. 150 N. Noble.
ROLL ISAAC H., wall paper, 16 S. Illinois, res. cor. Illi-
nois and Maryland.
Roller Jacob, blacksmith, bds. Andrew Dinks, W. North.
Rommel Henry, salesman Dessar Bros.
Romerill Charles E., plasterer, res. 99 W. Maryland.
Roop John, spinner Ohio P. W. Factory, bds. W. Kolb.
Rook Thomas, res. 67 N. West.
Rooker A. J., painter, res. 104 Indiana ave.
Rooker George, painter, bds. 164 N. West.
Rooker Samuel S., painter, res. 164 N. West.
Rooker J. S., painter, res. 106 Indiana ave.
Roos & Schmalzried, butchers, S. Illinois, bet. Georgia and
Union Depot.
Roos Jacob, (R. & Schmalzried,) 73 S. Illinois.
ROOT, BENNETT & CO., manufacturers and dealers in
stoves and tinware, 68 E. Washington.
Root Charles H., (R., Bennett & Co.,) bds. 80 N. Meridian.
Root Charles, assistant cook Crystal Palace Saloon, bds. 44
W. Washington.
Root Deloss, salesman R., Bennett & Co., res. 80 N. Meridian.
Root Jerome, B. R., Bennett & Co., bds. 80 N. Meridian.
Rose Augustus D., captain of police, res. 110 N. East.
Rose Charley, cabinet maker, bds. 81 Davis.
Rose Franklin, engineer I. & C. R. R., res. 50 S. East.
Rose James G., plumber, bds. W. L. Ramsey.
Rose Martin, carpenter, bds. 110 N. East.
Rosebrock John F., bds. 283 S. Delaware.
Rosebrock Hermon H., grocer, 283 S. Delaware, res. same.
ROSENBERG S., hat and cap store, 73 E. Washington, res.
same.

ROSENGARTEN HENRY, M. D., druggist, 1 Odd Fellows' Hall, res. 47 N. Delaware.

Rosengarten Louis, res. 46 S. East.

ROSENGARTEN SAMUEL, grocery and produce store, 78 E. Washington, res. Michigan Road.

Rosensteel Robert, butcher, res. 11 N. Liberty.

ROSENTHAL A., wines and liquors, 38 Louisiana, res. Missouri, bet. Maryland and Washington.

Rosenthal Henry, res. 89 S. East.

ROSENTHAL DR. ISAAC M., physician and surgeon, drugs and medicines, 30 S. Illinois, res. same.

Rosier Aaron, res. 132 W. New York.

Rosner H., cooper, res. W. North.

Ross Bascom, bookbinder, bds. American House.

ROSS J. H., coal merchant, res. 174 N. Tennessee.

Ross N. M., bds. American House.

Ross Robert, well-digger, res. 135 E. New York.

Rosson George W., brakeman M. & I. R. R., bds. Ray House.

Rothrock Valentine, foreman Osgood, Smith & Co., res. 14 N. Meridian.

Rourke Thomas, waiter Bates House.

Rouhette Arthur, laborer, 169 N. Noble.

Rubb W. E., student N. W. C. University and Journal carrier for north part of city, res. Ash.

Rubush Fletcher, carpenter, res. 59 N. Noble.

Rubush Jacob, brick mason, res. 62 N. East.

RUCKER JAMES S., physician and surgeon, res. 58 W. Vermont.

Rucker Thomas H., at Bryant's Commercial College, res. 168 N. Vermont.

Ruckle Nicholas R., printer Journal office, bds. Pyle House.

Rue William, gunsmith, res. 108 McCarty.

Ruff Joseph, barber, bds. 16 Georgia.

Rugg Samuel L., superintendent public instruction, res. 59 W. New York.

Rugh William G., res. 108 McCarty.

Rumann August, express wagon, 131 E. Washington.

Rumann Mrs. Natalie, milliner and dress maker, 131 E. Washington.

Rumel Jacob, at Rolling Mill, res. 162 S. Tennessee.

Rung Christian, butcher, bds. Delaware, near South.

Runnion Wm., (Hays & R,) bds. Macy House.

Rupley Michael H., printer Journal office, bds. Pyle House.

RUSCH FREDERICK P., flour, seed and grain store, 83 W. Washington.

Rusche Peter, stone cutter, res. Wyoming.

RUSCHHAU? T. AUGUSTUS, groceries and provisions, 220 E. Washington, res. same.

BATES HOUSE HAIR DRESSING SALOON,

No. 12 North Illinois Street, Under Bates House.

Cold, Warm and   **Shower Baths.**

E.C.HUSSEY—CO—ENG

HENNING & STELZELL, Proprietors

A. J. DANFORTH.   F. F. SIMPSON.

DANFORTH & SIMPSON,

Wholesale and Retail Dealers in

Groceries, Produce, &c.,

No. 3 Odd Fellows' Hall,

Indianapolis, Indiana.

Goods delivered to any part of the City free of charge.

ALBERT CHRISTY,

CARPENTER AND BUILDER,

Mississippi Street, Back of Negro Chapel,

INDIANAPOLIS,

Will execute all orders with neatness and dispatch.

RUSCHHAUPT & BALS, liquor dealers, 82 E. Washington.

Ruschhaupt Frederick. (R. & Bals,) res. 61 N. New Jersey.

Ruschhaupt William H., clerk Farmers' Hotel.

Ruschhaupt Wm., carpenter, res. 295 S. Delaware.

Russell Chas. S., conductor Indiana Central Railroad, bds. 95 Virginia ave.

Russell James, res. 115 W. Ohio.

Russell John S., carpenter, res. 284 S. Delaware.

Russell John, watchman, res. 284 S. Delaware.

Ruth Charles, assistant cook Crystal Palace Saloon.

Ruth Louis, clerk, bds. 168 Virginia ave.

Ruthenburg S., master machinist, res. 121 N. New Jersey.

Ryan Mrs. H., bds. 32 Kentucky ave.

Ryan James B., (C. A. Elliott & Co.,) res. 100 Mississippi.

Ryan John, laborer, res. 265 S. Delaware.

RYAN RICHARD J., attorney at law, office Elliott's Block, bds 32 Kentucky ave.

Ryan Thomas F., clerk, bds. 32 Kentucky ave.

S

Sabert W., engineer Jeffersonville Railroad, res. 115 S. Alabama.

SACKETT CYRUS O., printer Sentinel office, bds. 79½ E. Washington.

Sacks John P., cooper, bds. N. Illinois.

Sacks John, tanner, bds. California House.

Saetar C., cooper, res. 107 E. Washington.

Sahn Ludwig, carpenter, res. 88 Fort Wayne ave.

St. John E., clerk I. H. Roll, bds. 18 S. Illinois.

Sander John, carpenter, res. 148 N. Liberty.

Sanders Frederick, smith Bellefontaine shop, res. 99 Bluff road.

Sanders Jack, (col..) res. 178 W. North.

Sanders John, carpenter, res. 148 N. Liberty.

Sanders John F., cigar maker, bds. 148 N. Liberty.

Sanderson Fayette, weaver Ohio Woolen Factory, bds. National Hotel.

Sands Mrs. Susan, cook National Hotel.

Sandsherhoff Charles, express messenger Adams & Co. Ind. & Cin. R. R., bds. Farmers' Hotel.

Santo Edward, bar keeper Kansas Saloon, bds. 85 S. Illinois.

Sargent Arthur W., carpenter, res. 160 N. Pennsylvania.

Sargent Ezra, foreman Bellefontaine car shop, res. 115 E. Market.

Sashse Charles, currier Mooneys & Co., bds. California House.

Sauer John, laborer, res. 21 N. Railroad.
Saunders Charles, salesman J. B. Wilson, bds. J. S. Pratt.
Savomaer Christian, laborer, res. 164 E. Michigan.
Savomaer William, cooper, res. 187 N. Noble.
Sawyer John S., book-keeper Donaldson, Maxfield & Prine, bds. John Moffitt.
Sayer Philip, blacksmith, bds. S. E. cor. Alabama and Market.
Scales Joseph, stone mason, bds. Union House.
Scaper Simon, res. 67 alley, W. of N. Mississippi.
Schackel Christian F., checkman local freight T. H. & R. Railroad.
Schaffer Jacob, laborer, res. 212 S. Alabama.
Schaffhouser Andrew, barber, bds. S. Illinois.
Schafner Jacob C., laborer, res. 219 N. Noble.
Schaupt John, painter, res. 215 N. Alabama.
Scheessler Conrad, laborer, res. 152 N. New Jersey.
Scheigert Frederick, night police, res. 10 S. West.
Scheltmaer Charles, drayman, res. 193 E. St. Clair.
Schelar Henry, smith Bellefontaine R. R., res. 130 S. Alabama.
SCHIMMEL JOSEPH, grocery and vinegar factory, cor. Meridian and Bluff road, res. same.
Schindler Robert, porter H. A. Fletcher & Co., bds. 105 E. Washington.
Schindler Robert, physician, 244 E. Washington.
Schiveley Lewis H., millwright, 29 N. Liberty.
Schlantz Frederick, watchman, res. 89 Union.
Schlater John, teamster, bds. Union House.
Schley Allen, tinner, bds. 24 N. Pennsylvania.
Schley George, printer Journal office, res. 24 N. Pennsylvania.
Schley Mrs. Georgianna, res. 24 N. Pennsylvania.
SCHLEY JOHN, printer Sentinel office, bds. 24 N. Pennsylvania.
Schlotzhaner Valentine, cabinet maker, res. 75 N. Davidson.
Schmalzried C., (Roos & S.,) res. 73 S. Illinois.
Schmeeder P. H., tailor, bds. California House.
Schmidt Henry, bakery, groceries and lager beer saloon, S. side National road.
Schmidt John, watch maker, res. 184 S. Delaware.
Schmitt George, laborer, res. 95 N. Railroad.
Schmucker Lewis, cabinet maker Spiegel, Thoms & Co.
Schnadinger Nicholas, stone cutter, res. 89 Massachusetts ave.
Schnell T. M., telegraph operator, 1 N. Meridian, bds. Mrs. Morrison, cor. Pennsylvania and Market.

Schnell Zacharias, gardener, res. 76 E. Garden.
SCHNULL A. & H., grocers, produce and commission
    merchants, 83 E. Washington.
Schnull Augustus, (A. & H. S.,) res. N. Alabama, bet. Mar-
    ket and Ohio.
Schnull Henry, grocer, (A. & H. S.,) res. N. Alabama, bet.
    Market and Ohio.
Schoder John, tailor, bds. Jefferson House.
Schomberg William, shoemaker, shop 9, res. 11, N. New
    Jersey.
Schoop Miss ——, 26 Union.
Schoolcraft Mrs. Cinderilla, weaver Ohio Woolen Factory.
SCHOPPENHORST WM., groceries and provisions, 101
    E. Washington, res. same.
Schott F., cigar maker C. C. Hunt, bds. Farmers' Hotel.
SCHOTT JOSEPH, groceries, provisions and varieties, 117
    E. Washington, res. same.
Schove Frederick, laborer, res. 291 Virginia ave.
Schowe Frederick, carpenter, bds. Green, Green's addition.
Schrader Christopher, laborer, res. 130 N. Noble.
Schrader John A., blacksmith, res. rear of 68 N. Missis-
    sippi.
Schrader Rudolph, finisher Washington Foundry, bds. 148
    E. Market.
Schreder A., laborer, res. 144 N. Liberty.
Schreder Frederick, cooper, res. 192 N. Noble.
Schroeder Charles F., machinist, bds. 108 S. Alabama.
Schudericht Louis, clerk, bds. California House.
Schuller George, salesman New York Store.
Schulmeyer J., retired, res. 163 N. New Jersey.
Schulmeyer Louis, clerk William Hannaman.
Schulmeyer Philip, teamster, res. 144 E. Market.
Schultz Henry, foreman brewer, res. 35 N. Noble.
Schumm Julius, school teacher 2d ward school, res. 199 N.
    Alabama.
SCHUYLER FRANKLIN J., printer Sentinel office, bds.
    Mrs. Cook, N. Pennsylvania.
Schwarz Jacob, at Rolling Mill, res. 91 E. Washington.
Schwartz Mrs. Mary, res. 129 N. Railroad.
Schwear H., laborer, res. 146 N. Liberty.
Schwicho Charles, porter Fitzgibbon & Co., res. 78 Union.
Schweinhart Augustus, shoemaker, bds. North, bet. Noble
    and Liberty.
Schweinhart Edmund, shoemaker, res. North, bet. Liberty
    and Noble.
Schweinhart Peter, sr., grocer, 131 N. East.
Schweinhart Peter, jr., shoemaker, res. 129 N. East.
Schwomier Henry, cooper, res. 180 N. Noble.

Scollard Bart, tinner, bds. S. Delaware, opp. A. Wallace's
warehouse.
Scollard Nicholas, wagon maker, S. Delaware.
Scorader Charles F., machinist, bds. 108 S. Alabama.
Scott Adam, (S., Nicholson & Co.,) res. 122 E. Michigan.
Scott Amos, laborer, res. 87 N. Davidson.
Scott Frank, book binder, res. 110 N. Mississippi.
Scott John, clerk New York Store.
SCOTT, NICHOLSON & CO., stone cutters, S. Delaware,
bet. Washington and Maryland.
Scott T. E., M. D., (Dodge & S.,) 3 Glenns' Block.
Scudder Caleb, boarding house, cor. Market and Tennessee.
Scudder Henry, teamster, res. Blake.
Scudder Michael, carpenter, bds. 19 N. East.
Scudder M., carpenter, bds. Tully House, 79 S. Illinois.
Sewaemlein E., merchant tailor, 163 E. Washington.
Seamann Christian, laborer, res. 151 N. Noble.
Seaman Edwin, traveling agent, res. 20 S. Illinois.
Sears Andy, laborer, res. 17 S. Georgia.
Sears Andrew, laborer, 18 S. East.
Secrest Charles, brick mason, res. 205 S. Alabama.
Secrest Nathan, law student, bds. 205 S. Alabama.
Sechrist Henry, with William Daggett, bds. 22 S. Meridian.
See Abraham, carpenter, res. 194 Indiana ave.
Seele Henry C., laborer, res. 174 N. Liberty.
Segelken Mrs. Ann, house keeper Macy House.
Seibird H. L., tailor, res. 108 W. Vermont.
Seibert & Clinton, blacksmiths, 252 E. Washington.
Seibert Henry L., tailor, res. 71 W. Vermont.
Seibert Hiram, blacksmith, res. 91 S. East.
Seibert Samuel, (S. & Clinton,) res. 3 N. Liberty.
SEIDENSTICKER ADOLPH, attorney at law and notary
public, also editor Indiana Volksblatt, 95 E. Washing-
ton, res. 35 N. New Jersey.
Seigman William, carpenter, res. 216 E. Washington.
Sell P., wagon maker, bds. Pyle House.
Sellsmith Adolph, musician, res. 110 E. Ohio.
SEMMONS J. H. & Co., opticians, 19 S. Illinois.
Senior Mrs. P., washer and sewer, res. 90 Massachusetts
ave.
SENTINEL BUILDING, E. Washington, bet. Meridian
and Pennsylvania.
Seque William B., engineer Central Railroad, res. 61 E.
Market.
Serger A., clerk Moritz & Bro., bds. Palmer House.
Server Mrs. Caroline, res. 231 Indiana ave.
Server E., bds. 234 Indiana ave.
Server Frank, bds. 234 Indiana ave.

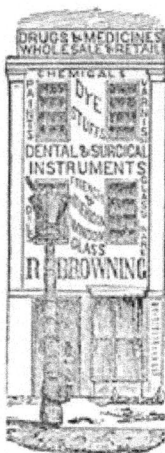

Server Gustus, clerk Mansur's pork house, bds. 234 Indiana ave.

Servison William, baggagemaster L. & I. R. R., bds. American House.

Severin Henry, grocer, cor. N. New Jersey and Fort Wayne ave, res. same.

Seward John, turner, 43 McCarty.

Sexton John R., gas fitter, bds. 22 Maryland.

Seybold Henry J., bds. 121 E. Ohio.

Seybold James H., (M. S. & Co.,) bds. 121 E. Ohio.

SEYBOLD M. & CO., marble dealers, 15 N. Pennsylvania.

Seybold M., (M. S. & Co.,) res. 121 E. Ohio.

Seybold Mahlon, wheat agent, res. 121 E. Ohio.

Shade Gottlieb, carriage maker, res. 52 N. Davidson.

Shade George, laborer, res. 52 N. Davidson.

Shade Reuben W., salesman New York Store.

Shea Jeremiah, res. Patterson, near North.

Shaff Abel, laborer, res. 51 N. Noble.

Shaffer Cornelius, hackman, res. 111 S. Tennessee.

Shaifehouser Andrew, barber, bds. near Union Depot.

Shaker C., laborer, res. 230 S. Alabama.

Shallman Isaac, clerk woolen factory, res. 242 W. Washington.

Shaler Henry, laborer, res. 139 S. Alabama.

Shappach H., shoemaker, res. 164 W. Washington.

Shanedorf Nicholas, teamster, res. 41 N. Noble.

Shanaberger David H., bds. 92 N. New Jersey.

Sharp E. B., clerk Mills, Alford & Co., bds. 79 N. Pennsylvania.

Sharp George, cigar maker, bds. Tremont House.

SHARPE JAMES M., secretary Indiana and Illinois Central Railway, 8 Blake's Row, 2d floor, res. 20 N. Meridian.

SHARPE JOSEPH K., wholesale leather and shoe dealer, 90 E. Washington, res. East, near Deaf and Dumb Asylum.

Sharpe Stephen, engineer Bates City Mills, res. 23 N. Noble.

SHARPE THOMAS H., Indianapolis Branch Banking Co., cor. Washington and Pennsylvania, res. 95 N. Pennsylvania.

Shaub George, shoemaker, res. 125 N. Noble.

Shaub Henry, bar keeper, res. 68 N. Noble.

Shaub John, laborer, res. 129 N. Noble.

Shaub Mrs., bds. 223 N. Noble.

Shauff Valentine, carpenter, res. 190 E. Market.

Shaup Peter, teamster, res. 123 N. Noble.

Shaup Henry, laborer, res. 137 N. Noble.

13

Shaw Augustus D., clerk, bds. 15 S. Alabama.
Shaw John, groceries and liquors, 228 E. Washington, res. same.
Shawber Christopher J., saddle maker, bds. 89 E. Market.
Shawver Alexander, carpenter, bds. S. Liberty.
Shawver Mrs. Mary, bds. S. Liberty.
Shea Cornelius, laborer, bds. 105 W. New York.
Shea John, laborer, res. 22 S. Liberty.
Shea John, laborer, res. 11 Railroad.
Shea Mrs. Mary, res. 108 Wabash.
Shea Michael, laborer, res. 55 E. St. Joseph.
Shea Patrick, laborer, res. 232 E. Washington.
Shea Rodger, res. 105 W. New York.
Shea Thomas, laborer, N. University ave.
Shean Donald, laborer, res. 38 E. Market.
Shean Geo. W., pump maker, res. 346 S. Delaware.
Sheckel Christian, laborer, res. 230 S. Alabama.
Sheehan Thomas, laborer, res. 201 E. Ohio.
Sheeks Hugh, student Bryant's Commercial College, bds. Mrs. Cook.
Sheets William, (S. & Braden,) res. cor. Ohio and Pennsylvania.
SHEETS & BRADEN, blank book manufactuers and dealers in stationery, 77 W. Washington.
Shellenberger John, pattern maker, res. 142 N. New Jersey.
Shepard Abner H., res. N. Noble.
Sherman Gustavus, (Kregelo, Blake & Co.,) res. 29 N. Meridian.
Sherman Paul, harness maker James Sulgrove, res. cor. Illinois and New York.
Sherlit Nicholas, brewer, res. 158 S. Liberty.
Sherer D., clerk, bds. 75 N. New Jersey.
Sherwood H. L., attorney at law, res. 45 N. Pennsylvania.
Shiffer Otho, machinist, res. W. Washington, lower end.
SHILDMEIER & MEYER, merchant tailors, 144 E. Washington.
Shildmeier Frederick, (S. & Meyer,) res. 144 E. Washington, up stairs.
Shilling Charles, at Bellefontaine freight depot, bds. Davidson.
Shipp Samuel M., at Bryant's Commercial College.
Shirling Nicholas, baker, res. 158 N. Liberty.
Shissler John B., clerk, bds. N. Pennsylvania.
Shmidt William, butcher, res. N. Davidson.
Shoels Lyman, American express messenger Indianapolis & St. Louis R. R., bds. Bates House.
Shrader Henry, clerk Robt. Browning, bds. 170 N. Mississippi.

Shreke Mrs. Mary, res. 143 N. Noble.
Shoemaker Frederick, cabinet maker, cor. New York and Mississippi.
Shoemaker George, bds. New York, cor. Mississippi.
Shoemaker Henry, laborer, res. 85 N. Noble.
Shoore John, breakman, bds. Union House.
Shopbach Henry, shoemaker, bds. G. Walk.
Shorer Jacob, res. 212 S. Alabama.
Short L. E., res. 46 S. Delaware.
SHOUPE FRANCIS A., attorney at law, office 95 E. Washington, res. 31 N. Meridian.
Shoup James M., res. 31 N. Meridian.
Shoup James, clerk B. F. Tuttle, bds. Mr. Kinder.
Shoutch George, brewer, bds. 135 W. Maryland.
Shortridge A. F., secretary Indianapolis Journal Co., res. 118 N. Illinois.
Shrader A., workman Bates City Mills, res. 144 N. Liberty.
Shrader Franklin, laborer, bds. 96 E. Louisiana.
Shrader Frederick, (Heimburgh & Co.,) res. 192 N. Noble.
Shrader Fred, shoemaker, bds. 68 N. Mississippi.
Shryock H., tailor Dessar Bros., res. 9 Elsworth.
Shucraft Silas, (S. & Gibbs,) res. 22 E. Lockibie.
SHUCRAFT & GIBBS, hair dressing saloon, under Palmer House.
Shuer John, laborer, res. 35 N. Noble.
Shupner Gottlieb, carpenter, res. 63 E. St. Joseph.
Shuhnocher F., cabinet maker Weaver & Williams, res. 95 cor. New York and Mississippi.
Shulmer Frederick, laborer, res. 57 E. St. Mary.
Shulmyer Jacob, laborer, bds. 169 N. New Jersey.
Shulmyer Louis, clerk Hannaman's drug store, E. Washington, bds. 169 N. New Jersey.
Shurr Leonard, watch maker, 64 N. Davidson.
Siaphoff Henry, cabinet maker, res. 68 Virginia ave.
Sibird David, blacksmith, res. 75 E. Market.
SIEGRIST REV. SIMON, (Ger. Catholic,) res. 46 S. Delaware.
Sierferts A., meat market, cor. Washington and Delaware, res. same.
Silver John, teamster, res. 51 N. Liberty.
Simcox John W., saddler, res. 138 N. East.
Simmelink William, carpenter, res. 157 E. Ohio.
Simmons Mrs. Anna, res. 137 N. Railroad.
SIMMONS GEORGE, printer Sentinel office, bds. 19 Circle.
Simmons Rev. James B., minister Baptist Church, S. Meridian, res. N. Pennsylvania.
Simon Peter, currier, res. cor. Market and Liberty.

Simond Frederick, cabinet maker, bds. Pennsylvania.
Simons Andy, laborer, res. extreme E. Washington.
Simons George, Adams' Express messenger J. & I. R. R., bds. Macy House.
Simpson Franklin F., (Danforth & S.,) res. 126 N. Pennsylvania.
Simpson James P., carpenter, res. 130 E. Ohio.
SIMPSON M. & R., groceries and provisions, 58 E. South.
Simpson Mathew, (M. & R. S.,) bds. Ray House.
Simpson N., groceries, flour and feed, 167 S. Delaware, res. same.
Simpson Richard, (M. & R. S.,) bds. Ray House.
Sims John Madison, (col.,) barber, 81½ E. Washington.
Sims William, 24 N. Mississippi.
Sin Augustus, varnisher, bds. S. Delaware.
Sinex William, (Beard & S.,) res. Richmond.
Singer L. F., American Express messenger Ind. Central R. R., bds. Bates House.
Sinker Edward T., (Dumont & S.,) res. 101 Virginia ave.
SINKER E. T., coal oil lamps, Meridian, S. of postoffice.
SINKING FUND OFFICE, junction of Virginia ave. and Pennsylvania.
Sipple L. P., conductor Bellefontaine R. R., bds. Bates House.
SIRRONIA L. D., hairdressing saloon, under American House.
Sittenheim Benjamin, salesman Glaser & Bro., bds. 15 N. East.
Skiles John W., conductor Bellefontaine R. R., bds. Bates House.
Skolley Matthew prop'r Indiana House, 31 Market.
Slate Benjamin F., carpenter, res. 126 E. Michigan.
Sleich wid. David, res. 24 N. Pennsylvania.
Sliach John, carpenter, bds. Union House.
Slippey Sylvester, book binder, bds. Pyle House.
Sloan George W., clerk R. Browning, res. 104 N. Meridian.
SLOAN & INGERSOLL, furniture and chair manufacturers, 4 Louisiana.
Sloan John, (S. & Ingersoll,) res. 83 S. Tennessee.
Sloan William I., cabinet maker, bds. 83 S. Tennessee.
Sloer Christian, shoemaker, res. 74 Fort Wayne ave.
Slasser Henry, res. 102 McCarty.
Small David, carpenter, res. 116 N. East.
Small Rev. Gilbert, Presbyterian Church, res. 40 N. Delaware.
Small Rody A., blacksmith, res. E. Washington.
Smallhalts John, laborer, res. 20 Garden.
Smallwood Mrs. Elizabeth, res. 52 N. East.

INDIANA
STATE JOURNAL
STEAM MAMMOTH
PRINTING
ESTABLISHMENT,

South-East Cor. Meridian and Circle Streets,
INDIANAPOLIS, INDIANA.

The Journal Office is prepared to do all kinds of

Book and Job Work

Neatly, promptly and accurately, being supplied with a number of fast
Presses, running by steam. Every description of Printing can be done
on short notice and quick time. We have in successful operation one of

GEO. P. GORDON'S FIRE FLY PRESSES.

CAPABLE OF PRINTING FROM 8,000 TO 20,000 CARDS PER HOUR.

We can furnish Printed Cards, when ordered in large quantities, at
cheaper rates than other establishments in Indiana can buy
the unprinted cards at Stationery Stores.

ADVERTISING.

The Daily and Weekly Journal furnish the best mediums in the State
for merchants and others to advertise their business through. It circu-
lates in every county of the State, and has the heaviest local circulation
of any paper published in Indianapolis.

JOURNAL COMPANY, Indianapolis, Ind.

Smallwood wid. James, res. 52 N. East.
Smallwood William, artist, res. 52 N. East.
Smicht Henry, 231 S. Pennsylvania.
Smidth E., watch maker W. H. Talbott & Co., res. 184 N. Delaware.
Smith Mrs. Annie, artist in hair, res. 143 E. New York.
Smith Anna M., notion store, 19 Alabama, res. same.
Smith Miss Anna, school teacher, res. 36 E. Market.
Smith C. H., 21 Chatham.
Smith Caleb B., (S. & S.,) res. cor. New York and California.
SMITH CHARLES C., attorney at law and notary public, office 95 E. Washington, res. 51 Ohio.
Smith Miss Catharine, dress maker, bds. 71 E. Market.
Smith Ebenezer, plasterer, bds. Pyle House.
Smith Ebenezer II., laborer. res. 111 St. Mary.
Smith Elisha M., carpenter, bds. 101 W. New York.
SMITH FRANCIS, (Delzell & S.,) attorney at law and notary public, 37 E. Washington, bds. Bates House.
Smith Frederick, groceries and provisions, 126 N. Mississippi, cor. Vermont, res. same.
Smith wid. George E., res. 59 N. New Jersey.
Smith Harrison, laborer, res. 146, cor. North and Blake.
Smith Henry, res. 4 E. Michigan.
Smith Horace E., law student Smith & Smith.
Smith Hugh, shoemaker, res. 19 N. Alabama.
Smith Hugh F., (S. & Stevenson,) res. Laurenceburg.
Smith James, last maker Osgood, Smith & Co., bds. 42 S. Meridian.
Smith Jas., brick yard, cor. East and McCarty, res. 267 East.
Smith John, boot and shoe maker, bds. North, bet. Pennsylvania and Maryland.
Smith John, res. 160 E. McCarty.
Smith John, stone cutter, res. S. side National road.
Smith John, butcher, res. 36 N. Spring.
Smith John, res. alley N. of W. North.
Smith John, shoemaker, res. 7 E. North.
Smith John, laborer, res. 265 S. Delaware.
Smith John C., carpenter, res. cor. St. Clair and James.
SMITH REV. JOHN C., (Meth. Epis.,) res. 115 N. New Jersey.
Smith John G., blacksmith, 36 Kentucky ave., res. 84 N. New Jersey.
Smith John I., American Express messenger L. & I. R. R., bds. Bates House.
Smith John S., carriage painter, bds. 7 W. Market.
Smith Jonathan, printer Sentinel office, bds. 20 N. Pennsylvania.

Smith Joseph, machinist, res. Fletcher's addition.
Smith Julius, watch maker, res. 184 N. Delaware.
Smith & La Rue, ornamental plasterers, 20 Kentucky ave.
Smith Leary, employee Bellefontaine R. R., res. 39 S. Meridian.
Smith Lewis C., turner, bds. Wm. Kolb.
Smith Mrs. Mary Ann, res. 95 E. Market.
Smith Mark, machinist, bds. National Hotel.
SMITH MRS. M. C., boarding Alvord's Block, S. Pennsylvania.
Smith M. T., (Duke & Smith,) res. near Christian University.
SMITH & MORGAN, merchant tailors, 35 E. Washington.
Smith Nathan, laborer, res. 144 E. McCarty.
Smith Nelson W., engineer, bds. E. Knight.
Smith Richard, teamster, 51 Union.
Smith Robert, tanner, res. S. New Jersey.
Smith Samuel F., (Osgood, S. & Co.,) res. 42 S. Meridian.
SMITH & SMITH, attorneys at law, 26 W. Washington, Ray's Building.
Smith Mrs. Sophia, dress maker, res. 86 E. Garden.
Smith Stephen, news agent and bill poster, res. 10 North.
SMITH & STEVENSON, coal, lumber and grain, 5 S. Delaware.
Smith Theodore, teamster, bds. 245 W. Washington.
Smith Thomas M., res. 126 E. Washington.
Smith Washington, teamster, res. 107 S. Alabama.
Smith Watt J., (S. &. S.,) notary public, bds. C. B. Smith.
Smith W. H., clerk J. S. Dunlop, bds. 84 N. New Jersey.
Smith Wilhelmina, 73 N. Pennsylvania.
Smith Rev. William C., presiding elder Wesley Chapel, res. 7 W. Market.
Smith William F., salesman R. Browning, bds. Mrs. Dana.
Smith William Q., clerk, bds. 21 S. Delaware.
Smith William, (S. & Morgan,) res. 37 N. Delaware.
Smith William, student Bryant's Commercial College, bds. 10 W. North.
Smith William, (Rexford & S.,) bds. 66 N. Mississippi.
Smithers William, clerk J. & J. Bradshaw, bds. 53 Indiana ave.
Smock M. L. J., res. 42 E. New York.
Smock Peter, clerk, res. 42 E. New York.
Smock Richard W., res. 227 S. Pennsylvania.
Smock William, laborer, res. 239 Massachusetts ave.
Snapp Mrs. Abigal, hair braider, res. 143 E. New York.
Snider Jacob, book-keeper, E. C. Mayhew & Co., bds. Tremont House.
Snider Conrad, laborer, res. 336 S. Delaware.

Snider Leonard, patentee, res. 149 N. Delaware.
Snow Miss ———, school teacher, bds. 14 N. Meridian.
Snyder David E., book-keeper Branch of the Bank of the State, bds. Jacob McChesney.
Socks Phillip, cooper, bds. 53 N. Illinois.
Socwell H. M., (Spencer & S.,) res. 14 N. New Jersey.
Soenke Charles, tanner and currier, res. above Union saloon, Washington.
Solomon Joseph, tobacconist, bds. Tremont House.
Soltee Wm., clerk, res. 24 S. Delaware.
Son wid Josiah, res. 111 S. New Jersey.
Sonderegger Fidel, clerk, res. 64 E. St. Joseph.
Sonnefeld Henry, carpenter, res. cor. Mississippi and South.
Southard A., cor. Vermont and Alabama.
Southard James P., res. 68 E. Vermont.
Southard M. R., salesman J. C. Yohn, res. cor. Illinois and St. Clair.
Southard M., 68 E. Vermont.
Southard J. P., res. 68 Vermont.
Spade Jacob, laborer, res. 177 N. Railroad.
Spaeth Christian, butcher, bds. Jefferson House.
SPANN & HALL, real estate, collecting and Insurance office, S. W. cor. Washington and Meridian.
Spann James R., groceries, provisions and meat store, 123 Indiana ave.
Spann John S., (S. & Hall,) res. 73 N. Pennsylvania.
Spangenberg Geo. D., shoemaker, res. 76 S. Noble.
Sparks Jesse, tailor, res. 69 Benton.
Sparks Wm., tailor, bds. Noble.
Spear Frederick, drayman, res. 103 E. South.
Spear wid. Prissilla (col.,) res. 63 S. Noble.
SPECKMAN & KRETSCH, dealers in cigars and tobacco, 57 S. Illinois, res. same.
Spencer E. S., general freight agent B. R. R. Line, bds. N. E. cor. Alabama and Washington.
Spencer George, foundryman, res. 213 N. Alabama.
Spencer James, (col.,) 135 N. Tennessee.
Spencer Milton, (S. & Socwell,) res. 24 N. New Jersey.
Spencer Rev. Oliver M., president Indiana Female College, res. N. Pennsylvanis.
SPENCER & SOCWELL, groceries and feed store, 202 E. Washington.
Spesser Charles, stone cutter, res. 267 S. Delaware.
Speth B., res. 146 S. Delaware.
Speth C., butcher, bds. Little's Hotel.
Spicer B. M., carpenter, res. 221 N. Tennessee.
Spicer Henry C., carpenter, bds. 221 N. Tennessee.
Spiegel Augustus, cabinet maker, res. 31 N. Liberty.

Spiegel Christian, (S., Thoms & Co.,) res. 180 E. Vermont.

SPIEGEL, THOMS & CO., furniture dealers and manufacturers, ware rooms 73 W. Washington, manufactory, 223 E. Washington.

Spilker Fred., laborer, res. 82 S. Noble.

Spillman Wesley L., at last and peg factory, res. 51 McCarty.

SPINNEY WILLIAM N., boots and shoes, 10 W. Washington.

Spinney William, moulder, bds. National Hotel.

Splain Maurice, laborer, res. 184 E. Market.

Splain Thomas, laborer, res. 29 N. Davidson.

Spond Frederick, turner, res. McCarty.

SPOTTS & THOMSON, Franklin Foundry, opp. I. &. C. freight Depot.

Spotts William, (S. & Thomson,) res. Fletcher's addition.

Spratt Joseph, plasterer, res. 60 N. Delaware.

SPRANDEL GEORGE, boot and shoemaker, 124 N. Mississippi, res. same.

Spreng Adam, stone cutter, bds. 16 Georgia.

Springer David, carpenter, res. 5. Chatham.

Springer James, tailor, res. 140 E. New York.

Springsteen George, brick mason, res. 37 N. East.

Springsteen Abram, brick mason, res. 37 N. East.

Springsteen Jefferson, City Marshal, res. 31 N. Spring.

Springsteen John, door and sash maker, res. 194 E. Ohio.

Sproule William K., (Fahnestock & Co.,) res. 18 and 22 S. Illinois.

Sprow Mrs. Louisa, res. 38 E. Pratt.

Squire P. J., 10 Cherry.

STAATS & ENGLISH, painters and glaziers, cor. Meridian and Washington.

Staats George D., (S. & English,) res. 6 E. Michigan.

Staff John, res. alley, bet. East and New Jersey.

Stagg Charles W., book-keeper Sheets & Braden, res. 76 W. New York.

Stahlin Martin, Arcadia saloon under Tremont House, res. 80 W. Georgia.

Stainkuhlar Henry, cooper, res. 91 Union.

Stanhilber Martin, driver for brewery, res. 270 E. Washington.

Stanton David, finisher, bds. W. H. Lingenfelter.

Stapp James H., (S. & Wright,) res. cor. Illinois and Fourth.

STAPP & WRIGHT, real estate, collecting and general intelligence office, 86 E. Washington.

Stareback Charles, carpenter, res. 203 S. Delaware.

Stark Gustavus, carpenter, res. 81 Fort Wayne ave.

Starling Samuel, clerk, res. 150 E. North.

Starr John, hostler J. Wood's livery stable, res. Wabash,
bet. New Jersey and East.
Starr John C., carpenter, 105 W. Market, res. 101 South.
STAUB J., clothing and gentlemen's furnishing goods, 59
E. Washington, res Noble, bet. New York and Vermont.
Staulb Frederick, carpenter, res. 99 N. Railroad.
Staufer John, switch tender, res. 98 S. Pennsylvania.
Steabler Michael, teamster, res. 45 N. Spring.
Steacy Joseph, carpenter, res. 127 W. Vermont.
Stedman E. P., M. D., physician, office 53 N. New Jersey,
res. same.
Stedman P., clerk I. & C. R. R. freight office, res. 147 Vir-
ginia ave.
Steele Thomas J., printer Sentinel Office, bds. 159 N. East.
Steele William H., carpenter, res. 159 N. East.
Steelsmith Simon, bds. South, bet. Delaware and Pennsyl-
vania.
Stegner John P., laborer, res. 243 S. Pennsylvania.
Steiber Charles, carpenter, res. 203 S. Delaware.
Stein Frederick, civil engineer, cor. Market and Cady.
Steiner Jacob, laborer, res. 158 N. East.
Steinmann Geo., tailor with J. Steinmann, 25 S. Meridian.
STEINMANN J., merchant tailor, 25 S. Meridian, res.
same.
Steinman William, book-keeper, bds. 21 S. Delaware.
Steinmiller George, cigar maker, bds. Farmers' Hotel.
Steinwinter Andrew, brewer, res. Wyoming.
Stelhorn Christian, carpenter, res. 176 N. Noble.
STELHORN FREDERICK, carpenter, res. 184 N. Noble.
Stelzell John, (Henning & S.,) res. 190 N. Illinois.
STERN REV. M. G. I., (German Reformed,) res. 15 N.
Alabama.
Sterding Frederick, res. 38 California.
Steubing Phillip, laborer, res. 119 N. Noble.
Stevens Abel, trader, res. 82 N. Tennessee.
STEVENS ALEX. D., printer Sentinel office, res. 142 Vir-
ginia ave.
Stevens Benjamin, cabinet maker, bds. Wm. Kolb.
Stevens Harrison, runner for Tremont House.
Stevens Dr. Isaac, bds. 171 S. New Jersey.
Stevens Levi B., brick maker, res. 261 S. East.
Stevens John, machinist, res. 66 Merrill.
STEVENS T. M., physician and surgeon, 172 E. Washing-
ton, up stairs, res. S. New Jersey.
STEVENSON C. S., cashier Branch of [the Bank of the
State of Indiana, res. 94 N. West.
Stevenson Rev. David, (Third Presb.,) res. 248 N. Illinois.
14

J. C. WORTH,

DEALER IN

PATENT RIGHTS,

99 NORTH MERIDIAN STREET,

Indianapolis, Ind.

To The Ladies.

MRS. M. S. THOMPSON,

PHYSICIAN & SURGEON,

Would respectfully say to the ladies of this city and vicinity, that the long experience she has had in connection with the formerly extensive practice of her husband, Dr. H. Thompson, has enabled her to treat disease in all its various forms, both acute and chronic, successfully; and also skillfully to assist woman in the most trying and perilous situation of her life. As Mrs. T. has never been so unfortunate as to lose any mother in parturition, and is not only competent, but has the facilities to treat the most difficult cases, with but one female assistant, she would therefore cheerfully invite all those who may wish for further information or acquaintance, to call on her at her residence.

Mrs. T., separate from the instructions she has received at a Medical Institution, has studied with and received private instruction from our most celebrated accoucheurs, especially in the safe administration of chloroform, in every case, without exception—in regard to which she will be happy to give satisfactory reference and testimonials. As her time and attention is given exclusively to her profession, she will be in readiness to attend calls day and night, at her office and residence, No. 20 North Illinois Street, first building north of the Bates House.

MISS E. LUEDERS,

TEACHER OF EMBROIDERY,

No. 16 South Illinois Street, Third Floor.

Embroidery and Needle-Work, in all its varieties, and Fancy Work generally, done to order, on reasonable terms.

Stevenson John, cooper, res. Canal.
Stevenson R., clerk Smith & S., res. 94 N. West.
Steward A., (col.,) 137 N. Tennessee.
Steward Thomas, (col.,) barber, bds. Kentucky ave., bet.
　Maryland and Georgia.
Stewart A., cook American House, bds. same.
Stewart Andrew, farmer, res. Elizabeth, bet. Blake and
　Dunlop.
STEWART & BOWEN, books and stationery, 18 W.
　Washington.
Stewart Charles G., clerk Stewart & Bowen, res. 99 N. New
　Jersey.
Stewart J. Austen, clerk McTaggart & Co., bds. 30 N. Illi-
　nois.
Stewart Jacob, employee McTaggart & Co., res. 191 S. New
　Jersey.
Stewart James, bds. Elizabeth.
Stewart Josiah, blacksmith Bellefontaine Railroad shop,
　res. 167 S. Noble.
Stewart Robert, book-keeper Moritz & Bro., bds. Bates
　House.
Stewart Robert R., foreman Witness office, 12½ S. Pennsyl-
　vania, res. same.
Stewart Thomas W., clerk American and U. S. Express Co.,
　bds. Bates House.
Stewart Rev. Thomas H., (Baptist,) res. 116 N. David-
　son.
Stewart wid. William, res. 99 N. New Jersey.
Stidely John B., teamster, bds. 65 Massachusetts ave.
Stiedel George, file maker, res. 55 N. Noble.
Stiger Fred, painter, res. 29 N. Liberty.
Stiegmann C., general store, 205 S. Delaware, res. same.
Stiles John, mason, res. E. Michigan.
Stilz J. George, (Birkenmeyer & Co.,) res. S. E. of city
　limits.
Stimebraker George, laborer, res. 7 Pearl.
Stimebraker Michael, res. Pearl.
Stirk Hammon, shoemaker, res. 172 N. Noble.
Stirk James, wheelwright, res. alley, bet. E. Ohio and New
　York.
Stoacker William, dyer and scourer, 18 Kentucky ave.
Stoddard Benj. F., clerk D. Braden, bds. 41 W. Michigan.
Stoelting Frederick, grocer, res. 163 Indiana ave.
Stokes Aaron, carpenter, bds. 107 S. Tennessee.
Stolte Henry, carpenter, 243 S. Delaware.
Stolte H. A., laborer, res. 135 E. McCarty.
Stolte William, clerk, res. 243 S. Delaware.
Stone H. L., student, bds. James.

Stone Timothy S., (V. K. Hendricks & Co.,) res. Worcester, Mass.

Stone W. O., clerk V. K. Hendricks & Co., bds. 99 N. Meridian.

Stoneman W. H., book-keeper Fitzgibbon & Co., bds. Samual Beck.

Stookey Charles, cooper, res. 27 N. Spring.

Stouff John, laborer, alley, bet. New Jersey and East.

Stout Benjamin G., (O. B. S. & Bros.,) bds. 19 W. Maryland.

Stout Carhart, coal dealer, res. 101 S. Tennessee.

Stout D. L., (R. C. & D. L. Stout,) bds. 19 W. Maryland.

Stout John R., (O. B. S. & Bros.,) bds. 19 W. Maryland.

Stout John, printer Sheets & Braden, res. cor. Tennessee and Louisiana.

Stout Mrs. L., res. 98 N. Meridian.

STOUT O. B. &. BROS., groceries, wholesale and retail, 42 W. Washington.

Stout Oliver B., (O. B. S. & Bros.,) bds. 19 W. Maryland.

Stout Oliver H., physician and surgeon, res. 19 W. Maryland.

STOUT R. C. & D. L., wholesale and retail grocers, 46 E. Washington.

Stout Richard C., (R. C. & D. L. S.,) res. 19 W. Maryland.

Stoven Thomas, res. 108 S. Tennessee.

Stover A. H., boarding, 118 N. Illinois.

Stowell Myron A., (Willard & S.,) res. 153 N. Illinois.

Stowers Mrs. Catherine, cor. Ohio and Tennessee.

Strachan Geo. C., salesman New York Store.

Strader Crist., laborer, res. 92 McCarty.

STRADER MARTIN V., cloaks and mantillas, 56 E. Washington, res. 32 N. Pennsylvania.

Straeghar Jacob J., carpenter, res. 121 Fort Wayne ave.

Strang Gabriel L., shoemaker, res. 97 N. Noble.

Strange William R., notary public Court House, res. 108 E. Vermont.

Stratton Joseph, machinist, bds. National Hotel.

Straub Albert, harness maker, res. 233 S. Pennsylvania.

Straub Fred., cook Union Saloon, E. Washington.

Strauhs Solomon, clerk Moritz & Bro., bds. Tremont House.

Strausner Frederick, tailor, res. 112 E. Washington.

Street J. W., (L. S. & Bro.,) res. 144 N. Illinois.

Street L., (L. S. & Bro.,) res. 132 N. Illinois.

STREET L. & BRO., staple and fancy dry goods, 56 E. Washington.

Streicher Jacob, carpenter, res. 121 Fort Wayne ave.

Strickland David H., paper maker, bds. National Hotel.

Strife David, tanner, bds. 180 E. New York.

Stringer Wesley, laborer, res. 266 Madison Railroad.

STRINGFIELD WOODFORD, attorney at law, office McOuat's Block, Kentucky ave.

Stucke Charles, (Heimburgh & Co.,) res. 27 Spring.

Stuckmeier John H., carpenter, res. 24 S. Alabama.

Stumpf George, laborer, res. 73 N. Davidson.

Stumpf John G., laborer, res. 155 N. Noble.

Stumpf Henry, laborer, res. 148 N. East.

Stumpf John H., laborer, res. 148 N. East.

Stumph Henry, stone mason, res. 228 N. Alabama.

Stumph John J., res. S. Illinois.

Styner Jacob, engineer on I. & C. R. R., bds. 46 S. Noble.

Sudbrock Francis H., laborer, res. 120 N. Davidson.

Suher Louis, saw grinder E. C. Atkins, res. 270 S. Delaware.

Sule Henry, laborer, res. 174 N. Liberty.

SULGROVE B. R., principal editor Indianapolis Journal Co., res. 87 W. South.

Sulgrove Eli C., harness maker, res. 117 N. Alabama.

SULGROVE & REYNOLDS, saddlery, hardware and trimmings, 20 W. Washington.

Sulgrove Jas., (S. & Reynolds,) res. 59 W. Maryland.

Sulgrove James W., clerk James Sulgrove.

SULGROVE JEROME B., harness maker and saddler, 44 E. Washington, res. 72 Kentucky ave.

SULGROVE JOHN M., harness maker Jas. Sulgrove.

Sulgrove Milton M., foreman Jas. Sulgrove, bds. 87 N. Pennsylvania.

Sullenberger Asher W., turner, res. 44 E. Pratt.

Sullivan Arthur, laborer, res. 209 S. Delaware.

Sullivan Mrs. A., res. 79 E. Market.

Sullivan Daniel, laborer, res. 73 E. Market.

Sullivan Henry, printer, bds. N. Meridian, cor. Pratt.

Sullivan James, carpenter, bds. 92 N. Meridian.

Sullivan John B., carpenter, res. 40 E. Pratt.

Sullivan John, railroad man, res. 73 S. Noble.

Sullivan John, laborer, res. 164 S. Mississippi.

Sullivan John, Bates House.

Sullivan Michael, laborer, 99 S. Louisiana.

Sullivan Ottis, laborer, res. 206 S. Delaware.

Sullivan Timothy, plasterer, res. 310 S. Delaware.

Sullivan Timothy, plasterer, res. 308 S. Delaware.

Sullivan W. H., clerk, bds. 156 N. Tennessee.

Sullivan William, sr., carpenter, res. 92 N. Meridian.

SULLIVAN WILLIAM, justice of the peace, 47 E. Washington, 2d floor, res. 107 N. Meridian.

Sumers Albert B., carpenter, res. 150 N. Mississippi.

Sumers B., cattle merchant, res. 144 E. McCarty.

Summer Augustus, laborer, 92 Union.

SUMMERS & WENTZ, confectionery and bakery, 144 W. Washington.
Summers A. B., (S. & Wentz,) bds. 144 W. Washington.
Surer Lewis, res. Wyoming.
Suse Godfrey, res. 148 New Jersey.
Suss Charles, tailor, station eating-house.
Sutherland Levi, carriage and wagon manufacturer, 162 Delaware, res. 112 McCarty.
SUTHERLAND JAMES, (Sutherland & McEvoy,) bds. Little's Hotel.
SUTHERLAND & McEVOY, State gazetteer, business and city directory publishers and compilers, office Sentinel Buildings, Indianapolis, and 50 Commercial street, St. Louis, Mo.
Sutphen Elias, fireman, res. E. Lord.
Sutphen James, engineer B. F. R. R., res. 99 S. New Jersey.
Sutton Joseph, plasterer, res. California.
Sutz Charles, tailor, bds. Railroad Exchange.
Swafford Edward, laborer, res. 217 N. New Jersey.
Swain James, clerk in postoffice, res. 29 N. Illinois.
Swammeier Christian, on Bellefontaine R. R., res. 164 N. Michigan.
Swartz Christian, teamster, res. 166 N. Noble.
Swartz Frederick W., clerk Munson & Johnston.
Swartz Jacob, baker Cincinnati Bakery, bds. 91 E. Washington.
Swear Crist., drayman, res. 101 E. South.
Sweeny Patrick, res. 241 S. Pennsylvania.
Sweeny John, carpenter, bds. 73 W. Maryland.
SWEETSER JAMES N., attorney at law, office Johnson buildings, 23 E. Washington, res. 50 N. Pennsylvania.
Sweicho Charles, laborer, 87 Union.
Sweinberger William, butcher, 73 S. Illinois.
Sweinhart Edmund, shoemaker, res. 68 E. St. Mary.
Sweinhart William, cutter, 3 W. Washington, res. 165 N. Alabama.
Sweir Gottlieb, laborer, res. 146 N. Liberty.
Swift Mrs. Mary, laundress, res. 51 E. Market.
Swigert Peter, house carpenter, Wabash, bet. New Jersey and East.
Swing Edward, butcher Bates House meat shop, res. 90 New York.
Syerup Henry, groceries, res. 119 N. East.
Sym James, cupola tender, res. 222 S. Alabama.
Symons Henry W., carpenter, res. 38 E. St. Clair.

T

Taff H., watchman, bds. 194 N. New Jersey.
Tagg H. B., blacksmith, bds. 84 N. New Jersey.
Taggart Samuel, machinist, res. 64 N. Mississippi.
Tague Geo. G., bds. 128 N. Alabama.
Talbott C. H., res. 66 Tennessee.
Talbott E. N., (Palmer & T.,) res. 90 N. Illinois.
TALBOTT JAMES W., merchant tailor, 3 W. Washington, res. 38 E. New York.
TALBOTT JOHN M., postmaster, res. 66 N. Tennessee.
TALBOTT JOHN T., directory publisher, bds. Palmer House.
Talbott Richard C., family groceries and produce, 101 W. Washington.
TALBOTT W. H. & CO., watches and jewelry, 24 E. Washington.
Talbott Washington H., (W. H. T. & Co.,) res. S. W. cor. Ohio and Meridian.
Talbott Wm., tinner, bds. 9 Ohio, cor. Meridian.
Talbott W., engineer Jeffersonville Railroad, res. 115 S. Alabama.
Talkington Robert, brick layer, res. 141 N. Noble.
Tallon John, machinist, res. 51 McCarty.
Tamma Frank, carpenter, res. 184 S. Alabama.
TANNER GORDEN, attorney at law and reporter Supreme Court, office McOuat's Block, bds. Palmer House.
Tanner John L., mattress maker, bds. 15 Indiana ave.
Tanney Martin, striker, res. 51 S. New Jersey.
Tanzy Mrs. Nancy, res. 100 E. Market.
Taonne Frederick, laborer, res. 238 Massachusetts ave.
TAPKING & BECKER, merchant tailors, 63 E. Washington.
Tapking Frederick H., clothier, E. Washington, res. 113 E. New York.
Tapking Frederick, (T. & Becker,) res. 113 E. New York.
Tapking John, chair maker, res. 65 N. New Jersey.
Tarlton James A., salesman Phillip Haynes, bds. 40 W. Washington.
TARKINGTON JOHN S., (Newcomb & T.,) res. 35 E. Ohio.
Tassling Leonard, works Washington Foundry, res. E. Washington.
Tattersall Joseph, stone cutter, res. 51 N. East.
Taylor Calvin, law student with N. B. Taylor, bds. 280 Massachusetts ave.

THE HARTFORD FIRE

INSURANCE CO.

OF HARTFORD, CONN.

INCORPORATED A. D. 1810.—CHARTER PERPETUAL.

CAPITAL, - - $500,000.

DIRECTORS:

H. HUNTINGTON,	CHAS. BOSSWELL,	JOB ALLYN,
ALBERT DAY,	HENRY KENEY,	JOHN P. BRACE,
JAMES GOODWIN,	CALVIN DAY,	CHAS. J. RUSS.

T. C. ALLYN, Secretary,   H. HUNTINGTON, Pres.
C. C. LYMAN, Assist. Sec.   WM. N. BOWERS, Actuary.

D. ALEXANDER, Gen'l Agt. for Western and South-Western States, Columbus, O.
JOHN GRAHAM, Ass't Agt. for Western and South-Western States, Columbus, O.

OFFICE OF AUDITOR OF STATE, INDIANA,
Indianapolis, February 13th, 1860.

To THE PEOPLE OF INDIANA:

The "Hartford Fire Insurance Company," having complied with the law of Indiana, by filing in this Office a statement of its condition on the first day of January, 1860, and having invited an examination of its affairs by this Department, I, John W. Dodd, Auditor of the State of Indiana, hereby certify that I have made a personal and thorough examination of the books and assets of the Company, at their Office in the City of Hartford, Connecticut, and that the Company own and have in their possession in cash, and in securities convertible at pleasure, nearly One Million of Dollars, applicable to the payment of losses—an amount corresponding with their official statement of January last. The Hartford Fire Insurance Company has been in existence for half a century. The high character of its officers for experience and probity—the promptness and fidelity with which it has met all it engagements—justly entitles it to the highest rank among the Insurance Companies of the country, and commends it to the patronage of the people of Indiana.

JOHN W. DODD, *Auditor of State.*

Insurance Policies in the Company issued by the undersigned upon as favorable terms as the nature of the risk will admit.

LOCKE & BROTHER,

Indianapolis, Ind.

Taylor David M., bds. 57 Massachusetts ave.
Taylor Isaac, carpenter, res. 170 S. Alabama.
Taylor Israel, book-keeper, res. 57 Massachusetts ave.
Taylor Mrs. Jane, seamstress, 82 Tennessee.
Taylor Mrs. Louisa, res. 7 Pearl.
TAYLOR N. B., attorney at law and notary public, 30½ W.
    Washington, up stairs, res. 109 N. Alabama.
Taylor Oliver, (col.,) bds. 107 W. North.
Taylor Mrs. Rebecka, seamstress, res. 177 N. Noble.
Taylor Riley, res. 146 W. Market.
Taylor Robert A., brick mason, res. 280 Massachusetts ave.
Taylor William H., tinner, bds. Mrs. Cook.
Taylor William L., American Express messenger Ind. Cen.,
    bds. American House.
TAYLOR, WRIGHT & HADLEY, wholesale grocers, 66 E.
    Washington.
Tawhead T. R., student N. W. C. University, bds. E. Clark.
Teal John, clerk in Hoosier Woolen Factory, lower end W.
    Washington.
TEAL NATHANIEL, physician and surgeon, 38½ W. Wash-
    ington, res. N. Illinois, N. of City limits.
Teamann Henry, blacksmith, res. Bluff Road, cor. McCarty.
Teaster Ernest, shoemaker, res. 133 N. Railroad.
Teats Frederick, 246 W. Washington.
Tebby Charles, res. 114 S. Noble.
Teckenbrock Wm., machinist, res. 187 S. Alabama.
Teder Henry, boot and shoemaker, res. 133 Railroad.
Teep Herman, striker, res. 271 Virginia ave.
Tegardner George, blacksmith, res. 180 S. Tennessee.
Teish John, cabinet maker Sloan & Ingersoll.
Telbutt Elizabeth, sewer, bds. 83 N. Alabama.
Telbert Charles, bds. Pennsylvania House.
Telli John, brakeman, bds. Union House.
TELLKAMPE JOHN, carriage blacksmith, Pearl, rear of
    Postoffice.
TEMPERANCE HALL, 30½ W. Washington, up stairs.
Teney Abraham, cooper, bds. cor. Market and Illinois.
TENEYCK J. & R. S., boots and shoes, 206 W. Washing-
    ton.
Teneyck John, shoemaker, res. 86 Indiana ave.
Teneyck John A., shoemaker, bds. California House.
Teneyck Nelson, boots and shoes, 260 W. Washington, bds.
    20 California.
Teneyck Richard F., shoemaker, res. 20 California.
Tentscher Frederick, cabinet maker, bds. E. Washington.
Terhune Charles, painter, 308 S. Delaware.
TERRE HAUTE & RICHMOND Railroad office and freight
    depot, Louisiana, bet. Tennessee and Mississippi.

Terrell Mrs. Frances, 2 Garden.
Terry Mrs. Jane, 221 S. Pennsylvania, cor. Merrill.
Tess John, cabinet maker, S. Delaware.
Testjoint John, laborer, bds. 306 S. Delaware.
Tetcomb Daniel, street superintendent, 45 N. Illinois.
Thalman Isaac, book-keeper Hoosier Woolen Factory, res.
    242 W. Washington.
Thalman John, (Grein & T.,) res. 214 E. Washington.
Tharp Caleb, res. 192 N. Illinois.
Thatew Amos, laborer, res. 13 Georgia.
Thayer Miss Aurellia A., res. 147 E. Market.
Thayer Daniel, collecting agent, res. 147 E. Market.
Thayer S., clerk G. E. West, bds. 145 E Market.
Theines Peter, porter, 35 N. Noble.
Theodore Thomas, brick mason, res. 125 N. East.
THE INDIANA AMERICAN, Semi-Weekly, T. A. Good-
    win, editor and proprietor, rear of Glenn's Block.
THE WITNESS, M. G. Clark, editor and proprietor, office
    Odd Fellows' Hall.
Thomas Benjamin, res. W. Market.
Thomas Benjamin, (col.,) servant, 34 E. Michigan.
Thomas E. J., American Express messenger L. & I. R. R.,
    bds. Bates House.
Thomas George, laborer, res. 61 N. Noble.
THOMAS GEORGE W., agent Grover & Baker's sewing
    machines, 46 W. Washington.
Thomas John, manager Indianapolis Rolling Mill, res. 57
    W. South.
Thomas Judge John H., bds. Pyle House.
Thomas Lewis L., carpenter, res. 155 W. Vermont.
THOMAS MRS. M. J., milliner and dress maker, 46 W.
    Washington.
Thompson Archibald, machinist, res. 157 S. Alabama.
Thompson Daniel, mason, 19 Willard.
Thompson Eli, res. 133 W. New York.
Thompson Gideon B., printer Sentinel Office, bds. 27 Indi-
    ana ave.
Thompson Henry, cigar maker, bds. Farmers' Hotel.
Thompson Hugh, bakery, 4 S. Meridian.
Thompson James, baker, 4 S. Meridian.
Thompson James, copyist, Co. clerk office, bds. Pyle House.
Thompson Jim, conductor P. & I. R. R., bds. American
    House.
THOMPSON MRS. MARY, accoucher, physician and sur-
    geon, res. 20 N. Illinois.
THOMPSON MRS. MARY, groceries and dry goods, 66 E.
    South, res. same.
THOMPSON MRS. MARY, news depot at Postoffice.

Thompson Milton, carpenter, res. 114 E. Michigan.
Thompson Richard, machinist I. & C. R. R., res. Oriental, bet National and Michigan Road.
THOMPSON & WOODBURN, physicians and surgeons, office 14 E. Market.
Thompson William C., (T. & Woodburn,) res. 58 N. Illinois.
Thompson William A. C., (Bartlett & Co.,) bds. Macy House.
Thompson William G., finisher, res. Indiana ave.
Thoms Frederick, (Spiegel, T. & Co.,) res. Noble, bet. Ohio and New York.
Thomson Hugh, machinist, bds. Michigan ave.
Thorn J., butcher, Cincinnati ave., cor. New Jersey.
Thornberry William, res. 134 N. Alabama.
Thornley Orian, machinist, res. 129 E. McCarty.
Thorpe John D., deputy Sheriff, office Court House, res. 39 E. Market.
Tickett John A., teamster, res. 178 N. East.
Tiernney Martin, blacksmith B. R. R. Shop, res. S. New Jersey.
Tilberry Mathew, teamster, res. 26 N. Delaware.
TILFORD A. L., matress maker, 192 N. Mississippi.
Tilford J. M., president Indiana Journal Co., res. 128 N. Tennessee.
Tilford J. W., clerk Journal Office, bds. 192 N. Mississippi.
Tilford Samuel E., res. 128 N. Tennessee.
Tilly Gilbert, marble cutter, bds. 223 W. Washington.
Tilly Herman, res. 188 S. Pennsylvania.
Tilly Joseph, physician, res. 128 S. Delaware.
TILLY THEODORE, soap manufacturer and dealer, res. 215 S. Pennsylvania.
TILLY WILLIAM, druggist, 81 E. Washington, res. 33 N. Alabama.
Tilton George W., painter, res. N. Pennsylvania.
Tilton Josiah S., painter, res. N. Pennsylvania.
Timmerman Herman, laborer, res. 153 N. Railroad.
TINDELL REV. GEORGE P., pastor 2d Presbyterian Chvrch, res. 54 W. Vermont.
Tiney Dennis, laborer, res. 95 S. Alabama.
Tinker John, teamster, 31 McCarty.
Tinsley Miss Lucy, music teacher, bds. 14 N. Meridian.
Toben Mat, with John Maloney, bds. 18 S. Meridian.
Tolan Eli, laborer, res. Wisconsin ave.
TOMLINSON & COX, druggists, 18 E. Washington.
Tomlinson James M., bds. 107 N. W. cor. Meridian and St. Clair.
Tomlinson Jesse D., carpenter, res. 157 N. Liberty.

15

Topp Frank, shoemaker, res. 91 Fort Wayne ave.
Topp Mrs. Frederica, res. 70 E. St. Joseph.
Toohey James F., dining-room clerk Bates House.
Tool John, laborer, bds. E. Washington.
Tool Martin, blacksmith, res. 177 S. East.
Torman John, carpenter, res. 248 Indiana ave.
TOUSEY & BYRAM, dry goods, 70 E. Washington.
TOUSEY GEORGE, president Branch of the Bank of the
    State of Indiana, N. E. cor. Meridian and Washington,
    res. 31 N. Delaware.
Tousey Homer, clerk, res. 110 N. New Jersey.
Tousey Jacob, porter Tousey & Byram.
Tousey Oliver, (T. & Byram,) res. 12 W. New York.
Tousey Zalmon, clerk Tousey & Byram, res. 90 N. Alabama.
Tousley Joseph H., bds. 183 E. Market.
Tout Henry, brick mason, res. 91 Indiana ave.
Township Library, Court House.
Tracy Mrs. Kate, 14 Garden.
TRAYESER GEORGE, piana forte manufacturer, cor.
    Washington and Alabama, res. 119 E. Washington.
Trask George K., stump puller, res. 117 N. Meridian.
Traub Conrad, laborer, res. 117 Fort Wayne ave.
Traut Israel, painter, res. 214 N. Alabama.
TRAUTMANN & CO., groceries and provisions, cor. East
    and North.
Trautmann Jacob, (T. & Co.,) res. 121 N. East.
Treisey Jacob, laborer, res. 15 Georgia.
TREMONT HOUSE, J. Rinkle, proprietor, cor. Illinois
    and Louisiana.
Trester John, expressman, res. 114 N. Mississippi.
Tretar John, white washer, res. E. St. Clair.
Trimble Joseph P., newspaper agent, bds. 33 W. Washing-
    ton.
Trimm Thomas, breakman I. & C. R. R., bds. 51 E. Louisi-
    ana.
Trindall Samuel, baggageman T. & R. R. R., bds. Palmer
    House.
Tripp Charles, runner Farmers' Hotel.
Troop James, currier Mooneys & Co., bds. Indiana House.
Trott John, baker Phillip Haynes, 40 W. Washington.
Trotter John, laborer, res. 170 N. Liberty.
Truksegs John, blacksmith, 62 Kentucky ave.
Trump Jacob, brick mason, res. 59 E. St. Joseph.
Truschaun Frederick, stone mason, res. 146 S. New Jersey.
Tull Thomas, res. 119 S. New Jersey.
Tull Martin, res. 177 East.
Tuller George W., student Bryant's Commercial College.
Tully William, proprietor Tully House, 79 S. Illinois.

Tumar Henry, carpenter, res. 65 N. Noble.
Turner Augustus, (col.,) barber, res. 67 W. Georgia.
Turner Barton, (col.,) res. 126 W. Ohio.
TURNERS' HALL, cor. Kentucky ave. and Tennessee.
Turner Hiram, carriage painter, bds. 27 E. Market.
Turner James, (col.,) rear 107 W. North.
Turner James, brick mason, res. 121 S. Alabama.
Turner William, brick mason, res. 65 Merrill.
TURNER WILLIAM H., produce and commission mer-
    chant, and agent for Maney's reapers and mowers, 74
    W. Washington, res. 18 N. New Jersey.
Turquin Martin, 138 E. New York.
Turtin Nathaniel, currier J. Fishback.
Tutewiler Charles, tinner, bds. 65 Massachusetts ave.
Tutewiler Henry, plasterer, res. 65 Massachusetts ave.
Tutewiler John W., clerk A. B. Willard & Co., bds. 65
    Massachusetts ave.
TUTTLE B. F., wholesale grocer, 27 W. Washington, and
    retail 34 N. Illinois, res. 16 W. Michigan.
Tuttle Dennis, 7 Madison ave.
Tuttle G. P., clerk B. F. Tuttle, res. New York, bet. Cali-
    fornia and Blackford.
Tuttle Henry, student Bryant's Commercial College, 154 N.
    Delaware.
Tuttle Henry, book agent, bds. Tully House.
Tuttle Orin, teamster, bds. cor. Vine and Huron.
Tweed Mrs. Carrie M., res. N. of State House.
Tyer George, freight conductor I. & C. R. R., res. 77 S. New
    .Jersey.
Tyler Charles, shoemaker, bds. 311 Virginia ave.

U

Uhl Peter, cigar maker C. M. Raschig, bds. Tremont House.
Uhlendorff George, bar tender Little House saloon.
Umphrey Miss Mary, milliner, bds. 39 N. Pennsylvania.
Underhill Frank, at flour mill, res. 43 E. Michigan.
UNION DEPOT, Louisiana, bet. Illinois and Meridian.
UNION HALL, (German,) 111 E. Washington.
UNITED STATES EXPRESS CO., office S. E. cor. Me-
    ridian and Washington, agent H. W. Daniels.
Unversall Andrew, butcher, res. 272 S. Delaware.
Unversall John, butcher, res. 112 Virginia ave.
Uphaus Henry, boot and shoe maker, res. 188 S. Delaware.
UPFOLD RIGHT REV. GEORGE, res. 51 N. Tennessee.
Uttinger Jacob, laborer, res. 215 N. New Jersey.

V

VAILE H. M., attorney at law, 21 E. Washington.
Vaile William, res. 176 S. Alabama.
Vaile William P., student, bds. 102 N. Alabama.
Vajen Charles D., clerk J. H. Vajen.
VAJEN JOHN H., hardware and cutlery, 21 W. Washington, res. 94 S. Illinois.
Valand William, laborer, Bluff road.
Vanbergen William, bds. 132 N. Tennessee.
Van Blaricum J. M., (Jones & Van B.,) res. 177 W. Washington.
Vance L. M., res. E. Washington.
Vance Thomas P., conductor I. P. & C. R. R., res. 53 N. Liberty.
Vandegrift Benjamin, printer Journal office, res. 85 N. Mississippi.
Vandegrift Benton C., student Bryant's Commercial College, bds. 33 Kentucky ave.
Vandegrift Henry, mail agent Jeffersonville Railroad, res. 33 Kentucky ave.
Vandegrift Jacob, (Kregelo, Blake & Co.,) res. 43 W. Michigan.
Vandegrift Millard, printer, bds. 85 N. Mississippi.
Vandergrift John, trunk maker Jas. Sulgrove.
Vane Christian, res. 270 S. Delaware.
Vanlaningham Lemuel, deputy county treasurer, res. 65 N. Alabama.
Vanlaningham Miss M., res. 198 N. New Jersey.
Vanneys Hezekiah, carpenter and builder, res. 192 E. Washington, up stairs.
Vasner Martin, shoemaker, bds. 35 South.
Vater Mrs. E. P., res. 41 Walnut.
Vater M., employee M. & I. R. R., bds. Ray House.
Vater Thomas J., brick mason, res. 45 Walnut.
Vaughan Jacob N., carpenter, res. 83 W. Maryland.
Vawter M., engineer, bds. 233 S. Delaware.
Vawter M., watchman Madison Depot, bds. Ray House.
Vayer William, res. 176 S. Alabama.
Veach J. V., res. 196 N. New Jersey.
Veach Nelson, carpenter, res. 132 E. St. Clair.
Veermann Christian, boot and shoe maker, bds. 174 E. Washington.
Vestell Abraham, (col.,) wood sawyer, res. 100 W. Michigan.
Vester Jonathan, (col.,) barber, 81½ E. Washington.
VICKERS WM. B., printer Sentinel office, res. 105 S. New Jersey.

Viera Harvey, (col.,) res. 138 W. Ohio.
Victor Catherine, washerwoman, res. 89 N. Alabama.
Vieweg August, tailor, 101 E. Washington, up stairs.
Vilant Christopher, 20 Union.
Vincent Henry B., laborer, res. 188 E. North.
Vincent William H., carpenter, res. 91 E. Davidson.
VINNEDGE & JONES, boots, shoes, hats and caps, 17 W.
   Washington.
Vinnedge J. A., (V & Jones,) res. 85 S. Tennessee.
Vinnedge Joseph D., clerk Vinnedge & Jones, bds. 85 S.
   Tennessee.
Vinton Almus E., (Hasselman & V.,) res. 30 N. Pennsyl-
   vania.
VOEGTLE JACOB, stoves and tinware, 177 E. Washing-
   ton, res. 111 E. New York.
Voight Frederick, driver F. Bolman, bds. 91 E. Washing-
   ton.
Voight Henry, clerk Murphy & Holliday, res. 113 W. Mich-
   igan.
VOLMER CHARLES, wholesale wines and liquors, 113 E.
   Washington, res. 144 W. Maryland.
VONNEGUT CLEMENS, hardware, hides and leather, 142
   E. Washington.
Voorhees Mrs. A. L., res. 97 N. Illinois.
Voorhees Mrs. Jane, res. 157 Massachusetts ave.
Voorhees Mrs. Mary, res. 82 N. Illinois.
VOORHEES PLATT, foreman Bates House meat shop, res.
   82 N. Illinois.
Voorhees William A., blacksmith, res. 157 Massachusetts
   ave.

W

Wachtsteller John, cook Blind Asylum, res. 207 N. Ala-
   bama.
Wade Robert, tailor, bds. Macy House.
Waddell John, clerk New York Store.
Waggoner John B., cigar maker, bds. A. Walk, Georgia.
Waggoner John, laborer, bds. Blackford.
Wagner Martin, shoemaker, bds. 35 South.
Wagner Mrs. M. J., teacher of drawing in Indianapolis Fe-
   male Institute, bds. 34 E. Michigan.
Wainwright Samuel, tinner, 5 E. New York.
Wakefield Mrs. Delila, bds. cor Ohio and Tennessee.
Walch William, laborer, 71 Madison ave.
Walden William, (col.,) white-washer, res. 131 N. West.
WALDO ELIJAH G. B., real estate, S. Illinois, res. Indi-
   ana ave.

Walesinski S., saloon, 27 N. Alabama, bds. cor. Alabama and
    Market.
Walk Anthony, shoemaker, 148 E. Market, res. same.
Walk Julius, watchmaker, 17 N. Illinois, bds. 16 Georgia.
Walk Louis, shoemaker, res. 16 W. Georgia.
Walker Charles M., bds. S. E. cor. New York and Me-
    ridian.
Walker II. A., track master Union R. R., res. 63 W. Louisi-
    ana,
Walker Jacob S., (W. & King,) res. 169 N. Illinois.
WALKER & KING, lumber dealers, cor. New York and
    Tennessee.
Walker T. R., salesman G. E. West, bds. American House.
Walker Wiley F., carpenter, res. 188 Indiana ave.
Walkup Andrew J., conductor, bds. American House.
Wall Thomas, carpenter, res. 118 N. Alabama.
Wall Thomas, laborer, res. E. Bates.
Wallace Alexander G., County Recorder, office Court House,
    res. 86 E. Market.
WALLACE ANDREW, wholesale grocer and commission
    merchant, cor. Virginia ave. and S. Delaware, res. 34
    N. Delaware.
Wallace Mrs. Beuleh, 79 Massachusetts ave.
Wallace Edward T., turner, bds. 71½ E. Washington.
Wallace George G., (W. R. Foster & Co.,) bds. 34 N. Dela-
    ware.
WALLACE & HARRISON, attorneys at law and notaries
    public, 30¼ W. Washington, up stairs.
WALLACE JAMES, copyist and canvasser, res. 176 N.
    New Jersey.
Wallace James A., res. 18 N. Delaware.
Wallace John, blacksmith, res. 65 N. New Jersey.
Wallace Samuel, brick mason, res. 176 N. New Jersey.
Wallace William, laborer, res. E. Georgia.
Wallace William, (W. & Harrison,) res. 121 N. Delaware.
WALLACE WILLIAM, deputy recorder, office Court
    House, res. 59 N. East.
Wallace William J., County Sheriff, office at jail, res. 18 N.
    Alabama.
Wallace W. P., 34 N. Delaware.
Wallace Mrs. Zerelda G., res. 139 N. New Jersey.
Wallach John, head salesman Moses Meyer, bds. 135 S. Ala-
    bama.
WALLACH JACOB L., notary public, office 85 E. Wash-
    ington, res. 18 N. Delaware.
Wallach Samuel, trader, res. 135 S. Alabama.
Waller Brenhard, boot and shoemaker, res. 124 N. Missis-
    sippi.

Wallick John F., manager W. U. Telegraph, office N. Meridian, bds. Bates House.

WALLINGFORD E. & CO., dealers in new and second-hand furniture, 61 E. Washington.

Wallingford E., (E. W. & Co.,) res. 100 N. East.

Wallwork James, cashier Glenn's Block, bds. Macy House.

WALPOLE ROBERT L., attorney at law, Johnson's Building, res. 8 Virginia ave.

Walsman Fred., saloon keeper and billiards, 55 S. Illinois.

Walson Charley, laborer, bds 20 N. Pennsylvania.

Walton William, at Rolling Mill, 13 Willard.

Walz Francis, laborer, bds. 20 N. Pennsylvania.

Wanderson James W., messenger American Express Co., res. 96 N. East.

WANDS ALEXANDER, boot and shoemaker, 12 S. Meridian, res. 131 N. Pennsylvania.

WANDS JOHN & SON, boot and shoemakers, 65 E. Washington.

Wands John, (J. W. & Son,) res. cor. McCarty and Greer.

Wands John, jr., (J. W. & Son,) res. cor. McCarty and Greer.

Wanger William, painter, res. 247 N. New Jersey.

Ward A. C., bds. 186 N. Pennsylvania.

WARD D. L., clerk American House.

Ward Ephriam G., salesman J. W. Talbott, res. Ohio, bet. Illinois and Tennessee.

Ward Gabriel, bds. 262 Indiana ave.

Ward Homer, conductor Bellefontaine R. R., Bates bds. House.

Ward John A., res. 17 Harris.

Ward Mrs. Lucinda, res. 262 Indiana ave.

Warden Jerry, laborer, 38 S. Illinois.

Ware James, carver, res. 169 S. Delaware.

Ware Richard, night police, bds. National Hotel.

Ware Robert, railroader, res. South, bet. Tennessee and Mississippi.

Ware William, cooper, res. 57 W. Georgia.

Warner Charles, res. 60 S. Louisiana.

Warner Charles, shoemaker, res. rear 48 Massachusetts ave.

Warner Charles G., printer, 100 W. Vermont.

Warner George, laborer, res. Madison ave.

Warner John, breakman, bds. Union House.

Warnock John, laborer, res. 54 S. Noble.

Warr James, machinist, res. 172 E. Ohio.

Warren George S., clerk, bds. Mrs. Kinder.

Warrick Henry, laborer, res. 23 E. Harrison.

Wartmann G., laborer, res. 238 S. Delaware.

Wash Mrs. Martha, 9 Massachusetts ave.

WASHINGTON FOUNDRY, Hasselman & Vinton, proprietors, near Union Depot.

Washington House, John Mattler, proprietor, 83 S. Meridian.

Washington William T., res. 50 Virginia ave.

Wasmuth Louis, tailor, bds. Kentucky ave., bet. Washington and Tennessee.

Watchtstetter Christian, boot and shoe maker, bds. 138 W. Washington.

Waters Charles R., printer Atlas office, res. 64, N. of Ohio, in alley.

WATERS JOHN G., city clerk, office Odd Fellows' Hall, res. 110 E. Market.

Waters Mrs. Sabel, res. 12 S. East.

Watgen Herman, clerk Robt. Browning, bds. 102 N. Illinois.

Watson Charley, hostler Wood & Foudray, bds. Mrs. Ferguson.

Watson Jehu M., machinist, res. 249 S. Delaware.

Watson Joseph S., printer, res. 129 W. Maryland.

Watson Samuel W., book-keeper Harrison's Bank, res. 12 W. North.

Waugh Richard C., bds. 105 N. Tennessee.

WAUGH WM., printer Sentinel office, bds. Little's Hotel.

Way Truman M., railroader, res. 70 S. East.

Waymouth Amos, blacksmith, res. 137 E. McCarty.

Weakley Patrick, at rolling mill, bds. 184 S. Tennessee.

Weakley Jonah A., turner, res. 97 W. New York.

Weakley W. J., clerk A. D. Atwood, res. 97 W. New York.

Wealzer William, (J. Ott & Co.,) 117 W. Washington.

Weasy Charles, machinist, res. 145 E. Ohio.

Weaver E. A., harness maker Sulgrove & Reynolds, res. 172 S. Alabama.

Weaver Rev. Elisha C., (col.,) M. E. Church, bds. 160 W. Georgia.

Weaver Frederick, laborer, res. 173 N. Railroad.

Weaver James P., book binder Sheets & Braden, bds. 147 N. Illinois.

WEAVER & WILLIAMS, undertakers, 72 W. Washington.

Weaver William W., (Weaver & Williams,) res. 147 N. Illinois.

Webb Miss Hannah A., dress maker and milliner, bds. 18 N. Illinois.

Webb Joseph, carpenter, bds. E. Knight.

Weber Adam, laborer, res. 180 S. Delaware.

Webster Geo. C., clerk W. Daggett, res. 22 S. Meridian.

Webster George, machinist, bds. W. Market.

Webster Joseph H., drayman, res. Strawberry Alley, cor. Broadway.

Wechler Judas, res. 46 S. East.

Wedman Frank, laborer, res. 266 S. Delaware.

Weekley Mrs. Mary, res. 67 N. New Jersey.

Weeks Charles H., printer John Fahnestock, bds. Little's Hotel.

WEEKS & COX, photographic artists, College Hall, E. Washington, cor. Pennsylvania.

Weeks Richard, laborer, res. 15 S. Alabama.

Weeks W. H., (W. & Cox,) bds. Mrs. Kinder.

Weeler Walter, foreman, 114 S. New Jersey.

Wehler Lukas, boot and shoe maker, res. 179 E. Washington.

Wehling Charles, wagon maker, New Jersey, near Cumberland.

Wehn Christian, tanner, res. 270 S. Delaware.

Weibel J. Edward, barber, Bates House shaving saloon.

Weiber Adam, res. S. Alabama.

Weikert John, clerk, res. 118 N. Alabama.

Weiland William, 69 Bluff road.

Weilleman Jacob, laborer, res. East.

Weils Samuel, res. 7 Chatham.

Weinberger Herman, confectioner, res. 60 S. Meridian.

WEINBERGER JOHN C., baker, 10 W. Louisiana, res. 60 S. Meridian.

WEIR J. W. & BRO., marble dealers, 13 Virginia ave.

Weise John, harness maker, Georgia, bet. Illinois and Meridian.

Welch Patrick, bell boy Bates House.

Welch Thomas, boiler maker, res. Sinker.

Weller Levi, railroad conductor, bds. 20 W. Michigan.

Wells Alexander, res. W. Market.

Wells Edmund, shoemaker, bds. 111 S. New Jersey.

Wells George, carpenter and joiner, res. 118 N. Mississippi.

Wells G. A., dentist, 19 E. Washington, res. 88 Virginia ave.

Wells John, carpenter, res. Michigan ave.

Wells William F., saw mill, Massachusetts ave., near limits, res. 85 E. New York.

Wenderath Julius, book-keeper, bds. 16 W. Georgia.

Wenger Michael, grocer, 20 N. Noble, res. same.

Wenner W. J., varnisher, res. McCarty.

Wentz C. A., res. 144 W. Washington.

Wentz W. W., res. 6 Alvord's Block, S. Pennsylvania.

Werbe Charles, clerk, bds. 16 W. Georgia.

Werbe C. G., clerk post office.

Werbe L. F., grocer and produce dealer, 185 W. Washington, res. same.

WERDEN E. & CO., books and stationery, wall paper, &c., 26 E. Washington.

Werden E., (E. W. & Co.,) bds. American House.

Werdeham Joseph, hair plater, res. W. Washington.

Wermer Jacob, varnisher, res. 40 N. Alabama.

Wernell Charles, blacksmith, bds. 85 E. Market.

WERT JOSEPH, boots and shoes, 6 S. Pennsylvania, res. 63 N. Alabama.

Werther Wm., (Boecher & W.,) res. Market, bet. Noble and Davidson.

Weslink Conrad, drayman, res. 158 E. Michigan.

Wesmaer Anthony, laborer, res. 148 E. Ohio.

West George, boots and shoes, 43 E. Washington, res. 60 N. Meridian.

West George H., clerk, res. 49 W Michigan.

West John, huckster, res. 170 N. Delaware.

West Nathaniel, (W. & Wilson,) bds. 86 N. Meridian.

WEST & WILSON, real estate agents, Ætna Buildings, 14 N. Pennsylvania.

WESTERN COMMERCIAL NURSERY, Fletcher, Williams & Loomis, proprietors, 14 S. Pennsylvania.

WESTERN UNION TELEGRAPH CO., 1 N. Meridian.

Westover Jonathan M., moulder, 123 E. McCarty.

Wexler David, laborer, res. 89 S. East.

Weyer James, res. 169 S. Delaware.

Wheatley John, (Fisher & W.,) bds. 39 S. Delaware.

Wheatley John W., student, bds. 33 N. East.

Wheatley Wm. M., (McCord & W.,) res. 24 N. West.

Wheeler Ephraim, (col.,) res. 107 W. North.

Whipple Charles W., machinist, res. 105 E. Vermont.

Whistler Geo., cigar maker, bds. Farmers' Hotel.

Whitaker Annis, bds. 59 Union.

Whitaker James, carpenter, bds. 59 Union.

Whitaker Jesse, bds. 59 Union.

Whitaker Francis, bds. 59 Union.

Whitcomb J., freight agent Jeffersonville R. R., bds. 41 S. Meridian.

White Alexander, cigar manufacturer, res. 22 S. Mississippi.

White Anderson, 147 N. Tennessee.

White James, (col.,) res. Harris.

White Jeremiah, (col.,) res. Elizabeth.

White Jesse, (col.,) res. 160 W. Georgia.

White John S., clerk James Hart & Co., bds. 113 East.

White Paul, laborer, res. 188 E. North.

WHITE RIVER VALLEY INSURANCE CO., Ray's Building, W. Washington.

White Stephen, (col.,) hod carrier, res. 96 alley E. of N. West.

Whitesell Henry, bds. 57 E. New York.

Whitehouse W. C., carpenter, bds. 141 W. Market.

Whiting R., American Express Indianapolis and St. Louis, bds. Bates House.

Whiteridge Samuel, house and sign painter, bds. 181 N. New Jersey.

WHITERIDGE WILLIAM, house and sign painter, 82 E. Washington, res. 181 N. New Jersey.

Whitsitt Courtland E., brick mason, bds. 244 Virginia ave.

Whitsitt Jesse, res. 244 Virginia ave.

Whitten Rev. Elijah, minister M. E. Church, res. N. Pennsylvania, bet. Second and Third.

Whitten James, res. 246 N. Pennsylvania.

Whittenburg Charles, salesman New York Store.

WICK WILLIAM W., attorney at law, office 4 Judah's Block, res. 58 N. East.

Wichmann Christ, at Rolling Mill, res. 91 E. Washington.

Wickert John, clerk, res. 118 N. Alabama.

Wies John, mason, bds. 152 N. New Jersey.

Wiegmann Christ, baker Cincinnati bakery, bds. 91 E. Washington.

Wigear William, cabinet maker, res. 124 S. Mississippi.

WIGGIM LYTLE, (W. & Morrow,) American House.

Wiggim R. D., steward American House.

WIGGINS & CHANDLER, agricultural works, 262 W. Washington, near Canal basin.

Wiggins Charles P., (W. & Chandler,) bds. Macy House.

Wiggins Henry, machinist Wiggins & Chandler, bds. Macy House.

Wikest John, clerk J. H. Vajen, res. New Jersey.

Wilcox John D., carmaker, 4 N. West.

Wilcox John, collar maker Sulgrove & Reynolds.

WILDE J. O., dealer in furniture, 71 S. Illinois, res. same.

Wiles Mrs. N. B., res. 50 S. Meridian.

Wiles Samuel G., 7 Chatham.

WILEY'S REAL ESTATE AGENCY, 10½ E. Washington, over Adams Express Co.

WILEY WILLIAM Y., real estate agent, stock broker, commissioner of deeds, &c., 10½ E. Washington, res. 32 E. New York.

Wilhelm Christopher, railroader, res. 156 S. Alabama.

Wilhelm Charles, car maker, res. Railroad.

Wilkerson D. S., res. 149 N. East.

Wilking Andrew, boot and shoemaker, res. 37 Noble.

Wilkins Henry, shoemaker, res. 39 N. Spring.

Wilkins John, res. 34 E. Market.

Wilkins John A., grocer, 32 E. Market.

Wilkins W. C., bds. Macy House.

Wilkinson Daniel S., butcher, res. 149 N. East.
Wilkinson William B., laborer, res. 138 E. Ohio.
WILLKISON WM , livery and sale stable, 10 Pearl, res. 119 S. Alabama.
Will John F., currier, 46 E. Ohio.
WILLARD ASHBEL P., Governor of the State of Indiana, office State House, res. cor. Market and Illinois.
WILLARD A. B. & CO., dry goods and fancy goods, 8 E. Washington.
Willard A. B., (A. B. W. & Co.,) res. 66 E. New York.
Willard A. G., (A. B. W. & Co.,) res. 103 N. Alabama.
Willard Charles, laborer, Union.
WILLARD & STOWELL, music and musical instruments, 4 Bates House.
Willets Jacob S., dairyman, res. Massachusetts ave.
Willet Wm., clerk A. Wallace, bds. 48 E. Maryland.
Willgast Daniel, teamster, 166 S. Illinois.
Williams Augustus, laborer, 15 McCarty.
Williams Charles, (Weaver & W.,) res. 20 W. Michigan.
WILLIAMS C. H., agent Wheeler & Wilson's sewing machines, 19 W. Washington, res. 98 West.
Williams Daniel G., clerk Elias Werden & Co., bds. 34 E. Michigan.
WILLIAMS DAVID, agent for McCormick's reaper, 70 E. Washington, res. 82 N. New Jersey.
Williams Mrs. Ellen, (col.,) bds. 78 Missouri.
Williams Miss E. A., principal Indiana Female Institute, 34 E. Michigan.
Williams George W., dentist, 23 Indiana ave., res. same.
Williams Rev. Gibbon, D. D., superintendent Female Institute, res. 34 E. Michigan.
Williams George, with J. W. Harris, Farmers' and Drovers' Hotel.
Williams Hubbard, painter, cor. Noble and Huron.
Williams Jacob T., bookbinder, res. 46 California.
Williams John, laborer, res. S. Missouri, near Rolling Mill.
Williams Martin, (Fletcher, W. & Loomis,) res. Michigan Road, 3½ miles North.
Williams Owen, general business agent, res. 134 N. Illinois.
Williams Samuel, (col.,) res. 129 N. West.
Williams Mrs. Susan, boarding, res. 125 E. New York.
Williams William, brick mason, 182 S. Tennessee.
Williams William, tailor, res. Stephen, near Virginia ave.
Williamson Mrs. Catherine, bds. 75 W. Vermont.
WILLIAMSON & HAUGH, iron railing manufacturers, 2 N. Delaware.
Williamson Levi B., (W. & Haugh,) res. 118 E. Vermont.
16

WILLIAMSON & LEE, editors and publishers Herald and
    Era, Locomotive Building, 1st door.
Williamson Marshall, lumber merchant, res. 117 E. Market.
Willis Clark, plasterer, res. 50 N. East.
Willis John, brick layer, res. 142 E. Walnut.
Wilman Henry, cooper, bds. 91 Union.
Wilmington Levi, at peg and last factory, bds. 14 N. Me-
    ridian.
Wilmot Horace Q., book binder, bds. 115 N. Pennsylvania.
WILMOT SAMUEL, hats, caps and furs, 8 W. Washing-
    ton, res. 115 N. Pennsylvania.
Wilmot Theodore, salesman Samuel Wilmot.
Wilson A. A., foreman pressroom Indianapolis Journal Co.,
    bds. 85 S. Pennsylvania.
Wilson Charles G., carriage painter, res. 174 S. Mississippi.
Wilson Colman J., telegraph operator, 1 N. Meridian, res.
    15 S. Illinois.
Wilson David, res. 55 S. Pennsylvania.
Wilson Edward, res. 170 W. Market.
WILSON MRS. ELIZA, millinery and dress making, 18
    N. Illinois, res. same.
Wilson George W., Adams' Express messenger, bds. Palmer
    House.
Wilson Harmon E., marble dealer, res. 45 N. Noble.
Wilson James E., carpenter, res. 50 Indiana ave.
Wilson wid. James, res. 15 S. Illinois.
Wilson Jeremiah, teamster, res. 230 N. New Jersey.
Wilson John S., blacksmith, res. S. side National road.
Wilson John F., brick mason and plasterer, res. 115 Mc-
    Carty.
Wilson John, pump maker, res. 95 E. Market.
Wilson John E., laborer, res. 128 W. Georgia.
Wilson John M., baker, bds. 4 S. Meridian.
Wilson John, laborer, res. 174 N. East.
WILSON JOSEPH B., hardware and cutlery, 4 W. Wash-
    ington, res. 266 N. Illinois.
Wilson Lamdon, (col.,) barber, bds. Macy House.
Wilson L. D., bds. W. end North.
Wilson Oliver M., attorney at law and notary public, cor.
    Washington and Meridian, bds. 63 W. Maryland.
Wilson Patrick, watchman M. & I. R. R., bds. Ray House.
Wilson Richard, book-keeper, res. 19 S. Illinois.
Wilson Sandford B., res. S. side National road.
Wilson Thomas, showman, bds. 212 W. Washington.
Wilson Thomas, last maker, bds. 114 S. New Jersey.
Wilson Thomas, res. 266 N. Illinois.
Wilson William, watchman Madison R. R., bds. Ray House.
Wilson William, bds. Mrs. Dana, W. Market.

Wilson Rev William, pastor Robert's Chapel, res. 35 N. Pennsylvania.
Winchell Mrs. Elizabeth, tailoress, res. 36 N. Noble.
Winchell John J., blacksmith, res. 36 N. Noble.
Wingate Ferdinand, res. 151 Virginia ave.
Wingate W. L., clerk Andrew May, res. 31 East.
Wingate William L., res. 91 Virginia ave.
Winslow J., (col.,) teamster, res. 146 W. North.
Winsor Samuel, machinist, bds. 99 E. Bates.
Winter Anthony, laborer, res. corporation line, bet. Alabama and New Jersey.
Winter D. E., house painter, 9 Virginia ave., res. 20 N. Pennsylvania.
Winthrope John, res. 169 W. Washington.
Wise Adam S., (Youngerman & W.,) res. 83 E. Washington.
Wise Henry, laborer, res. 103 N. Railroad.
Wise John, saddler Hinesley & Hereth, res. 16 Georgia.
Wise William, dealer in ale, res. 46, cor. Tennessee and Walnut.
Wisenthal Hermon, dealer in rags, &c., res. 173 E. Washington.
Wishmier Christian, saw mill, res. 189 N. Davidson.
Wishmier Henry, shoemaker, res. 51 S. Illinois.
Wiseman Mrs. B. A., res. 83 N. Pennsylvania.
Wiseman Mrs. Margaret, res. 243 W. Washington.
Wiseman Simon, teamster, 245 W. Washington.
Wiss George, tailor, bds. Union Hotel.
Wissert John, baker, res. 25 N. Alabama.
WISSERT MRS. S. S., cap and dress maker, 25. N. Alabama.
Wittenberg Charles, clerk New York Store, res. 111 E. Ohio.
Witthoft Henry, (Myers & W.,) res. 171 E. Washington.
Woerner Phillip, grocer and baker, 78 W. Washington.
Wolf W. S., student N. W. C. University, bds. D. S. Wilkerson.
WOLF JACOB, saloon and oysters, 162 E. Washington, res. same.
Wolfe Phillip, proprietor Cincinnati House, 124 S. Delaware.
Wolfe John, breakman I. & C. R. R., bds. 70 S. Noble.
Wolfram C. A., pressman Locomotive Office, bds. 101 N. New Jersey.
Wolfram Christopher, tinner, res. 101 N. New Jersey.
Wolfram Mrs. Sarah, res. 101 N. New Jersey.
Wonderle Henry, brickmason, res. 41 N. Davidson.
Wonnell Charles, blacksmith, bds. 85 E. Market.
Wonnell John A., carpenter, res. 39 California.
Wood Alexander, groceries and provisions, cor. Illinois and Vermont, res. same.

WOOD A. D., wholesale and retail hardware, 71 E. Washington, also proprietor City hardware store, 12 W. Washsngton, res. 164 N. New Jersey.

Wood Benjamin, blacksmith, res. Stringtown.

Wood Mrs. Elizabeth, 20 S. East.

Wood E. A., butcher, res. 157 E. Washington.

WOOD & FOUDRAY, livery and sale stables, 10 N. Pennsylvania.

WOOD JAMES A., American Express messenger Ind. Cen., bds. Bates House.

Wood James, City engineer, office 3 Blake's Building, res. 127 N. Illinois.

Wood James N., assistant City engineer, office 3 Blake's Building, bds. 127 N. Illinois.

Wood John B., clock repairer, 51 N. Illinois.

Wood John F., at City hardware store, 12 W. Washington, res. 145 N. New Jersey.

Wood John G., carpenter, res. 168 N. Delaware.

Wood John M.. (W. & Foudray,) res. 53 N. Pennsylvania.

Wood Nelson R., carpenter, 60 Indiana ave.

Wood Mrs. Sarah, 55 N. Pennsylvania.

Wood wid. Stephen, 20 S. East.

Wood William, (W. & Foudray,) res. 140 N. Pennsylvania.

Wood William D., saddle maker, bds. 120 N. Illinois.

Woods James, res. 116 W. New York.

Woods R., 83 N. New Jersey.

WOODALL AQUILLA P., clerk Adams' Express Co., bds. Macy House.

Woodburn James H., (Thompson & W.,) bds. 32 N. Pennsylvania.

WOODBURY JOSIAH G., attorney at law, McOuat's Block, bds. 21 S. Delaware.

Woodcock Charles, marble polisher, bds. Mrs. Nash.

Woodford Mrs. Margaret, (col.,) res. 65 S. Noble.

Woodford Mrs. Betsey, (col.,) 139 W. Washington.

Woodin Almon M., printer Atlas office, bds. Little's Hotel.

Woodruff Mrs. Adeline, res. N. University.

WOOLF M., wholesale wines and liquors, S. Illinois, bet. Maryland and Georgia, res. 100 N. Illinois.

Woodford Mrs. Nancy, M. D., for the cure of fits, res. 60 N. Delaware.

Woollen William I., res. 35 E. Michigan.

WOOLLEN WILLIAM M., groceries and provisions, 82 W. Vermont, res. same.

Woolson Frank, laborer, bds. 120 New York.

WORLAND WILLIAM, groceries and feed, 37 Virginia ave., res. same.

WORTH ALEXANDER, sec'y I. & C. R. R., res. 33 N.
  Delaware.
WORTH I. C., patent right dealer, res. 99 N. Meridian.
Worth Robert G., telegraph operator B. R. R. office, bds.
  Ray House.
Wren Edward, wagon maker, res. 51 S. New Jersey.
Wren John, carpenter, res. 192 S. Delaware.
WRIGHT ARTHUR L., deputy county treasurer, bds. 82
  E. Vermont.
WRIGHT AUGUSTUS S., (M. D.,) homeopathist, office 28
  N. Illinois, res. 136 N. Illinois.
Wright Charles A., (Stapp & W.,) bds. 44 N. Pennsylvania.
Wright C. E., res. near Deaf and Dumb Asylum.
Wright Rev. Charles P., (M. E.,) res. 91 N. Noble.
Wright Miss F., teacher Indianapolis Female Institute, bds.
  34 E. Michigan.
Wright Francis H., currier. res. 82 E. Vermont.
Wright Hiram, 122 Benton.
Wright Jacob T., county auditor, bds. 57 Massachusetts
  ave.
Wright Mrs. Lucy, (col.,) res. N. Meridian.
WRIGHT DR. MANSUR H., (Parry & Wright,) office 12
  E. Market, bds. 23 N. Meridian.
Wright Richard M., shoemaker, res. 50 N. Delaware.
WRIGHT WILLIAM G., pump manufacturer, Maryland,
  res. cor. Huron and Pine.
Wright William G., butcher, 54 South, bet. Delaware and
  Pennsylvania, res. same.
Wright William H., clerk Geo. T. Browning, res. 39 E.
  Michigan.
Wright Willis W., groceries and provisions, cor. Washing-
  ton and Delaware.
Wust John, turner, 97 Fort Wayne ave.
Wygant William D., res. 76 W. Maryland.
Wyland August, tailor, res. 125 N. Noble.
Wysong Christopher, boarding house, 72 S. Illinois.

Y

Yager Charles, brewer, Wyoming, res. 240 S. Alabama.
YANDES & CO., hide and leather dealers, 38 E. Washing-
  ton.
YANDES DANIEL, SEN., (Y. & Co.,) res. 64 N. Pennsyl-
  vania.
Yandes Daniel, jr., (Y. & Co.,) res. 137 Virginia ave.
Yandes Geo. B., clerk Yandes & Co., bds. 64 N. Pennsyl-
  vania.
Yandes James W., res. 12 E. Vermont.

YANDES SIMON, attorney at law, 23 E. Washington.
YEAGER CHRISTIAN, dry goods and groceries, 215 E.
    Washington, res. same.
Yeager William, cooper, res. 154 N. Noble.
Yewell Solomon, book-keeper, res. 103 S. New Jersey.
YOHN JAMES C., dry goods, 17 E. Washington, res. 74
    N. Delaware.
Yorger Natz, butcher, bds. 15 Indiana ave.
Young Charles P., machinist Bellefontaine R. R. shop.
Young George D., machinist, res. 68 S. New Jersey.
Young Harrison P., student N. W. C. University, res. 44 N.
    Pennsylvania.
Young Isaac, clerk C. F. Hagerhorst, bds. 115 S. Tennessee.
Young Jesse, machinist Bellefontaine R. R. shop.
Young Jesse, (col.,) Y. & Revels, bds. cor. Michigan and
    Tennessee.
YOUNG MEN'S CHRISTIAN ASSOCIATION, rooms
    Ray's Block, W. Washington.
YOUNG & REVELS, hair dressing saloon, Tremont House.
Young Mrs. Sarah, res. N. Alabama.
Youngerman Charles, blacksmith and wagon maker, 12 N.
    Delaware.
Youngerman Charles F., stone cutter, res. 168 S. Dela-
    ware.
Youngerman C. W., (Y. & Wise,) bds. 134 E. Washington.
YOUNGERMAN GEORGE B., groceries and provisions,
    209 E. Washington, res. same.
Youngerman Geo. M., blacksmith, bds. 14 and 16 N. Dela-
    ware.
Youngerman Mrs., bds. 84 Massachusetts ave.
YOUNGERMAN & WISE, blacksmiths, 122 S. Delaware.
Youtsey Thomas, employee Osgood, Smith & Co., res. 226
    S. East.

Z

Zahringer Longelein, cabinet maker, res. 121 N. Noble.
Zeachs Godfrey, shoemaker, res. 148 S. New Jersey.
Zeien Peter, assistant engineer, bds. near Madison Depot.
Zeigler Nelson, clerk Boston Store, bds. 71 N. Meridian
ZEIGLER WILLIAM, proprietor Boston Store, 5 E.
    Washington, res. 71 N. Meridian.
Zellers Henry, mattress maker, bds. E. Knight.
Zeppenfeld Ernst, tanner, bds. California House.
Zimmerman Benjamin, shoemaker, bds. 112 S. New Jersey.
Zimmerman Benjamin, laborer, 59 Union.
Zimmerman Christopher, patent roofing, res. 22 N. Liberty.
Zimmerman Jas., carpenter, bds. 22 N. Liberty.

PEORIA

MARINE AND FIRE

INSURANCE CO.

CHARTERED, A. D. 1841.

No. 39 Main St., Peoria, Ill.

CAPITAL, $500,000.

This Company continues to issue Policies on

Marine, Inland Navigation

TRANSPORTATION AND FIRE RISKS,

AT REASONABLE RATES.

DIRECTORS.

ISAAC UNDERHILL	PEORIA.
RICHARD GREGG	PEORIA.
SAMUEL HOWE	CHICAGO.
C. HOLLAND	PEORIA.
P. HOLLAND	PEORIA.
JACOB GALE	PEORIA.
A. G. TYNG	PAORIA.
SILAS RAMSEY	PEORIA.
S. PULSIFER	PEORIA.
H. N. WHEELER	PEORIA.
WILLIAM R PHELPS	PEORIA.
IRA I. FENN	PEORIA.
L. HOLLAND	PEORIA.

OFFICERS.

ISAAC UNDERHILL,   **ALEX. G. TYNG,**
President.   Vice Pres.
C. HOLLAND, SECRETARY.

C. B. DAVIS, AGENT,

INDIANAPOLIS, IND.

BUSINESS MIRROR,

Containing the Name and Location of every Business Man in the City, under the particular Trade or Profession in which he is engaged.

Accouchers and Midwives.

Bohme Mrs. Mary, 22 S Alabama
Custer L. N., res. 19 N East
Foley Mary, bds. 40 S Illinois
Leonard Mrs. Abigail, 60 N Delaware
Thompson Mrs. M., 20 N Illinois

Agents, Ale and Porter.

Blaes Nicholas, 66 S Delaware
Wise William, 46 Tennessee

Agents, Book.

Kile, Cleveland & Co., opposite Union Depot

Agents, Insurance.

Blake C., 95 E Washington
Bryant Benjamin, 111 W South
Covington George B, office 14 and 16 S Meridian
Covington Samuel F, secretary Indianapolis Insurance Co., office 14 S Meridian
Davis Charles B, Odd Fellows' Hall, 2d floor
Dunlop J S, N W cor. Washington and Meridian
Gatling R J, Blackford's Building
Henderson Wm., Ætna Building
Igoe Martin, 70 E Washington
Locke & Bro., Blackford's Building
Spann & Hall, cor. Washington and Meridian
Seidensticker A, 95 E Washington

Agents, Patent Right.

Boyd David M, 37 S Meridian
Brown John L., 12 S Pennsylvania
Detrick J D, Circle
Fisher & Wheatley, 6 S Meridian, opposite post office
Gee R S & Co., Ætna Buildings, N Pennsylvania
Redstone Albert E, opposite post office
Worth I C, 99 N Meridian

Agents, Real Estate.

Detzell & Smith, 37 E Washington, up stairs
Dunlop John S, jr., office Dunlop's Block, cor. Washington and Meridian

Eldridge, McMillin & Biddle, 39 W Washington
Gatling Richard J, office Blackford's Buildings
McKernan & Pierce, 39½ W Washington
O'Neal Richard, 12 S Pennsylvania
Phipps Isaac N, 28 E Market
Spann & Hall, S W cor. Washington and Meridian
Stapp & Wright, 86 E Washington
Waldo Elijah G B, S Illinois
West & Wilson, real estate agents, Ætna Buildings, 14 N Pennsylvania
Wiley William Y., 10½ E. Washington.

Agents, Sewing Machine.

Ames James, (Grover & Baker,) cor. Washington and Kentucky ave.
Fridley Mrs Susan, (Kelsey & Co.'s) bds. 6 N Meridian
Hall E A, 2 Odd Fellows' Hall
Henderson Duncan, res. 52 Bates
McIver John C, (Braman & Co.'s,) 6½ W Washington
Rockwell R E, (Forest City,) 2 Ray's Building
Thomas George W, (Grover & Baker's,) 46 W Washington

Agricultural Implements.

Beard & Sinex, N E cor. Washington and Tennessee
Braden David, 84 W Washington
Birkenmayer P S & Co., 74 E Washington
Buist Thos., 60 W Washington
Dawson William, 250 K Washington
Park Theron, 86 W Washington
Spotts & Thompson, S Delaware
Wiggins & Chandler, 262 W Washington, near Canal basin
Turner William, 74 W Washington

Architects.

(See also Carpenters and Builders.)

Bohlen D A, Ætna Buildings, N Pennsylvania
Costigan Francis, Oriental House, S Illinois
Curzon Joseph, res. 218 N Illinois
Hirsching Theodore, bds. 61 N Illinois

Hodgson Isaac, room 5 Glenns' Block
May Edwin, 18 E Market

Artists.

Adams Mrs J G, Blake's Buildings, 2d floor
Bruening E & J, 6 E Washington, up stairs
Cox Jacob, 2 Blake's Building
Dunlap James B, bds. Dr Dunlap
Gulick Samuel W, box 167 post office
Hays B S, 32½ E Washington
McEvoy H N, (landscape,) Little's Hotel
Reed Fishe P, 6 Ray's Building
Smallwood William, res. 52 N East

Attorneys at Law.

Barbour & Howland, 19 E Washington
Beal John A, 6 Glenns' Block
Bedford W R, 35 E Washington
Bowles Thomas H, office 19 E Washington
Brown Ignatius, 19½ E Washington
Caven John, over 19 E Washington
Coburn John, 15½ E Washington
Conner & Fishback, S W cor. Pennsylvania and Washington, up stairs
Coulon Charles, 97 E Washington
Deford Wm. R, 35½ E Washington
Dumont & Torbest, junction of Pennsylvania and Virginia ave.
Duncan R B, S cor. Washington and Meridian, up stairs
Dunham & Tanner, 6 McOuat's Block
Edgar James W, 2 McOuat's Block
Elliott Byron K, 24½ E Washington
Ellsworth, Colley & Redstone, office 10 S Meridian
Ferguson Kirby, Sentinel Building
Gordon George E, Odd Fellows' Hall
Gordon & Beal, 6 Glenns' Block, E Washington.
Hall Reginald H, 24½ E Washington
Hall R C, 82 E Washington
Hamilton John W, Court House
Henderson William, office 14 N Pennsylvania
Hines C C, office Johnson's Building, E Washington
Holladay Elias G, Ætna Building.
Igoe Martin, 70 E Washington
Ketcham & Coffin, Blackford's Building
Kiger Harry, S E cor. Washington and Meridian
McCarty Nicholas, 70 E Washington
McDonald & Porter, Yohn's Block
McDonald & Roache, McOuat's Block
McKenzie Wm. A, 30½ W Washington
Macy David, 10½ E Washington, up stairs
Major Stephen, res. W of city
Milner J, 84 E Washington
Morris Samuel, 24½ E Washington
Morrison & Ray, 26 E Washington, up stairs
Newcomb & Tarkington, 24 E Washington, up stairs
Olmstead G L, Blackford's Building
O'Neal Hugh, Ætna Building, N Pennsylvania
Patterson William, 30 W Washington, up stairs
Perrin George K, bds. Pyle House
Porter Albert G., 109 N Delaware
Rand Frederick, 26½ E Washington
Ryan R J, cor. Meridian and Maryland
Seidensticker Adolph, 95 E Washington
Sherwood H L, 21 E Washington
Shoupe Francis A, 95 E Washington

Smith Charles C, 95 E Washington
Smith Francis, 37 E Washington
Smith & Smith, 26 W Washington, Ray's Building.
Stringfield Woodford, McOuat's Block.
Sweetser James N, 23 E Washington
Tanner Gordon, McOuat's Block
Taylor N B, 30½ W Washington
Yaile H. M, 21 E Washington
Walpole R L, Johnson's Building
Wallace & Harrison, 30½ W Washington, up stairs
Wick William W, office 4 Judah's Block
Wilson O M, cor. Washington and Meridian
Woodbury J G, McOuat's Block
Yandes Simon, 23 E Washington.

Auction and Commission.

Bell Thaddeus D, 15 W Washington
Burrows G. W, 6 W Washington
Duke & Smith, 8 S Meridian
Eldridge, McMillin & Riddle, 39 W Washington
Gott & Featherston, 48 E Washington
Hunt Aaron L, with Gott & Featherston.

Bakers.

Bollman Frederick, 91 E Washington
Brown John W, 150 N New Jersey
Finton F, 77 Fort Wayne ave.
Foos T J, 84 N Mississippi
Gray William, 64 South
Grain & Thalman, 214 E Washington
Haynes Phillip, 40 W Washington
Knauff Adam, 248 W Washington
Knaus S, N side E Washington
Kaestle Jacob, 201 E Washington
Kuhn William, 181 E Washington
Metzger A & J, 11 N Pennsylvania
Rentsch Harmon, 134 S Illinois
Summers & Wentz, 144 W Washington
Thompson Hugh, 4 S Meridian
Weinberger John C, 10 Louisiana
Youngerman Geo., 209 E Washington.

Bankers.

Fletcher Stoughton A, sen., 30 E Washington
Harrison A & J C S, 19 E Washington
Indianapolis Branch Banking Co., S W cor. Washington and Pennsylvania

Banks.

Bank of the State of Indiana, cor. Illinois and Kentucky ave; branch cor. Washington and Meridian

Barbers.

Fey R, basement Little's Hotel
Fisher & Ringle, Louisiana, cor. Illinois
Gutig Henry, cor. Washington and Pennsylvania
Gulliver William, Blake's Row
Henning & Stelzell, Bates House, N Illinois
Leiminger & Ferling, Blackford's Building
Miller R, cor. South and East
Revels Thos. W, (col.,) N. Tremont House
Rider Henry, (col.) 81½ E Washington
Shucraft & Gibbs, under Palmer House
Stronia L D, under American House
Turner Augustus, (col.,) res. 67 W Georgia
Vester Jonathan, (col.,) 81½ E Washington
Young & Revels, Tremont House

Beef and Pork Packers.

McTaggart Israel, 23 N Illinois
Mauser W & I, 14 S Meridian

Bell Hanger and Locksmith.

Reinhardt Joseph, S. Illinois.

Billiard Saloons.

Balcke C, 175 E Washington
Bot Henry, 109 E Washington
Bussey John, opp. Union Depot
Emmen egger I, 113 E Washington
Imbery A, 86 E Washington
Larg L 11 E Washington
Morcninger D & C, 121 E Washington
Montgomery C H, Washington Hall
Walsman F, 32 S Illinois

Bill Posters.

Hedges & Hurlin, office Sentinel Building
Smith Stephen, 10 North

Blacksmiths.

Berryman John, E Washington, near 1 mits
Brutner John, 3 N Noble
Clinton Wharton, 252 E Washington
Gates John, 14 S New Jersey
Gei-el Henry, 8 Delaware
Gorham John M, 76 Indiana ave.
Jones & Vanbl ricum, 8 E Mar land
McVey David, 203 W Washington
Ma-kham Thomas, 26 S Pennsylvania
Smith John G, 36 Kentucky ave.
Te tkampe John, Pearl, rear of postoffice
Wise & Co., 122 S Delaware
Youngerman & Wise, 122 S Delaware

Blank Book Manufacturers.

Bingham & Doughty, Sentinel Building
Campbell & Bro., 37 E Washington
Douglass & Palmer, 36½ E Washington
Sheets & Braden, 77 W Washington

Boarding Houses.

Beck Samuel, 24 S Delaware
B exley Nathanie, 132 S Delaware
Brigh Mrs Eliza, 27 Indiana ave
Coen John, 107 S Tennessee
Crook Mr Julia, 44 N Pennsylvania
Dana M s Ames W. 10 W Market
Donahan Mrs Barbara, 74 N Tennessee
Ferguson wid. Andrew, 20 N Pennsylvania
Hahn Andrew, 8 East
Hanrahan Patrick, 184 S Tennessee
Jeffrey Mrs Mary B, 15 W Washington
Kelly James, (col,) 145 W Washington
Kinster Mrs M W, 79½ E Washington
Knigt Elijah, 8 Illinois
Kolb Wm, 30 Kentucky ave.
Lawton Mrs Susan A, 71 W Maryland
Miller Mrs Sarah, 12 Kentucky ave.
Morgan rs H, 51 E Louisiana
Scudder Caleb cor. Market and Tennessee
Smith Mrs. M C, Alvord's Block, 8 Pennsylvania
Stover A H, 118 N Illinois
Wysong C, 72 S Illinois.

Boiler Manufacturers.

Dumont & Sinker, 8 Pennsylvania

Bonnet Bleachers.

Conaty James B, 22 S Illinois
Copeland J W, 7 S Meridian
Parker Mrs, 134 E Washington

Bookbinders.

Bingham & Doughty, Sentinel Building
Campbell W H & Bro., 37 E Washington
Douglass & Palmer, 36½ E Washington
Grove Charl s H, 125 E Washington
Lieber Herman, 14 N Pennsylvania
Sheets & Braden, 77 W Washington

Booksellers and Stationers.

Asher & Co., Odd Fellows' Hall
Lieber H, 14 N Pennsylvania
Merrill & Co., 15 E Washing on
Perrine Charles O, Union Depot
Stewart & Bowen, 18 W Washington
Werden E & Co., 26 E Washington

Boots and Shoes, Wholesale.

Hendricks & Co., 76 W Washington
Mayhew E C & Co., 8 Louisiana, opp. Union Depot
Sharpe J K, 90 E Washington
Vinnedge & Jones, 17 E Washington

Boots and Shoes, Retail.

Aldag Charles, 133 E Washington
Biddle & Cooper, 79 E Washington
Bruner Charles. 38 W Washington
Buche Frederick, 93 S Illinois
Bur ring Charles, 176 E Washington
Busch Christian, 138 W Washington
Calmyer Henry, 155 S Alabama
Castello John, 5 W Washington
Cutley Wm B, 128 E Washington
Dugan Thomas, 4th story Blake's Row
Edgar & Frazee, Glenn's Block E Washington
Elliott Samuel W. 28 E Washington
Grout Joseph B, 26 W Maryland
Hafner A & F, 103 W Washington
Karle Christian, 79 E Washington
Karle Joseph, 64 E Washington
Kisner John G, 51 S Illinois
Knolle A & Son, 52 E Washington
Koch H H. 53 E South
Lahmann Frederick H, E Washington
Lancaster Washington, 128 Illinois
Lebbene Charles, opp. Madison Railroad Depot
Luebking Charles H. 194 E Washington
Mayhew E C & Co., 5 W Washington
Mathwig John. Illinois
Molony John, 11 S Meridian
Murphy Timothy. 4 W Market
Preis John, 218 E Washington
Rehling Charles, 176 E Washington
Resener Christian F, E Washington
Richter Adolphus I, 161 E Washington
Riemenschneider Herman, 179 E Washington
Robbins & Myers, 51 Blake's Row
Sharpe Joseph K. 90 E Washington
Smith John. North, bet. Pennsylvania and Maryland
Spinney William N, 10 W Washington
Sprandel George, 124 N Mississippi
Teneyck Nelson, 260 W Washington
Teneyck J & R S, 206 W Washington
Vinnedge & Jones, 17 W Washington
Wands Alexander, 128 Meridian
Wands John & Son, 65 E Washington
Wehler Lukas, 179 E Washington
Wert Joseph, 6 S Pennsylvania
West George, 43 E Washington

Bowling Alleys.

Bush Jacob, 248 E Washington

Kollmeyer J C., 138 E Washington
Laird Wm H, Georgia, bet. Illinois and Meridian

Brass and Bell Founders.

Davis J. W. & Co., 96 S Delaware
Garratt Joseph, Union track, near Delaware

Brewers.

Imbery Augustus, near Madison Depot
Jacquet A, 278 E Washington
Jaeger & Schmid, Wyoming, bet. Alabama and New Jersey

Brick Makers.

Feudman William, Nebraska
Hand & Stevens, Nebraska
Hubbard William, Miller, E of Merrill
Johnson O W, 172 E South
McNabb Stephen, near Lawrenceburg Depot
Smith Jas, cor East and McCarty

Brokers, Bill or Note.

Cain John, 8½ E Washington
Fletcher S A & Co., 30 E Washington
Gatling R J, Blackford's Building
Holloway C B, 6½ W Washington
Kline Henry, 77 S Illinois
McKernan & Pierce, 39½ W Washington
West & Wilson, Ætna Building
Wiley Wm Y, 10 E Washington

Building Stone.

Scott, Nicholson & Co., 31 Virginia ave.

Butchers.

Boecher & Werther, 175 S Delaware
Cook Richard, 5 N Illinois
Davids & Rigg, 67 S Illinois
Hahn Louis, 104 W Washington
Heizer J, 131 E Market
McTaggart & Dougherty, Bates House, 15 N Illinois
Morningstar Peter, N Pennsylvania, near Odd Fellows' Hall
Nicolai L, 39 E New York
Pourder & Borst, cor. E Washington and Pennsylvania
Roos & Schmalzried, S Illinois, bet. Georgia and Union Depot
Sierferts A, cor. Washington and Delaware
Wood E A, 157 E Washington
Wright Wm G, 54 South

Butter and Egg Packers.

Holmes & Neil, 184 E Washington

Cancer Doctors.

Howard & Conwell, 52 S Illinois

Carpenters and Builders.

Avery John L, 124 N Alabama
Behymer Daniel, N Delaware
Boerum Joseph S, 204 N Illinois
Bray John S, N Delaware
Brouse Andrew & Sons, 56 E New York
Bundy John, 156 E New York
Bunte John B, New Jersey, near Ohio
Byrket & Beam, 60 S Tennessee
Carter H, Georgia, W of Canal
Coffman Jacob, S New Jersey, near Merrill.
Copeland Jesse, 47 E Market
Dickman F & Co., Wabash, near Liberty
Eden & Copeland, 27 E Market

Emerson R B, 141 W Market
Fatout J L & M R, cor. Mississippi and Indiana ave
Fearnley John, 11 S Illinois
Feary & Low, 18 S New Jersey
Gamble James, Broadway alley, near New Jersey,
Gilkey O B, N Delaware
Helwig Charles, 113 E Ohio
McDonough D B, E Vermont
Rafert & Brothers, 105 N Illinois
Rickards Thomas, cor. Delaware and Maryland.
Stacey Joseph, 127 W Vermont
Stethorn Frederick, 184 N Noble
Seigert Peter, Wabash, bet. New Jersey and East
Wells George, 118 N Mississippi
Wonnell J A, 74 Indiana ave

Carpets and Matting.

Coffin & Morton, 3 Odd Fellows' Hall
Fletcher H A & Co., 26 and 28 W Washington.
Glenn W & H & Co., Glenns' Block
Tousey & Byram, 70 E Washington

Carriage Manufacturers.

Buster Samuel M., 38 Kentucky ave
Clarke Stephen A, N Pennsylvania
Drew Samuel W, E Market Square
Gaston Hiram K, 23 N Illinois
Lowe George, 40 N Pennsylvania
Sutherland Levi, 162 Delaware

China, Glass and Queensware.

Hawthorne & Buchanan, 83 E Washington
Lindley Jacob, 16 W Washington
Middlemas D C, 107 W Washington

Cigars and Tobacco.

Dietrich Wm, 63 E Washington
Donaldson, Maxfield & Prine, 71 W Washington
Heidlinger John A, 10 N Illinois and 3 Palmer House
Henninger Charles & Co., 42 E Washington
Hunt Charles C, 61½ E Washington
Lichtenhein & Son, 85 E Washington
Meyer George F, 35 W Washington
Otten Deitrich, 159 E Washington
Raschig Charles M, 15 E Washington
Reinkin Henry, 93 Fort Wayne ave
Speckman & Kretsch, 57 S Illinois

Clothiers.

(See also Merchant Tailors.)

Criqui Michael, 138 E Washington
Dessar Brothers, 4 E Washington and 6 Meridian
Dernham M, 1 W Washington
Franco D, 2 Palmer House
Glaser & Bro., 2 Bates House
Gœpper F, 15 E Washington
Gramling J & P, 41 E Washington
Hall E A, 2 Odd Fellows' Hall
McGinnis Owen, 39 E Washington
Moritz & Bro., Blackford's Building, and 19 W Washington
Myer Moses, 2 W Washington
Staub J, 59 E Washington
Tapking & Becker, 63 E Washington

Coal Dealers.

Burk John, 148 N Tennessee
Jordan J & J, 50 South
Lowden James, opp. Madison Railroad, or 21 W Washington
Ross J H, 42 W Washington
Smith & Stevenson, 5 S Delaware
Stout C, 101 S Tennessee

Coal Oil Lamp Dealer.

Sinker E T, Meridian, S of postoffice

Commercial Colleges.

Bryant's Commercial College. T J Bryant, principal, Ramsay's Block, S Illinois
Hayden's Commercial College, S W cor. Washington and Meridian, J C Hayden, principal

Commission Merchants.

Bradshaw & Glazier, 16 Meridian, cor Pearl
Fitzgibbon M. & Co., opp. Union Depot
Gallup W P & E P, 74 W Washington
Gott & Fenhrson, 48 E Washington
Hanna V C, cor. Alabama and L Uisiana
Holland John W, 72 E Washington
Jordan J & J, 50 South
Kirland P 73 S Meridian
May Andrew, 85 E Warrington
Middlemas D C, 107 E Washington
Schmull A & H. 83 E Washington
Turner Wm H, 74 W Washington

Commissioner of Deeds.

Wiley William Y, 10 E Washington

Confectioners.

Cunningham Fred P, 43 N Illinois
Daggett W, 22 S Meridian
Haynes Phillip, 40 W Washington
Hull John E, 76 E Washington
Kliber John L, 81 E Washington
Metzger A & J, 11 N Pennsylvania
Parsette James, 15 Illinois
Summers & Wentz, 144 W Washington
Weinberger John C, 10 W Louisiana

Coopers.

Burton G H, 78 N Mississippi
Heimburgh & Co., alley, cor. N Liberty, bet. Washington and Market
May Andrew, 58 S East.

Coppersmiths.

Cottrell & Knight, 94 S Delaware

Daguerrean Artists.

Bruening E & J, E Washington, next door to Hausman's Bazaar
Crane J D, 19½ W Washington
Fish A A, cor. Washington and Meridian
Hays & Reunion, 32½ E Washington
Perdue H, 39½ W Washington
Purcell C W, 8 Ray's Block, W Washington
Weeks & Cox, E Washington, cor. Pennsylvania

Dentists.

Frink Dr. S C, Yohn's block, 4 N Meridian
Hunt P G C, 7 W Maryland
Johnston Dr. John F, 11 W Maryland
Kendrick Oscar H, 132 N Davidson
Moffitt John
Nichols T M, 24 S Meridian
Wells G A, 19 E Washington

17

Dress Makers.

(See Milliners and Dress Makers.)

Drugs and Medicines.

Browning Robert, 22 W Washington
Hanlin & Barnitt, 172 E Washington
Hausaman Wm, 49 E Washington
Lowery Wiley M, 49 Massachusetts ave
Ludden & Co., 14 N Illinois
Perkins & Coon, 14 W Washington
Pope J P, 33 W Washington
Rosenthal Isaac M, 30 S Illinois
Roesch Charles, 163 E Washington
Rosengarten Henry, M D, 1 Odd Fellows' Hall
Tilly Wm. 81 E Washington
Tomlinson & Cox, 8 E Washington

Dry Goods, Retail.

Bradley J & J. 81 E Washington
Coffin & Morton, 3 Odd Fellows' Hall
Fletcher H A & Co., 26 and 28 Ray's block, W Washington
Gilligan Miss M A, 5 Bates House
Glenn W & H & Co, Glenn's block, E Washington
Houpt Robert, 209 Alabama
Kirlin James, 36 W Washington
Koller & Cook, 169 E Washington
Ostermeyer Frederick, 258 E Washington
Palmer & Talbott, 37 E Washington
Stiermann C, 265 S Delaware
Street L & Brother. 56 E Washington
Tousey & Byram, 70 E Washington
Yohn James C, 17 E Washington
Zeigler Wm, 5 E Washington

Dry Goods, Wholesale.

Crossland Jacob A, 75 W Washington
Fletcher H A & Co., 26 and 28 Ray's block
Glenn W & H & Co., Glenn's block, E Washington
Palmer & Talbott, 37 E Washington

Dyers and Scourers.

Bouchet Ed, 174 W Washington
Budence Henry, 158 W Washington
Goodwin A, 56 E Market
Harris Joseph, 38 S Illinois
Harris J, jr., 19 S Meridian
Heal & Call, 17 S Meridian
Kalisch B, 11 N Illinois
Stoacker Wm, 18 Kentucky ave

Edge Tool Manufacturer.

Kellogg Newton, W Washington, near river

Embroideries.

Lennett Ferdinand G. 16 S Illinois, up stairs
Lennett Sarah E. 16 S Illinois, up stairs
Luele's Eliza, 16 S Illinois, 3d floor

Engraver on Wood, &c.

Fahnestock John, 19 W Washington

Express Companies.

Adams Express Co, John H Ohr, agent, 12 E Washington
American Express Co., H V Daniels, agent, S E cor Washington and Meridian
Great Western Dispatch, T A Lewis, agent, office at A Wallace's, cor. Virginia ave and Delaware

United States Express Co., H W Danie's, agent, S E cor. Washington and Meridian

Fancy Articles.

Binz Simon, jr., 32 W Washington
Crossland J A, 61 W Washington
Coffin & Morton. 3 Odd Fellows' Hall
Fahnestock & Co., 18 and 22 · Illinois
Fletcher H A & Co., 26 and 28 W Washington
Gilligan M A, 5 Bates House
Glenn W & H & Co., Glenn's block, E Washington
Hausmann H & Co., 6 E Washington
Klotz & Pfafflin, 29 W Washington
Langbein Joseph, 160 E Washington
Parker Edgar, 17 S Illinois

File Maker.

Stiedel George, 55 N Noble

Flour and Feed Dealers.

Barnitt & Brother. 170 E Washington
Bradshaw & Glazier, 16 S Meridian
Carlisle & Dixon, 208 W Washington
Danforth & Simpson, 3 Odd Fellows' Hall
Fortesque W M, 165 E Washington
Heckman C, 266 E Washington
Jordan J & J, 50 South
Kelley & Petrew, Virginia ave
Loran Leonard, near Madison Depot
Rusch Frederick P., flour, seed and grain store, 83 W Washington

Flouring Mills.

Bates City Mills, J A P Anderson, proprietors, 282 E Washington
Capital Mills, B P Finney, proprietor, cor. Canal and Market
Patterson S J, W Washington, near river bank

Foundries and Machine Shops.

Davis I & Co., 98 S Delaware
Dumont & Sinker, 8 Pennsylvania, E of Union Depot
Hasselman & Vinton, Washington Foundry, opp. Union Depot
Spelts & Thomson, Franklin Foundry, opp. I. & C. freight depot

Furniture Dealers and Cabinet Makers.

Purgtorf F, 199 E Washington
Goebel John G, 82 W Washington
Jose Nicholai, 21 S Meridian
Myers & Witthoft, 171 E Washington
Ott John & Co., 147 W Washington
Ramsay John F, 21 S Illinois
Sloan & Ingersoll. 4 Louisiana
Spiegel, Thoms & Co, ware rooms 73 W Washington
Walingford E & Co., 61 E Washington
Wilde J O, 71 S Illinois

Gas and Steam Pipe Fitters.

Duck John C., 22 Kentucky ave
Mahoney James, 36 N Illinois
Ramsey & Banning, 85 W Washington

Gilder and Picture Framer.

Lieber Herman, Ætna building, N Pennsylvania

Grocers, Wholesale.

Avery L S, 24 W Washington
Bradshaw J & J, 25 W Washington
Danforth & Simpson, 3 and 5 Odd Fellows' Hall, N Pennsylvania
Elliott C A & Co , 34 S Meridian, cor. Maryland
Fitzgibbon M & Co., 77 S Meridian
Hart James & Co., 84 E Washington
Holland John W. 72 E Washington
Jones Wilson & Co., N E cor Meridian and Maryland
Jordan Thomas, 9 W Washington
Kirland P., 72 S Meridian
Langenberg Henry H, 134, cor. W Washington and Mississippi
Mills Alfred & Co., 26 E Washington
Stout O H & Brother 42 W Washington
Stout R C & D L, 46 E Washington
Tuttle B F 27 W Washington
Wallace Andrew, cor. S Delaware and Virginia ave

Grocers, Retail.

Allen Stephen, cor. Illinois and Indiana ave
Avels Mrs Margaret. 277 S Delaware
Avery Leonard S, 24 W Washington
Barnitt & Brother, 170 E Washington
Bartlett Joseph L. 133 S Tennessee
Basty John H, 31 N Alabama
Bell Miletus & Co., 46 Fort Wayne ave
Braco Charles, cor. North & N Alabama
Bradshaw J & J 25 W Washington
Brenker August, 94 E New York
Bretz Adam, cor. Illinois and Louisiana
Breuniner Augustus. 168 Virginia ave
Butsch Geo M, 153 S Delaware
Caric· J M, cor Tennessee and Indiana ave
Carlisle & Dixon. 208 W Washington
Catterson A. 347 S Alabama
Coburn & Lingenfelter, S E cor. Delaware and New York
Corzelmann Conrad. W Washington
Chim A & Brother, 118 Virginia ave
Crall & Brothers, 55 W Washington, Blake's Commercial Row
Crockett Robt. (col.,) N Tennessee, bet. Illinois and Mississippi
Cuncoubman Conrad, W Washington, near river
Danforth & Simpson, 3 and 5 Odd Fellows' Hall
Dobyns B D, cor. St. Clair and Fort Wayne ave
Dougherty Charles. 245 S Delaware
Dosras Charles. S W cor. Vermont and Massachusetts ave
Duncan John, 174 E Washington
Ellerbeg S, 190 S Delaware
Emmerich & Reese 91 W Washington
Ettir glaugh Charles, 180 South
Exline George A. 151 N East
Fiscus Wm. 174 E Washington
Fortesque W M, 165 E Washington
Foster Wm R & Co, 21 N Alabama
George James. 143 W Washington
Gold Adam, W Washington, opp. Woolen Factory
Hagerhorst Christian F, 28 S Illinois, cor. Maryland
Hansen Charles, 50 Bluff road
Hanway Samuel, cor. E Washington and Virginia ave
Hart Jas & Co., 84 E Washington
Heinrich Charles, 61 Madison ave
Binde Miss M E, under Little's Hotel

Hlade P J, Massachusetts ave, cor. Delaware
Hofmeister Nicholas, 82 N Noble
Hohl Christian, 77 E Washington
Ittenbach Gerhard & Co , 180 S Delaware
Johnson Wm, 167 S Tennessee
Jordan T, 9 W Washington
Kamm Gottlieb, 322 Virginia ave
Keely Wm H, 19 N Noble
Kemper Charles, 12 McCarty
Kettenbach Henry, 207 Massachusetts ave
Kingsbury John R, 181 Massachusetts ave
Kirlin James, 36 W Washington
Kobb John A, 69 S Illinois
Koeniger George, 60 South
Kolb J A, 8 Illinois, bet. Georgia and Union Depot
King G, 24 E Georgia
Kuhlmann E H L, 187 W Washington
Liman Charles, 317 Virginia ave
Langlein Joseph, 160 E Washington
Langenberg Henry, 162 W Washington
Lawrence Arthur W, 164 E Ohio
Littner C H & Co, cor. Illinois and Indiana ave
Loucks Cornelius, 165 Virginia ave
McWorkman & Brother, cor. Pennsylvania and North
Mead James, 166 S Illinois
Middlemas David C & Co., 167 W Washington
Miller Henry, 165 N Noble
Mills, Alford & Co, 36 E Washington
Piel Wm F, 240 E Washington
Perrott Samuel & Son, 200 W Washington
Presel & Stoelting, cor. North and West
Reese Henry, 91 and 93 W Washington
Rentsch Edward, 126 S Illinois
Rolewald Henry, 288 Indiana ave
Rosebrock Herman H, 283 S Delaware
Rosegarten Samuel, 78 E Washington
Ruschhaupt T Augustus, 220 E Washington
Schimmel Joseph, cor. Meridian and Bluff road
Schmidt Henry, S side National road
Se null A & H 83 E Washington
Scheppenhorst Wm, 101 E Washington
Schutt Joseph, 117 E Washington
Schweinhart Peter, sr., 131 N East
Shaw John, 228 E Washington
Simpson M & R, 58 E South
Simpson N, 167 S Delaware
Smith Frederick, 126 N Mississippi
Spaan James R, 123 Indiana ave
Spencer & Soell, 212 E Washington
Stoelting Frederick, 163 Indiana ave
Stout O B & Brothers, 42 W Washington
Stout R C & D L, 46 E Washington
Sweeup Henry, 119 N East
Talbott Richard C, 101 W Washington
Thomson Mrs Mary, 66 E South
Tuttle B F, 27 W Washington and 34 N Illinois
Trautmann & Co., cor. East and North
Wallace Andrew, cor. Virginia ave and S Delaware
Werbe L F, 185 W Washington
Wenger Michael, 20 N Noble
Wilkins John A, 32 E Market
Werner P, 78 W Washington
Wood A, cor. Illinois and Vermont
Woollen Wm M, 82 W Vermont
Worland Wm, 37 Virginia ave
Wright W W, cor. Washington and Delaware
Yeager C, 215 E Washington
Youngerman G B, 209 E Washington

Guns and Pistols, Manufacturers and Dealers.

Beck Christian, 15 S Meridian
Beck Jacob, 86 E Washington
Parker Edgar, 17 S Illinois
McLaughlin John A, 254 E Washington

Hardware and Cutlery.

City Hardware Store, 12 W Washington
Kellogg H S, 66 E Washington
Pottage B, 76 W Washington
Vajen J H, 21 W Washington
Vonnegut Clem, 142 E Washington
Wilson J B 4 W Washington
Wood A D, 71 E Washington

Hats, Caps and Furs.

Bamberger H, 16 E Washington
Hickok & Starr, 30 W Washington
Reed Benjamin F, 22 E Washington
Rosenberg S, 73 E Washington
Wilmot S, 8 W Washington

Hide and Leather Dealers.

(See also Tanners.)

Fishback John, 30 S Meridian
Mooneys & Co., 75 S Meridian
Sharpe J K, 95 E Washington
Vonnegut C, 142 E Washington
Yandes & Co., 38 E Washington

Hosiery and Trimmings.

McCollin Phillip G, 7 N Meridian

Hotels and Proprietors.

American House, Wiggim & Morrow, proprietors Louisiana, opp. Union Depot.
Bates House, William Juds n, proprietor, cor. Illinois and Washington
Batty House, J H Batty, proprietor, 31 N Alabama
California House, 126 S Illinois
Cincinnati House, P Wolfe, proprietor, Delaware, bet. South and Louisiana
East Street House, Henry Hahn, proprietor, East, near Penn Depot.
Farmers' Hotel, H Buehrig, proprietor, 61 S Illinois
Farmers' and Drovers' Hotel, J Harris, proprietor, 212 W Washington
Galt House, John Hebele, proprietor, 98 S Illinois
Indiana House, 31 E Market
Jefferson House, South, near Madison Depot
Jackson House, near Madison Depot
Little's Hotel, A R Hyde, proprietor, cor. Washington and New Jersey
Macy House, A S Kingsley, proprietor, cor. Mark t and Illinois
National Hotel, D Bender, proprietor, 217 W Washington
Oriental House, F Costigan, proprietor, S Illinois, bet. Maryland and Georgia
Palmer House, Jesse D Carmichael, cor. Washington and Illinois
Pattison House, 31 N. Alabama
Pennsylvania House, 268 E Washington, cor. East.
Pyle House, John Pyle, proprietor, cor. Maryland and Illinois
Ray House, Ray & Lambert, proprietors, cor. South and Delaware
Tremont House, J Riddle, proprietor, cor. Illinois and Louisiana

Tully House, Wm. Tully, proprietor, 79 S
Illinois
Washington House, John Mattler, proprietor,
83 S Meridian

Ice Dealers.

Buckhart Jackson, 146 N. Mississippi
Pitts George W., res. 78 Indiana ave.

Insurance Companies, (Home.)

German Mutual Insurance Co. of Indiana,
25 E Washington
Indianapolis Insurance Co., office 14 and 16
Meridian
Indianapolis Life Insurance Co., office 14 S
Meridian
Rising Sun Insurance Co., 14 and 16 S Me-
ridian
White River Valley Insurance Co., Ray's
Block.

Insurance Companies, (Foreign.)

Ætna, (Fire,) Ætna Ins., Building, N Penn-
sylvania bet Washington and Market
British Commercial, (Life,) Blackford's Build-
ing
Charter Oak, (Fire,) Odd Fellows' Hall
Charter Oak, (Life,) Blackford's Building
City, (Fire,) Blackford's Building
Commercial, (Fire,) cor. Washington and
Meridian
Connecticut Mutual, (Life,) 70 E Washington
Conway, (Fire,) Odd Fellows' Hall
Fulton, (Fire,) New York, 70 E Washington
Hanover, (Fire,) Odd Fellows' Hall
Hartford, (Fire,) Blackford's Building
Home, (Fire,) Blackford's Building
Humphrey, (Fire,) Blackford's Building
Knickerbocker, (Life,) cor. Washington and
Meridian
Manhattan, (Life,) Odd Fellows' Hall
Madison, (Fire,) cor. Washington and Me-
ridian
Massasoit, A Graydon, agent
Merchants, Blackford's Building
New England, (Life,) Blackford's Building
New England, (Fire,) cor. Washington and
Meridian
North American, (Fire,) Ætna Insurance
Building
Park, (Fire,) cor. Washington and Meridian
Peoria Odd Fellows' Hall
Phœnix, Hartford, Richards' Building
Phœnix, (Fire,) Brooklyn, N Y., 70 E Wash-
ington
Quaker City, cor. Washington and Meridian
Springfield, Alex. Graydon, agent

Iron Railing.

Dumont & Slutes, 8 Pennsylvania
Williamson & Haugh, 2 N Delaware

Iron and Steel.

Bulst Thomas, 70 W Washington
Kellogg H S, 66 E Washington
Murphy & Holliday, 34 E Washington
Pottage B, 72 W Washington

Justices of the Peace.

Coulon Charles, 97 E Washington
Curtis Andrew, 39 E Washington
Faber Charles, 1 N Meridian
Sullivan William, 47 E Washington

Lard, Oil, Soap and Candles.

Busby & Stiches, office 9 W Washington
Tilly H & Co., Bluff Road

Last and Peg Manufacturers.

Osgood, Smith & Co., 180 S Illinois

Lightning Rods, (Copper.)

Locke & Muns n, 1 Blackford's Building
Hall William, S W cor. Washington and
Meridian

Lime and Cement.

Burnam George, Central Depot
Butsch Valentine, N of the M. and I. Rail
road Depot

Livery, Sale and Boarding.

Allen & Hinesley, rear of Palmer House
Brinkman & Bucksot, 17 S Delaware
Citizens' Livery Stable, William Wilkison,
proprietor, 10 Pearl
Herman & Greensteiner, 114 E Market
Johnston Oliver, Pearl, bet. Meridian and
Illinois
Land's Jacob, 18 E Maryland
North Cape Myron, 24 S Pennsylvania
Patterson J M, 34 E Maryland
Wood & Fondray, 10 N Pennsylvania

Loan Offices.

Cain John, 8½ E Washington
Holloway C B, 6½ W Washington, up stairs
Kline Henry, 77 S Illinois

Locksmith.

Reinhardt Joseph, Illinois, S of Washington

Lumber, Lath and Shingles.

Brown P, 275 Massachusetts ave.
Byers & Beam, 60 S. Tennessee
Kregelo, Blake & Co., cor. Canal and New
York
McCord & Wheatley, 119 S Delaware
Mars & J & Co., 146 Washington
Walker & King, cor. New York and Tennes-
see

Marble Workers.

Dame Jaso, 67 E Washington
Downey Michael, cor. Washington and Ala-
bama
James Seth C, 104 S Illinois
Keys Wm. A, 26 S Meridian
Richards & Goddard, cor. Market and Ten-
nessee
Seybold M & Co, 15 N Pennsylvania
Weir J W & Bro., 13 Virginia ave.

Merchant Tailors.

Bodantz H, 158 W Washington
Criqui M, 158 E Washington
Dernhim M, 1 W Washington
Wesear Bros., 2 E Washington
Franco D, 2 Palmer House
Gerstner & Rogge, 164 E Washington
Glasser & Bros., 2 Bates House
Gupper F, 15 E Washington
Gramling J & P, 41 E Washington
Hall E A, 2 Odd Fellows' Hall
Hotz & Co., Illinois, near Georgia
McGinnis O, 39 E. Washington
Moritz & Bro., 3 E Washington and 19 W
Washington
Sewxembein E, 163 E Washington
Stillmeir & Meyer, 144 E Washington
Smith & Morgan, 35 E Washington
Steinmann J, 25 S Meridian

Tapking & Bec'er, 63 E Washington
Talbott James W, 3 W Washington

Milliners and Dress Makers.

Aldene Madame, 118 N Illinois
Baker Miss Sarah A, 20 S Illinois
Baker Mrs. *nea, 20 S Illinois
Ca·seberry Mrs. M, 184 · sss chnsettsave
Copeland Joshua W, 7 S Meridian
Dawson Mi s E, 3 E Michigan road
Dietrich Mrs. M, 63 E Washingt n
Fahnestock Miss C S K & Co., 22 S Illinois
Farrell Miss K 21 S Delaware
Fiscus Mrs. Elizabeth, 174 E Washington
Hani Mrs Mary A, 11 Indiana ave
Heely Ann, 11 Alabama
Huey Miss Sinesia, 18 N Illinois
Humphrey Miss Mary. 39 N Pennsylvania
Johnson Miss Maria, 3 N Meridian
Kelly Mrs. A·n, 3 N Meridian
Kirk Mrs E, 39 N Pennsy vania
L wman Mrs. N, 58 E st. Clair
Matthews Mrs Marg ret, 124 E Market
Pratt Mrs. L A, Dunlop's Row, N Meridian
Rumann Mrs Natalie, 131 E Wa h ngton
Smith Miss Catharine, 71 E Ma ket
Smith Mrs. Sophia, 86 E Gard n
Thomas Mrs. M J, 46 W Washington
Webb Miss Hannah A, 18 N Illinois
Wilson Mrs. E, 18 N Illinois
Wissart Mrs. S S, 25 N Alabama

Model Builders.

McDonald Currin E, Sentinel Building
McLean & Gummer, cor. Maryland and Meridian
Perine & Mayhew, 1 3d floor Blake's Building, cor. Washington and Kentucky ave.

Money Broker.

Wiley Wm Y, 10½ E Washington, up stairs.

Music and Musical Instruments.

Ames James, cor. W Washington
Willard & Stowell, 4 Bates House

News Depots.

Perrine Charl s O, Union Depot
Thompson Mrs. M, at postoffice

Newspapers and Periodicals.

Christian Record, E Goodwin, proprietor, Journal Office
Herald & Era, Williamson & Lee, edi'ors and publishers, cor. Washington and Meridian
Indiana American, T A Go dwin, proprie or, rear of Glenn's Block.
Indiana Farmer, (weekly,) J N Ray, editor and publisher, office over postoffice
Indiana Free Press, (German,) R Henninger, proprietor, 83 E Washin ton
Indiana State Sentinel, daily and weekly, Bingham & Doughty, proprietors, 16, 18, and 20, E W ashington
Indiana Se ool Journal, O Phelps, editor, Sentinel O fce
Indiana Volksblatt, Julius Boetticher, proprietor, 199 E Washington
Indi napoli daily and weekly Jourr al, published by Indianapolis Journal Co., 8 8 Pennsylvania, new building Circle, cor. Meridian
Locomotive, (weekly,) Elder & Harkness, proprietors, 2 S Meridian

Repository, (co ·.,) Elijah Weaver, Journal Office.
The Witness, M G Clark, e 'itor an l proprietor, office Odd Fellows' Hall

Notaries Public.

Bowles Thomas H. 10 E Washington
Brown Ignatius, 19½ E Was ington
Coburn Joh , Johns n'n Bud ling, E Washington, bet. Me idian and Pennsylvania
Comn r & Fish ack, College Hall Buil ing
Deford W lliam R, 35 E W s ington, 2d floor
Dunlop John S, cor. Washington and Meridian, up stairs
Elliot B K. 24½, E Washington
Fergus n K, Sentinel Building
Grubbs D W, S W cor. Washington and Meridian
Hall C W, 39 W Washi gton, 2 d floor
Hines C C, Johnso 's Building
Holloway C B, W Wash n ton, bet. Meridian and Il inois
Howland Livingston, 13 E Washington
Milner J, 84 E W shington
Morris Samuel V, 24½ E Washington, up stairs
O'Neal Hugh, 45 E Washington
Patterson Wi liams. 7 W Washington
Persin George K, College Hall Building, 45 E Washingt n
Seidensticker A. 95 E Washington
Sherw ed H L, 21 E Washington
Smith Watt J, R·y's Building
Smith C C, 95 E Washin ton
Smi h Francis. 37 E Washingt n
Strange W R, Court House
Taylor N B, 33½ W Washington
Vaile H M, 21 E Washington
Wallach J L, opp. Court House, E Washington.
Wallace & Harrison. Temperance Hall
Wilson O M, 95 E Washington
Woodbury J G, McOuat's Block, Kentucky ave
Wiley Wm Y, 10½ E Washington

Nurseries.

Fletcher, Williams and Loomis, 14 S Pennsylvania
Hill, Goldsmith & Co., 81 E Washington

Occulist and Aurist.

Gustin L, cor. Lou'siana and Illinois

Opticians.

Moses Lucius W, 20 E Washington
Semmons J H & Co., 19 S Illinois

Paint and Color Works.

Beck & Moffitt, 87 E Washington

Painters and Glaziers.

Baker & Kelly, cor. Washington and Meridian
Beale Joshua, 133 Virginia ave.
Blain James W, 31 S Delaware
Cook M R, cor. Meridian and Maryland
Fertig Frank, 4 E Washington
Hulings John P, 12½ S Pennsylvania
Knotts Nim K, 35 ½ E Washington
Long b D, 28 S Meridian
Maker George W, S W cor. Washington and Meridian
McAdams H H. 35 E Washington
Osgood J B, 24 Kentucky ave.

Styles & English, cor. Meridian and Washington
Whiteridge William, 82 E Washington

Paper Box Maker.

Grobe Charles H, 125 E Washington

Patent Medicines.

Brell Chester H, 5 N Meridian
Frost J M & Co., 5 N Meridian
Roberts Dwight, 6 Louisiana

Patent Solicitors.

Bussell Dr. E T, 19 S Mississippi
Ellsworth, Colley & Redstone, 10 S Meridian
Okey Joseph B, 144 N East

Physicians.

Abbett Lawson, 20 Virginia ave.
Arnold & Davis, 40½ Louisiana, up stairs
Baine Thomas, 68 Blackford
Bell Milens, 124 N Delaware
Bobbs J S, 172 E Washington, up stairs
Boyd J T, 28 N Illinois
Brown Clay, 23 S Meridian
Bullard Talbot, 23 S Meridian
Bulla d W R, with Dr. T Bullard
Cawd H H B, 180 S Pennsylvania
Cook Stephen S. 34 Ellsworth
Corliss C T. 53 Maryland
Darrach G M, 41 N New Jersey
Dicki son James L. 241 S Alabama
Dodge & Scott, 3 Glenn's Block
Donezhy John T, 26 E Washington, up stairs
Dorsay Nicholas, 46 and 48 N Pennsylvania
Dougherty Zadok, California, W side near Market
Dunlap John M, Indiana Hospital for the Insane
Dunlap L, 12 Virginia ave
Elenby James, 21 S Delaware
Elliott Thomas D, 28 N Illinois
Ewing J, 53 S Pennsylvania
Fahnestock Samuel, 19 W Washington
Fishback Charles, office 146 Virginia ave.
Funkhouser David. 5 S Meridian
Gaston John M, S E cor. New York and New Jersey
Given John, 25 Ramsay's Block
Gustin Levi, cor. Louisiana and Illinois
Homburg Konradin, 24½ E Washington
Howard & Conwell, 52 S Illinois
Jameson & Funkhouser, 5 S Meridian
Kee'y Isaac I, 62 E Michigan
Kendrick Wm H, 33 N East
Kitchen J M, S W cor. Washington and Meridian
Klein Emel, 100 E New York
Lowery George D, 164 N Noble
Ludden Benjamin M, 14 N Illinois
Lynch Michael, Virginia ave., near Washington
McCann Samuel D, 29 N East
Mears George W, 14 Circle
Merrill John F, 156 W Washington
Musgrove Phillip B, bds. N Tennessee
Newcomer F S, 14 Circle
Parry & Wright, 12 E Market
Parvin Theophilus, 69 N Alabama
Pleasants John, 30 E Market
Rhoads John W, 25 Ramsay's Block
Rosenthal Isaac M, 30 S Illinois
Rucker James S, 58 W Vermont
Schindler Robert, 244 E Washington
Stedman E P, 53 N New Jersey
Stevens T M, 172 E Washington

Stout Oliver H, 19 W Maryland
Teal Nathaniel, 38½ W Washington
Thompson & Woodburn, 14 E Market
Tilly Jo ep , 108 S D lawere
Wright Augustus, 28 N Illinois

Piano Fortes.

Ames James, cor. Washington and Kentucky ave
Fraezser George, cor Washington and Alabama, up stairs
Willard & Stowell, 4 Bates House

Planing Mills.

Byrkit & Beam, 60 S Tennessee
Hall George W. cor. East and Georgia
Kregelo, Blake & Co., cor. Canal and New York

Plasterers.

Hartman Mathew, 108 N Alabama
Northway John, 143 E North
Smith & LaRue, 20 Kentucky ave

Plumbers.

Dunn John C, 22 Kentucky ave
Ramsey & Hanning, 85 W Washington

Portrait Painters.

Adams Mrs. J G, 4 Blake's building
Cox Jacob, 2 Blake's building
Hays S B, 32 E Washington
Neimeyer John H, over A B Willard & Co.

Professors of Music.

Brummer Charles, 33 N Alabama
Ewald Robert, Little's Hotel
Grenh Benjamin F, N Illinois
Hines Edward, bds. 18 N East
Hunter Bell , 125 E New York
Lord Julia F, 89 E Ohio
Pearsall Peter R, 16 S Tennessee

Printers, Book and Job.

Bingham & Doughty, Sentinel buildings
Bowticher J, 132 E Washington
Cameron Wm S, 8 E Pearl
Elder & Hark ss, 28 S Meridian
Fahnestock John, 19 W Washington
Journal Company, 10 S Pennsylvania

Publishers, Book.

Asher & Co., Odd Fellows' Hall, up stairs
Bingham & Doughty, Sentinel building
Haws Geo W, Sentinel building
Sutherland & McEvoy, E Washington
Talcott John T, bds Palmer House

Pump Makers.

Childers John P, 151 S Noble
Hall Lytel, E Vermont, near Massachusetts ave
Basket & Kyle, Pearl, rear of Post office
Wright W G, Maryland

Real Estate Agents.

(See Agents, Real Estate.)

Real Estate Auctioneers.

Wiley Wm Y, 10½ E Washington

Restaurants.

Beck Edward, Crystal Palace, 44 W Washington
Dieta Adam, Paradise Garden, 65 Fort Wayne ave

Dietz Geo & Co, Washington Hall, 78 and 80 W Washington
Dunn Thomas B, 7 N Illinois
Eastman Henry, cor. Illinois and Louisiana
Flagg Seth A. Magnolia, 9 S Illinois
Heidenreich C ristopher, 168 E Washington
Hug Martin, Capital, 14 E Washington
Leslie John, Pearl, Little's Hotel
Lang Lewis, 17 E Washington
Rhodius George, National, 27 S Meridian
Wolf Jacob, 162 E Washington

Rolling Mill.

Indianapolis Rolling Mill Co., cor. Merrill and Mississippi

Saddle and Harness Makers.

Andra John, 196 E Washington
Blair James M, 87 W Washington
Hinesley & Hereth, 34 W Washington
Nicolai Charles, 264 E Washington
Sulgrove Jerome B, 44 E Washington
Sulgrove & Reynolds, 20 W Washington

Saddlery Hardware.

Hinesley & Hereth, 34 W Washington
Sulgrove & Reynolds, 20 W Washington
Sulgrove J B, 44 E Washington

Saloons.

Balcke Charles, 175 E Washington
Ballweg Fredericl, 95 W Washington
Bates House Saloon, N Illinois
Beck Edward, 44 W Washington
Beebe R, 23 W Washington
Blaes N, 66 S Delaware
Bott Henry, 109 E Washington
Buehrig H. Farmers' Hotel
Buscher Henry, 51 E South
Bradema yer Henry, 312 Virginia ave
Beinelm yer John C, 75 E Washington
Bussey John, 38 Louisiana
Dess'er John, South, near Madison Depot
Dickmann Carl, 166 E Washington
Dietz Geo & Co , 78 and 80 W Washington
Dunn T B, 7 N Ill nois
Eiff & Regenaur, 25 S Meridian
Emmenegger Matthias, 101 and 113 E Washington
Ewrick John L, 12 W Louisiana
Frenzel John P, 85 S Illinois
Heidenreich C, 168 E Washington
Holl C, 77 E Washington
Hoppe George, 81 S Meridian
Hug Martin, 14 E Washington
Imbery Aug stus, 26 E Washington
Johnson Benjamin F, basement Palmer House
Kistner Adam, California House
Kollmeyer John C, 138 E Washington
Lang Lewis, 11 E Washington
Leslie John, under Little's Hotel
Mattler John, 83 S Meridian
Mosch T H, Apollo Garden
Momberger D & C, 121 E Washington
Miller Charles T, S side National road
Naltner A, 117 S Tennessee
Newcomer Christian, 13 W Washington
Petrie John, 222 E Washington
Rassmann Charles, 119 E Washington
Regensuer Wm, 25 S Meridian
Renard E, 276 E Washington
Stahlin Martin, under Tremont House
Walesinski S, 27 N Alabama
Waleman Fred, 55 S Ill nois
Wolf Jacob, 162 E Washington

Sash, Doors and Blinds.

Behymer Daniel, 6 N Delaware
Byrkit & Beam, cor. Georgia and Tennessee
Hill Geo W, cor. East and Georgia
Kreadlo, Blake & Co., cor. New York and Canal

Saw Manufacturers.

Atkins Elias C, 155 S Illinois
Coffin Nathan T, E of Union Depot

Saw Mills.

Hill G W, cor. East and Georgia
Stevens G D, near Madison Depot
Wells Wm F, Massachusetts ave, near limits
Wishmier C, 199 N Davidson

Seed Stores.

Birkenmeyer P S & Co , 74 E Washington
Braden D, 84 W Washington

Silver Smiths.

Bacon Robert D, rear of 24 E Washington
Covert Isaac, 83½ W Washington
Higgins Wm B, 136 N Alabama

Stair Builder.

Chester A A, cor. Pennsylvania and Union

Stock Broker.

Wiley Wm Y, 10½ E Washington

Stoneware.

Middlemas D C, 167 W Washington

Surveyors.

Allen Charles F, 8 Blake's block
Harper John L, 263 Washington
Hosbrook Daniel B, 168 N Mississippi
Stein Frederick, cor. Market and Cady
Wood James. 3 Blake's building
Wood James N, 3 Blake's building

Tanners.

Creasser Wm, E Washington, E of Pogue's Run
Hoffman Henry, bet. Washington and Maryland
Patterson T T N, 71 N Alabama

Tea Dealers.

(See also Grocers.)

Daggett W, 22 S Meridian
Donaldson, Maxfield & Prine, 71 W Washington
Heiddinger J A, 10 Bates House
Kirland P, 73 S Meridian
Muir James, 33 W Market

Telegraph Office.

Western Union, 1 N Meridian

Tinware and Stoves.

Cox Charles, 11 W Washington
Frankem Isaac L, 9 Virginia ave
Goldsberry Livington D, 182 E Washington
Kevill Robert L, 70 E Louisiana
McGuat R L & A W, 69 W Washington
Munson & Johnston, 62 E Washington
Pottage Benjamin, 76 W Washington
Rexford & Smith, 11 S Illinois.

Root, Bennett & Co., 64 E Washington
Voegtle Jacob, 177 E Washington

Trunk Manufacturers.

Becker H, 30 W Washington
Sulgrove & Reynolds, 20 W Washington

Turner.

Kolb Louis, Georgia, near Pennsylvania

Umbrella Maker.

Mayer John F, 69 E Washington

Undertakers.

Burgtorf Frederick, 129 E Washington
Herrmon & Greensteianer, 114 E Market
Long Matthew, 98 S Meridian
Weaver & Williams, 72 W Washington

Vinegar Manufacturers.

Dink Andrew, 135 Indiana ave
Ludlow Cyrus, near Madison Depot

Wagon Manufacturers.

Jones & Van Blaricum, 6, 8, 10 and 12 E Maryland
Montague Wm, 12 N Delaware
Munsell Henry, Wabash alley, bet. Liberty and Noble
Richmann & Buchanan, 211 E Washington
Youngermann & Wise, 122 S Delaware

Wall Papers.

Roll Isaac H 16 S Illinois
Werden E & Co , 26 E Washington

Watches and Jewelry.

Bingham W P & Co., 2 E Washington
Daumont S H, 9 S Meridian

Draeger Charles, 103 E Washington
Feller George, 17 N Illinois
Fergus n C A & Co., 7 W Washington
French C G, 57 W Washington
McLene Jeremiah, 1 Bates House
Roch M, 80 W Washington
Talbott W H & Co , 24 E Washington

Well Diggers.

Donovan Peter, 197 E New York
Ross Robert, res. 135 E New York

Wines and Liquors.

Buscher & Co., 140 W Washington
Emmerich & Reese, 91 and 93 W Washington
Hart James & Co., 84 E Washington
Jaquet Adolph, 278 E Washington
Kirland P, 73 S Meridian
Leier Anton, 140 E Washington
Middlemas D C, 107 W Washington
Mueller John, 212 E Washington
Rosenthal A, 38 Louisiana
Raschbaupt & Bals, 82 E Washington
Volme Charles, 113 E Washington
Woolf M, 8 Illinois, near Georgia

Wood and Willow Ware.

Klotz & Pfafflin, 29 W Washington

Woolen Factories.

Geisendorff G W & Co., 268 W Washington
Merritt & Coughlen, S side W Washington, near river

Yankee Notions and Toys.

Fing S, jr., 32 W Washington
Crosland J A, 75 W Washington
Hausmann H & Co., 6 E Washington
Klotz & Pfafflin, 29 W Washington
Parker Edgar, 17 S Illinois.

CHARTER OAK

FIRE AND MARINE

INSURANCE CO.

Hartford, Connecticut.

Cash Capital, $300.000.

BOARD OF DIRECTORS.

Ralph Gillett,	Mason Gross,	A. D. Euson,
Barzillai Hudson,	William W. House,	Albert F. Day,
Wareham Griswold,	Alonzo W. Birge,	J. B. Russell,
Phillip Ripley,	Charles Forbes,	R. C. Osborn,
Roswell Brown.	H. K. W. Welch,	J. H. Sprague.

JOSEPH H. SPRAGUE,   **RALPH GILLETT,**

Secretary.   President.

LOSSES EQUITABLY ADJUSTED AND PROMPTLY PAID IN CASH

BY

C. B. DAVIS, AGENT,

Indianapolis, - - - - Indiana.

CITY GOVERNMENT.

ANNUAL ELECTION SECOND TUESDAY IN MAY. COUNCIL MEETS EVERY OTHER SATURDAY NIGHT.

CITY OFFICERS FOR 1860.

Mayor—S. D. Maxwell.

Treasurer, James M. Jameson; *Clerk*, John G. Waters; *Marshal*, Jefferson Springsteen; *Deputy Marshal*, J. J. Bisbing; *City Engineer*, James Wood, sr.; *Assistant Engineer*, James Wood, jr.; *Street Commissioner*, Henry Colestock; *Market Master*, Charles John; *Assessor*, R. W. Robinson; *City Attorney*, B. K. Elliott.

COUNCILMEN.

First Ward, Sims A. Colley, Samuel Seiberts.
Second Ward, T. P. Haughey, Andrew Wallace.
Third Ward, J. S. Pratt, Jacob Vandegrift.
Fourth Ward, Eric Locke, George W. Guisendorff.
Fifth Ward, E. H. Kuhlmann, Stephen McNabb.
Sixth Ward, Alexander Metzger, Hermann Tilly.
Seventh Ward, Thos. Cottrell, Charles Richmann.

WATCHMEN.

Captain, A. D. Rose, Thos. Amos, Halden Davis, Charles Carter, Richard Ware, Frederick Shergart, John S. Russell, Hubbard Adams, Hannibal Taffee, John Farrell.
Sealer of Weights and Measures, Cyrus W. Butterfield.
Keeper of Cemetery, G. W. Allred.
School Trustees, David S. Beaty, John Love, D. V. Cully.

CENTER TOWNSHIP OFFICERS.

Constables, David W. Loucks, Robert B. Barbee, John Hanna, Edward Davis; *Trustee*, Jacob Nieman.

MARION COUNTY OFFICERS.

Judge of Common Pleas Court, John Coburn; *Clerk of Circuit and Common Pleas Court*, John C. New; *Principal Deputy*, Fred. Knefler; *Sheriff*, John Wallace; *Recorder*, Alexander G. Wallace; *Deputy*, Wm. J. Wallace; *Coroner*, John Moffitt; *Treasurer*, Thomas D. Barker; *Deputy*, Samuel Vanlandingham; *Auditor*, Jacob W. Wright; *Deputy Auditor*, Warren L. Lockhart; *Surveyor*, Royal Mayhew; *Prosecuting Attorney Court of Common Pleas*, James N. Sweetzer; *Commissioners*, Levi A. Hardesty, Thomas Johnson, Samuel Moore.

COURTS.

UNITED STATES CIRCUIT COURT.

Held at the State House on the third Mondays of November and May in each year.
Circuit Judge, John McLean. *Circuit Clerk*, Horace Bassett.

UNITED STATES DISTRICT COURT.

Held at the State House on the third Mondays of November and May in each year. Clerk's office at State Bank building.
District Judge, Elisha M. Huntington; *District Clerk*, John H. Rea; *District Attorney*, Daniel W. Voorhees.

UNITED STATES MARSHALL.

Marshal, John L. Robinson; office State Bank buildings. *Deputy Marshals*, Geo. McOuat, Samuel Barbour, C. W. Seely; *United States Commissioners*, John H. Rea, Reginald H. Hall, H. C. Newcomb.

SUPREME COURT.

Court meets in State House fourth Mondays in May and November.
Judges, Andrew Davidson, J. L. Worden, James M. Hanna, Samuel E. Perkins; *Clerk*, William B. Beach; *Sheriff*, Henry H. Nelson.

MARION CIRCUIT COURT.

Meets at Court House, Indianapolis, fourth Mondays in March and September.
Judge Fifth Judicial Circuit, Fabius M. Finch; *Clerk*, John C. New; *Prosecuting Attorney*, W. P. Fishback.

MARION COURT OF COMMON PLEAS.

Meets at the Court House, Indianapolis, second Mondays in February, June, August and December.
Judge, J. Coburn; *Clerk*, John C. New; *Prosecuting Attorney*, James N. Sweetzer.

INDIANAPOLIS STEAM FIRE DEPARTMENT.

Established on the principle of regular and specified compensation to all employed under the auspices of this department.

Chief Engineer, Joseph W. Davis.

Company No. 1, hand engine, New Jersey, N. of Washington. Chas. Richmond, Capt.

Company No. 2, steam engine, Washington, W. of West.

Company No. 3, South, bet. Delaware and Alabama.

MILITARY.

INDIANAPOLIS CITY GREYS.

Organized August 12, 1857. Place of meeting, Military Hall, E. Washington street. Drill meetings every Tuesday evening. Business meeting, 1st Monday evening of each month. Number of members, 83.

OFFICERS.

E. Hartwell, *Commandant;* W. F. Harris, *1st Lieutenant;* R. S. Foster, *2d Lieutenant;* B. K. Elliott, *3d Lieutenant;* T. F. Holland, *4th Lieutenant;* Geo. Butler, *1st Sergeant;* D. W. Carlisle, *2d Sergeant;* E. C. Brundage, *3d Sergeant;* S. W. Elliott, *4th Sergeant;* C. S Butterfield, *5th Sergeant;* James O. Brown, *1st Corporal;* W. F. Oglesby, *2d Corporal;* T. S. Campbell, *3d Corporal;* J. N. Mayhew, *4th Corporal;* Thomas McBaker, *Quartermaster;* Geo. Rodius, *Ensign;* S W Elliott, *Secretary;* Capt. E. Hartwell, *Treasurer.*

CITY GREYS ARTILLERY COMPANY.

F. A. Colestock, *Captain;* L. Demoss, *Lieutenant;* H. D. Carlisle, *Sergeant;* B. K. Elliott, *Secretary;* Wm. Reeves, *Treasurer.*

INDIANAPOLIS NATIONAL GUARDS.

Organized March 11th, 1856. Place of meeting, Ætna Insurance Building, N. Pennsylvania street. Number of members, 84.

OFFICERS.

Irwin Harrison, *Commandant;* Winston P. Noble, *1st Lieutenant;* Harvey Bates, jr., *2d Lieutenant;* James Drum, *3d Lieutenant;* Charles Coulon, *4th Lieutenant;* John Lindley, *Ensign;* W. W Darnall, *1st Sergeant;* George Sloan, *2d Sergeant;* Dorman N. Davidson, *3d Sergeant;* L. Adams, *4th Sergeant;* Captain North, *Drum Major;* E. G. Ward, *1st Corporal;* David Braden, *2d Corporal;* L. R. Garner, *3d Corporal;* Jas. Moore *4th Corporal;* John Fashestock, *Secretary;* Winston P.

Noble, *Treasurer;* Jacob Vandegrift, *Quartermaster;* J. R. Bracken, *Commissary;* John Kitchen, *Surgeon.*

MARION LIGHT DRAGOONS.
Organized August, 1858. Number of members, 50.

OFFICERS.

John Love, *Commandant;* H. H. Dodd, 1st *Lieutenant;* J. W. Murphy, *2d Lieutenant;* Francis Cunningham, *Secretary;* Harrison Dodd, *Treasurer;*

INDIANAPOLIS ROLLING MILL COMPANY.
J. M. Lord, *President and Superintendent;* C. B. Parkman, *Secretary;* W. O. Rockwood, *Treasurer;* John Thomas, *manager.*

INDIANAPOLIS GAS LIGHT AND COKE COMPANY.
Established in 1850. Works located on Pennsylvania street. Office 3 W. Washington street, 2d floor, near the corner of Meridian.
Board of Directors.—D. V. Culley, E. J. Peck, I. Mansur, S. A. Fletcher, jr., D. S. Beaty.

OFFICERS.

C. I. Brown, *Superintendent;* D. S. Beaty, *President and Secretary;* S. A. Fletcher, sr., *Treasurer.*

INDIANAPOLIS BUILDING, LOAN FUND AND SAVINGS ASSOCIATION.
Directors.—Wm. Y. Wiley, D. V. Culley, L. S. Newell, J. B. McChesney, James M. Sharpe, Chas. G. French, Ed. T. Sinker, Samuel Wilmot, Andrew Wallace, Josiah R. Griffith.

OFFICERS.

Wm. Y. Wiley, *President;* David V. Culley, *Vice President;* C. B. Davis, *Secretary;* S. A. Fletcher, *Treasurer;* John Cavin, *Attorney;* Andrew Wallace, *Surveyor.*

BANKS.
BANK OF THE STATE OF INDIANA.
Office cor. Illinois and Kentucky avenue; capital paid in, $3,051,750.
Hugh McCulloch, *President;* James M. Ray, *Cashier.*

BANK OF THE STATE OF INDIANA, BRANCH AT INDIANAPOLIS.
Office N. E. cor. Meridian and E. Washington streets. Capital, $200,000.
George Tousey, *President;* C. S. Stevenson, *Cashier.*

BANKERS.

Indianapolis Branch Banking Company, corner Pennsylvania and Washington streets.
C. Fletcher, *President;* Thomas H. Sharpe, *Cashier.*
Fletcher S. A., No. 30 E. Washington street.
Harrison A. & J. C. S., No. 19 E. Washington street.

HALLS AND PUBLIC BUILDINGS.

Ætna Building, N. Pennsylvania.
Odd Fellows' Hall, cor. Washington and Pennsylvania.
Masonic Hall, cor. of Washington and Tennessee.
College Hall, S. W. cor. Washington and Pennsylvania.
Temperance Hall, Washington, N. side, bet. Meridian and Illinois.
Washington Hall, Washington, E. of Tennessee.
Union Hall, Washington, opp. Court House.
Military Hall, Washington, bet. Meridian and Pennsylvania.
Court House, Washington, bet. Delaware and Alabama.
State House, Washington, bet. Tennessee and Mississippi.
Metropolitan Hall, cor. Washington and Tennessee.
Sons of Malta Hall, Washington, bet Meridian and Pennsylvania.

POST OFFICE.

Office on Meridian street, near corner of Washington. Office opens at 7½ A. M., and closes at 7½ P. M. On Sunday from 9 to 10 A. M.
Postmaster, John M. Talbott. *Clerks,* James McCready, James Swain, James Russell, E. C. Boyd, E. A. Elder, J. L. Fish, C. G. Werbe, J. B. Morrison, H. McWorkman, George Sweetser, N. J. Dorsey, Richard Slater, James Diver, B. F Riley, John Brennan, William A Morrison.
Special Agent, William Garver.

LITERARY INSTITUTIONS.
YOUNG MEN'S CHRISTIAN ASSOCIATION.

Organized November, 1854. Room No. 7 Ray's Block, W. Washington, up stairs.
President, Benjamin Harrison; *Vice Presidents,* one member from each Christian denomination; *Recording Secretary,* Wm. H. Smith; *Corresponding Secretary,* Charles W. Moores; *Treasurer,* Chas. G. Stewart; *Librarian,* Dr. A. S. Wright.
This association has a library of over one thousand well selected works.

The regular meeting of the association is held at their rooms on the third Monday evening of each month.

The Reading Room is open from 7 o'clock A. M. to 9 o'clock P. M.

Books can be taken from the Library between 8 and 9 o'clock A. M., or from one to 3 o'clock P. M., by calling on the librarian, Dr. A. S. Wright.

Any person of good moral character may become a member of the association by the payment, in advance, of $1 00 a year.

IRVING ASSOCIATION.

Organized December 15, 1859.

OFFICERS.

President, C. H. Williams; *Vice President,* S. Allamon; *Secretary,* L. H. Crall; *Treasurer,* S. C. Frink; *Finance Committee,* L. H. Crall and I. Klingensmith.

The object of this association is the promotion of literature and science, by means of popular lectures, &c.

Meets at the President's office, No. 19 W. Washington.

METROPOLITAN LITERARY INSTITUTE.

Meets every Tuesday evening at rooms Fletcher's Building.

OFFICERS.

President, Thos. J. Vater; *Vice President,* B. F. Copeland; *Secretary,* Francis Smith; *Treasurer,* J. H. Newmeyer; *Reviewer,* Rolin Defrees; *Critic,* T. J. Vater.

INDIANAPOLIS CHESS CLUB.

Meets for practice on Monday, Wednesday and Friday evenings of each week at No. 1 Blackford's Building, up stairs.

President, Capt. John Love; *Secretary,* Z. Lichtenhein; *Treasurer,* A. E. Vater.

CHURCHES AND PASTORS.

First Presbyterian, N. E. cor. Circle and Market, Rev. Thos. M. Cunningham, bds. 170 N. Illinois.

Second Presbyterian, N. W. cor. Circle and Market, Rev. G. P. Tindall, 12 E. Vermont.

Third Presbyterian, cor. Illinois and Ohio, Rev. David Stevenson, 248 N. Illinois.

Fourth Presbyterian, cor. Market and Delaware, Rev. — Brooks.

Associate Reformed Presbyterian, Ohio, W. of Delaware, Rev. Gilbert Small, bds. 78 Massachusetts ave.

Wesley Chapel, (Methodist,) S. side of Circle, Elijah T. Fletcher, 2 Circle.

Robert's Chapel, (Methodist,) cor. Pennsylvania and Market, Rev. William Wilson, adjoining church.

Strange Chapel, (Methodist,) Tennessee, S. of Vermont, Rev. Wm. Graham, adjoining church.

Asbury Chapel, (Methodist,) New Jersey, S. of Louisiana, Rev. E. D. Long, 104 Virginia ave.

German, (Methodist,) Ohio, E. of New Jersey, Rev. Miller, adjoining church.

African, (Methodist,) Georgia, bet. Canal and Mississippi, Rev. E. Weaver, N. Tennessee.

North Street, (Methodist,) North, W. of Alabama, Rev. John Hill, 143 N. Pennsylvania.

Episcopalian (Christ Church,) N. E. cor. Meridian and Circle. Rev. Joseph C. Talbott, adjoining church, Circle.

Baptist, cor. Meridian and Maryland, Rev. James B. Simmons, N. Pennsylvania, opp. Blind Asylum.

African Baptist, Missouri, near New York, Rev. M. Broyles, 199 W. North.

Christian Church, cor. Ohio and Delaware, Rev. Perry Hall.

First Evangelical Lutheran, cor. Alabama and New York, Rev. Kunkleman, bds. 167 N. Alabama.

Second Evangelical Lutheran, Pennsylvania, bet. St. Clair and Pratt.

German United Evangelical, Ohio, bet. Illinois and Meridian, Rev. Edward Kuester, basement of church.

German Lutheran, Alabama, S. of Washington, Rev. Chas. Fricke, 13 N. East.

Congregationalist, N. W. cor. Circle and Meridian, Rev. N. A. Hyde, bds. 56 N. Meridian.

German Reformed, Alabama, S. of Market, Rev. M. J. I. Stern, at church.

United Brethren, cor. New Jersey and Ohio, Rev. C. W. Witt, bds. 62 N. East.

St. John's, (Catholic,) Georgia, bet. Tennessee and Illinois, Rev. Bessonies, adjoining church.

St. Mary's, (Catholic,) Maryland, bet. Pennsylvania and Delaware, Rev. Simon Seirist, 46 S. Delaware.

German Evangelical, New Jersey, bet. Market and Ohio, Rev. M. Hoehn, back of church.

Universalist, College Hall, W. C. Brooks, Alvord's Block.

Friend's Church, (Hicksite,) Delaware, bet. Michigan and North.

Friend's Church, (Orthodox,) cor. Delaware and St. Clair, David Tatum and wife, Massachusetts ave.

Jewish Synagogue, 97 E. Washington, up stairs, Rev.

18

Judah Wezhsler Rabbi, Maryland, bet. Pennsylvania and Virginia ave.

INDIANAPOLIS FEMALE INSTITUTE.

North-east corner of Pennsylvania and Michigan streets.

BOARD OF INSTRUCTION.

Rev. Gibbon Williams, Superintendent.

Miss E. A. Williams, Principal, and Teacher of Mental and Moral Science, and Latin.

Miss Georgiana Nicholas, Teacher of Mathematics and Modern Languages.

Miss M. J. Ball, Teacher of Natural Sciences and Penmanship.

Miss Francis A. Wright, Teacher of the Preparatory Department.

Miss S. J. Ingersoll, Teacher of Music.

Miss Gussie Ford, Assistant Teacher of Music.

Miss M. S. Wagner, Teacher of Drawing.

The year will be divided into two sessions of 20 weeks each—the first commencing the 1st day of September, 1860, and the second on the 26th January, 1861. There will be a vacation of one week at Christmas, and one in the Spring, commencing the 6th of April.

McLEAN'S FEMALE SEMINARY.

27 North Meridian. C. G. McLean, Principal.

ST. JOHN'S ACADEMY—CATHOLIC.

Adjoining the Catholic Church, conducted by the Sisters of Providence.

NORTH-WESTERN CHRISTIAN UNIVERSITY.

This institution is located about one mile and a half N. E. of the Governor's Circle.

BOARD OF DIRECTORS.

Ovid Butler, *President*; Jeremiah Smith, Benj. F. Reeve, Benj. Eranklin, Geo. W. Branham, Wm. H. Craig, Chauncey Butler, John B. New, Robert B. Duncan, John Young, Elijah Goodwin, John O'Kane, A. D. Hamrick, Wm. S. Pickerell, Benj. Craig, D. C. Stover, James Ford, L. H. Jameson, Jacob Wright, Geo. Campbell, W. W. Thrasher.

Ovid Butler, jr., *Secretary;* Elijah Goodwin, *Tresasurer;* A. R. Benton, *Treasurer of Iastitution.*

FACULTY.

President, S. K. Hoshour, A. M.

Professor of Ethics and Intellectual Science, S. K. Hoshour, A. M.

Professor of Natural Science, R. T. Brown, A. M., M. D.
Professor of Ancient Languages and Literature, A. R. Benton, A. M.
Professor of Mathematics and Civil Engineering, G. W. Hoss, A. M.
Professor of English and Normal School, Madison Evans, A. M.
Professor of Modern Languages, S. K. Hoshour, A. M.

TEACHERS OF ENGLISH PREPARATORY SCHOOL.

Mrs. N. Burns, and Mrs. E. J. Price.

NEWSPAPERS AND PERIODICALS.

Indiana State Sentinel, Daily and Weekly, Bingham & Doughty, proprietors, No. 18 E. Washington, Democratic.

Indiana State Journal, Daily and Weekly, Journal Co., proprietors, No. 10 S. Pennsylvania, Republican.

Locomotive, Saturdays, Elder & Harkness, proprietors, No. 2 S. Meridian, Independent.

Volksblatt, (German,) Saturdays, Boetticher & Seidensticker, proprietors, No. 130 E. Washington, Democratic.

Freie Presse, (German,) Thursdays, Richard Henninger, proprietor, No. 66½ E. Washington, Republican.

Indiana American, Wednesdays and Saturdays, T. A. Goodwin, proprietor, rear of Glenn's Block, Republican.

Herald and Era, Saturdays, Williamson & Lee, proprietors, Locomotive Building, 1st door, Universalist.

Witness, Wednesdays, M. G. Clarke, proprietor, Odd Fellows' Hall, Baptist.

Christian Record, Monthly, Elijah Goodwin, proprietor, Journal Office, Christian.

Indiana Farmer, Weekly, J. N. Ray, proprietor, over postoffice, Agricultural.

Indiana School Journal, Monthly, O. Phelps, proprietor, Sentinel Office, Educational.

Repository, (col.,) Quarterly, Elijah Weaver, proprietor, Journal Office, Literature and Religion.

LIBRARIES.

STATE LIBRARY.

State House. James R. Bryant, Librarian. Number of volumes, 20,000. For the use of Judges, State officers, professional men, &c. Office hours from 9 till 4.

CENTER TOWNSHIP LIBRARY.

Court House. Number of volumes, 1,000. Alex. Graydon, Librarian. Open on Saturdays form 2 till 5 P. M. Terms free.

MARION COUNTY LIBRARY.

Under the charge of nine trustees. This institution was organized under the special law of 1843.
John W. Hamilton, *Librarian.* Number of volumes, 1,650. Office at Court House. Terms 75 cents a year for two books, 50 cents for one book. Open on Saturdays from 9 till 3.

TELEGRAPH.

Western Union Telegraph Company. Office No. 1 N. Meridian.

STATE BENEVOLENT INSTITUTIONS.

INDIANA INSTITUTION FOR THE EDUCATION OF THE BLIND.

Located half a mile N. of Washington street, between Meridian and Pennsylvania streets.

OFFICERS.

President, W. H. Talbott; *Trustees,* Harvey G. Hazlerigg, Michael Fitzgibbon.
Superintendent, J. McWorkman, M. D.
Literary Teachers, Granville M. Ballard, Miss Eliza W. Bowman.
Matron, Mrs. Juliette McWorkman.
Teacher of Music, Miss Gertrude McColloch.
Physician, Livingston Dunlap, M. D.
Teacher in Work Shop, Milton C. Holman.

INDIANA INSTITUTION FOR THE EDUCATION OF THE DEAF AND DUMB.

Located on E. Washington street, near City limits.

OFFICERS.

Board of Trustees, W. H. Talbott, *President:* Jno. M. Kitchen, M. D., Thomas W. Woolen.

INTELLECTUAL DEPARTMENT.

Superintendent, Thomas Mac Intire, A. M.
Instructors, Wm. Willard, H. S. Gillet, A. M., W. A. Latham, A. M., M. D., W. H. De Motte, A. M., Phillip A. Emery, A. M., B. R. Nordyke, W. S. Marshall, A. B.

DOMESTIC DEPARTMENT.

Physician, Livingston Dunlap, M. D.
Matron, Miss Julia A. Taylor.
Assistant Matron, Miss L. B. Paige.
Steward, William R. Hogshire.

INDUSTRIAL DEPARTMENT.

Master of Shoe Shop, James Davis.
Master of Cabinet Shop, S. F. Kahle.
Gardener, George McClain.

INDIANA HOSPITAL FOR THE INSANE.

This Institution is located on a farm of 160 acres of land, three miles west of the City on the National road. The first law for its establishment was enacted by the General Assembly during the session of 1843–4. The farm was purchased of N. Bolton, Esq., for $5,300, in the fall of 1845. It was open for the reception of patients, November, 1849. The cost, thus far, has been about three hundred thousand dollars. There has been over fifteen hundred insane patients admitted to its Wards.

OFFICERS OF THE HOSPITAL, 1860.

Commissioners, W. H. Talbott, *President;* Edwin J. Peck, Henry Brady.

RESIDENT OFFICERS.

Superintendent, James S. Athon, M. D.
Assistant Physicians, Henry F. Barnes, M. D., John M. Dunlap, M. D.
Steward, Moses Hunter.
Matron, Mrs. Esther McLaughlin.

MASONIC ORDERS.

GRAND ENCAMPMENT OF KNIGHTS TEMPLAR.

The next Annual Conclave of the Grand Commandery of Knights Templar of the State of Indiana, will be held at Indianapolis, on the first Wednesday (5th) of December, 1860.

GRAND OFFICERS FOR THE YEAR 1860.

Rev. Sir William Pelan, of Connersville, R. E. Grand Commander; Rev. Sir John W. Sullivan, of Jeffersonville, V. E. D. G. Commander; Sir Harvey G. Hazelrigg, of Thorntown, Grand Generalissimo; Sir John A. Hutton, of New Albany, Grand Captain General; Rev. Sir Lewis Dale, of New Castle, Grand Prelate; Sir Isaac Jenkinson, of Fort Wayne, Grand Senior Warden; Sir Martin Frybarger, of Connersville, Grand Junior Warden; Sir Charles Fisher, of Indianapolis, Grand Treasurer; Sir Francis King, of Indianapolis, Grand Recorder; Sir William G. Cooper, of Reynolds, Grand Standard Bearer; Sir Joseph Johnson, of Fort Wayne, Grand Sword Bearer; Sir William G. Terrell, of Lafayette, Grand Warder; Sir Henry Colestock, of Indianapolis, Grand Sentinel.

GRAND COUNCIL OF ROYAL AND SELECT MASTERS.

The Grand Council of Royal and Select Masters of the State of Indiana, will hold the next annual communication at Indianapolis, at 9 o'clock A M., on the Tuesday (22d) before the fourth Monday of May, 1860.

GRAND OFFICERS.

Comp. William Hacker, of Shelbyville, Grand Puissant; Comp. William W. Lynde, of Centreville, Deputy G. Puissant; Comp. Horace Coleman, of Logansport, Gr. T. I. Gr. Master; Comp. Thomas Pattison, of Aurora, Gr. P. C. of Work; Comp. Martin Frybarger, of Connersville, Gr. Capt. Guards; Comp. P. G. C. Hunt, of Indianapolis, G. Treasurer; Comp. Francis King, of Indianapolis, Gr. Recorder; Comp. Daniel K. Hays, of Attica, Gr. Chaplain; Comp. Henry Colestock, of Indianapolis, Gr. S. and Sentinel.

GRAND CHAPTER OF STATE OF INDIANA.

The Grand Royal Arch Chapter, of the State of Indiana, will hold its next annual communication at Indianapolis, at 2 o'clock P. M., on the Tuesday (22d) before the fourth Monday of May, 1860.

GRAND OFFICERS.

M. E. Daniel K. Hays, of Attica, G. H. Priest; E. Geo. W. Porter, of New Albany, D. G. H. Priest; E. Chauncy Charter, of Logansport, G. King; E. James R. Mendenhall, of Richmond, G. Scribe; E. Rev. F. A. Hardin, of Muncie, G. Chaplain; E. Phineas G. C. Hunt, of Indianapolis, G. Treasurer; E. Francis King, G. Secretary; Comp. Thomas Pattison, of Aurora, G. Capt. Host; Comp. Horace Coleman, of Logansport, G. R. A. Captain; Comp. Henry Colestock, of Indianapolis, G. Guard.

GRAND LODGE OF THE STATE OF INDIANA.

The Grand Lodge of Indiana holds its annual communication at the Masonic Hall, in the city of Indianapolis, at 2 o'clock P. M., on the fourth Monday (28th) of May, 1860.

GRAND OFFICERS.

M. W. Alexander C. Downey, of Rising Sun, G. Master; R. W. Mahlon D. Manson, of Crawfordsville, D. G. Master; R. W. William N. Doughty, of Laurel, S. G. Warden; R. W. John B. Fravel, of Laporte, J. G. Warden; R. W. Chas. Fisher, of Indianapolis, Grand Treasurer; R. W. Francis King, of Indianapolis, Grand Secretary; Bro. Rev. William Pelan, of Connersville, G. Chaplain; Bro. William J. Millard, jr., of Millersville, G. Lecturer; Bro. Ebenezer Morehouse, of Madison, G. Marshal; Bro. Daniel K. Hays, of Attica, S. G. Deacon; Bro. William W. Clinedenst, of Centreville, J. G. Deacon; Bro. Henry Colestock, of Indianapolis, G. Tyler.

RAPER ENCAMPMENT, No. 1.

Total number of members 49; date of charter, October 16th, 1850; stated meetings fourth Wednesday in each month.

OFFICERS.

M. E. Sir Ephraim Colestock, G. Commander; M. E. Sir William Sullivan, Generalissimo; M. E. Sir John M. Bramwell, Capt. General; M. E. Sir Francis King, Prelate; M. E. Sir Martin Igoe, Senior Warden; M. E. Sir A. D. Gall, Junior Warden; M. E. Sir Samuel Campbell, Treasurer; M. E. Sir Charles Fisher, Recorder; M. E. Sir William H. Lingenfelter, Standard Bearer; M. E. Sir John D. Morris, Sword Bearer; M. E. Sir David McWorkman, Warder; M. E. Sir Henry Colestock, Sentinel.

COUNCIL.

Indianapolis Council, No. 2, at Indianapolis.

Francis King, T. I. G. M.; Ephraim Colestock, D. T. G. M.; Barton D. Jones, P. C. W.; Israel Conklin; C. G.; John L. Bramwell, Treasurer; Chas. Fisher, Recorder; Henry Colestock, Steward and Sentinel.

CHAPTER.

Indianapolis Chapter, No. 5, at Indianapolis, meets first Friday of each month; number of members 84.

OFFICERS.

John L. Bramwell, H. P.; Ephraim Colestock, K.; Samuel Campbell, S.; Francis King, C. of H.; Israel Conklin, P. S.; James H. Seybold, R. A. C.; Richard Richards, G. M. 3. V.; Hermon Weinberger, G. M. 2. V.; Roger Parry, G. M. 1. V.; James Sulgrove, T. R.; Charles Fisher Sec'y; Henry Colestock, Guard.

MARION LODGE, No. 35.

Chartered 1853. Meets at Masonic Hall third Wednesday in each month.

J. M. Bramwell, W. M.; Israel Conklin, S. W.; B. D. Jones, jr., J. W.; Moses Wolf, T.; F. King, Sec'y; Richard Richards, S. D.; Jas. M. Jameson, J. D.; Henry Colestock, Tyler.

CENTER LODGE, No. 23.

Number of members 100. Chartered October, 1846. Meets at Masonic Hall first Wednesday in each month.

J. M. Tomlinson, W. M.; Wm. Warman, S. W.; Peter
Ritter, J. W.; I. H. Roll, Treasurer; Chas. Fisher, Sec'y;
Wm. Nichols, S. D.; John C. Weinberger, J. D.; H. Cole-
stock, Tyler.

CONCORDIA LODGE, No 178.

Chartered May, 1855. Meets at Masonic Hall the second
Wednesday in each month.

Geo. F. Meyer, W. M.; Frank Damme, S. W.; Jacob
Reinacker, J. W.; Chas. John, Treasurer; Albert Reisner,
Sec'y; Adam Spring, S. D.; Godleif Kamm, J. D.; H. Cole-
stock, Tyler.

INDEPENDENT ORDER OF ODD FELLOWS.

R. W. G. ENCAMPMENT, I. O. O. F., OF INDIANA.

The R. W. Grand Encampment, I. O. O. F., of Indiana, was
instituted on the 10th of December, 1847, and convenes at
Odd Fellows' Hall, Indianapolis, on the third Monday
preceding the third Tuesday of May and November of
each year.

OFFICERS.

Thomas B. McCarty, M. W. G. Patriarch, Wabash; R. C.
S. Maccoun, M. E. G. High Priest, Danville; John T. Saun-
ders, R. W. G. Senior Warden, Jeffersonville; A. J. Power,
R. W. G. Junior Warden, Warsaw; E. H. Barry, R. W. G.
Scribe, Indianapolis; T. P. Haughey, R. W. G. Treasurer,
Indianapolis; Christopher Toler, W. G. Sentinel, Madison;
Jacob T. Williams, Dep. G. Sentinel, Indianapolis; Chris
Miller, Lafayette, J. S. Harvey, Jeffersonville, G. Reps. G.
L. U. S; John H. Stailey, Rochester, David Ferguson, Win-
chester, Alt. G. Reps.

PAST GRAND PATRIARCHS.

Christian Bueher, of No. 2; Isaac H. Taylor, of No. 2;
Daniel Moss, of No. 27; J. S. Harvey, of No. 5; Jacob P.
Chapman, of No. 5; Job B. Eldridge, of No. 10; E. H. Barry, of No. 12; Lewis Humphreys, of No. 9; Chris Miller,
of No. 6; J. H. Stailey, of No. 24.

PAST GRAND HIGH PRIESTS.

Casper Markle, of No. 11; W. P. Applegate, of No. 33;
George B. Jocelyn, of No. 1; Thos. P. Gunnell, of No. 38;
David Ferguson, of No. 50.

GRAND LODGE OF INDIANA.

The R. W. Grand Lodge of I. O. O. F., of Indiana, was instituted on the 14th of August, 1837, and convenes at

MUNSON'S
COPPER TUBULAR

LIGHTNING ROD
WITH
SPIRAL FLANCES.

[SEE NEXT PAGE.

Odd Fellows' Hall, Indianapolis, on the third Tuesday of May and November in each year.

OFFICERS.

Thomas Underwood, M. W. Grand Master, Lafayette; James Burgess, R. W. D. Grand Warden, Danville; J. H. Popp, R. W. Grand Warden, Richmond; E. H. Barry, R. W. Grand Secretary, Indianapolis; T. P. Haughey, R. W. Grand Treasurer, Indianapolis; Milton Herndon, G. Rep. G. L. U. S., Crawfordsville; George B. Roberts, G. Rep. G. L. U. S., La Porte; L. M. Campbell, Alt. G. Rep., Danville; J. L. McLaughlin, Alt. G. Rep., Lebanon; Rev. I. M. Westfall, R. W. Grand Chaplain, Lafayette; W. H. Schlater, R. W. Grand Marshal, Centreville; F. R. A. Jeter, R. W. Grand Conductor, Brookville; Chris Toler, R. W. Grand Guardian, Madison; A. W. Fuqua, W. Grand Herald, Indianapolis; S. Levin, Grand Messenger, Logansport.

METROPOLITAN ENCAMPMENT, No. 5, I. O. O. F.

Meets every first and third Monday of each month.

Benjamin F. Foster, Chief Patriarch; Roger Parry, High Priest; Stephen Sharpe, Senior Warden; A. W. Branham, Junior Warden; Samuel Frazer, Scribe; Horace A. Fletcher, Treasurer; John G. Waters, Per. Scribe.

MARION ENCAMPMENT, No. 35, I. O. O. F.

Meets every second and fourth Monday of each month.

S. C. Morgan, Chief Patriarch; Richard C. Stout, High Priest; W. H. Lingenfelter, Senior Warden; Andrew J. Hinesley, Junior Warden; Zalmon Tousey, Scribe; George G. Holman Treasurer.

GERMAN TEUTONIA ENCAMPMENT, No 56, I. O. O. F.

Meets every second and fourth Friday of each month.

Frederick Ruschhaupt, Chief Patriarch; John Brinkman, High Priest; Frederick Burgtorf, Senior Warden; John Stumph, Junior Warden; John Kistner, Scribe; Joseph Karle, Treasurer,

CENTER LODGE, No. 13, I. O. O. F.

Meets every Tuesday evening.

Stephen McNabb, Noble Grand; Wm. J. Woolen, Vice Grand; Benjamin F. Bryant, Recording Secretary; John G. Waters, Permanent Secretary; Horace A. Fletcher, Treasurer.

PHILOXENIAN LODGE, No. 44, I. O. O. F.

Meets every Wednesday evening.

Theophilus Parvin, Noble Grand; Thomas J. Vater, Vice

Grand; S. C. Morgan, Recording Secretary; Joseph S. Watson, Permanent Secretary; Joseph R. Haugh, Treasurer.

GERMANIA LODGE, No. 129, I. O. O. F.

Meets every Thursday Evening.

Charles Richmann, Noble Grand; John Brinckmeyer, Vice Grand; Tobias Bender, Recording Secretary; G. F. Henning, Permanent Secretary; John Kistner, Treasurer.

CAPITAL LODGE, No. 124, I. O. O. F.

Meets every Friday evening.

Geo. P. C. Brown, Noble Grand; W. L. Lingenfelter, Vice Grand; Zalmon Tousey, Recording Secretary; Theodore P. Haughey, Permanent Secretary; Benjamin R. McCord, Treasurer.

INDEPENDENT ORDER OF SONS OF MALTA.

CORTEZ LODGE, NO. 1.

Supreme Grand Council for the State of Indiana. Organized May 26th, 1859. Place of meeting, at Hall, N. side of Washington, bet. Meridian and Pennsylvania.

GRAND OFFICERS.

H. Otis, S. G. Commander; A. H. Conner, S. V. G. Commander; A. P. Willard, G. B. J. A.; A. A. Hammond, G. R. J. A.; E. Hartwell, S. G. Treasurer.; Samuel W. Gulick, S. G. D. D.; James Sweetser, S. G. C.; L. H. Dodd, S. G. C.; C. J. Dobbs, S. of G.; S. W. Elliott, S. G. S.; J. Kitchen, M. D., S. G. S.; Barton Jones, G. T. J. A.

UNITED OLD ORDER OF DRUIDS.

OCTAVIAN GRAVE, No. 3.

Meets every Monday night. Hall, E. Washington opp. Court House.

OLD GERMAN LODGE OF HARAGURIS.

FREYA LODGE, No. 81, A. D. O. H.

Meets every Tuesday evening. Hall, E. Washington, opp. Court House.

OFFICERS.

John Mueller, O. B.; Fred Stein, Per. Secretary; David Steif, U. B.; John B. Stumph, Treasurer; Charles Bruner, Secretary; Ad. Seidensticker, District Deputy.

TEMPERANCE ORDERS.
GRAND TEMPLE OF HONOR OF INDIANA.
Meets annually in May. The next session will be held in Lafayette.

OLIVER TEMPLE OF HONOR, No. 6.
Meets at Temperance Hall, every Monday evening.

GRAND DIVISION OF SONS OF TEMPERANCE OF INDIANA.
The annual session is held at Indianapolis in November, and the semi-annual session in April, at whatever point the Grand Division may designate.

WASHINGTON DIVISION No. 1.
Organized April 20th, 1846, meets at Temperance Hall, every Friday evening.

MARION DIVISION No. 76.
Organized January, 1858, meets every Tuesday night, at Wright's Hall, opposite Little's Hotel.

METROPOLITAN DIVISION No. 410.
Organized April, 1859, meets every Wednesday night, at Temperance Hall.

GRAND LODGE I. O. G. T., OF INDIANA.
Meets annually in Indianapolis, in October.

INDIANAPOLIS TYPOGRAPHICAL UNION No. 1.
Meets last Saturday in each Month.

OFFICERS.

John H. Randall, *President;* John Schley, *Vice President;* John Eskew, *Corresponding Secretary;* M. H. Halpin, *Recording Secretary;* Henry Nobbe, *Treasurer;* Theophilus McClure, *Guardian.*

Executive Committee.—Charles P. Hutchinson, S. L. Johnson, James Appleton, Wm. M. Meridith, C. S. Butterfield, A. M. Woodin, Michael Broden.

RAILROADS.
BELLEFONTAINE LINE.
In full operation. Whole length, 202 miles. Indianapolis, Pittsburgh and Cleveland Railroad Co. From Indianapolis to Columbus.

OFFICERS.

President and Superintendent, John Brough; *Assistent Superintendent,* John Camby; *General Ticket Agent.* J. F. Boyd; *Treasurer,* Edward King; *Auditor,* W. H. Otis.

Office Meridian and Louisiana streets, N. E. corner.

EVANSVILLE, INDIANAPOLIS AND CLEVELAND STRAIGHT LINE RAILROAD COMPANY.

Office No. 3, Post Office Building.

OFFICERS.

President, Jeremiah Smith; *Secretary and Treasurer*, James Greene.

INDIANA & ILLINOIS CENTRAL R. W. COMPANY.

Whole length of line, 149 miles from Indianapolis to Decatur, Illinois. About $500,000, have been already expended on this Road.

Office in Blake's Building.

OFFICERS.

President, Edmund Clarke; *Secretary and Treasurer*, J. M. Sharpe.

INDIANAPOLIS AND CINCINNATI RAILROAD.

In full operation. Running from Indianapolis to Cincinnati, via. Lawrenceburgh, without change of cars. Making use of the Ohio and Mississippi broad guage track from Lawrenceburgh to Cincinnati.

OFFICERS.

President and Superintendent, H. C. Lord; *Assistant Sup't.*, J. W. Mills; *General Ticket Agent*, W. H. L. Noble; *General Freight Agent*, John W. Check; *Treasurer*, W. O. Rockwood; *Secretary*, A. Worth; *Master Machinist*, R. Meek.

General offices, south Delaware street, one square north of South street.

INDIANA CENTRAL RAILWAY.

In full operation. Running from Indianapolis to Cincinnati and Dayton, via. Richmond.

OFFICERS.

President, John S. Newman; *Vice President*, Charles Parry; *Superintendent*, Henry L. Pope; *Road Master*, John L. Shank; *Secretary and Treasurer*, Samuel Hannah; *General Ticket Agent*, Horace Parrott; *General Freight Agent*, William A. Bradshaw.

General office, corner Delaware street, and Virginia ave. Freight office, one square on Delaware street.

JEFFERSONVILLE RAILROAD.

In full operation from Indianapolis to Jeffersonville. Length of Road, 103 miles.

OFFICERS.

President, D. Ricketts; *Superintendent*, A. S. Crothers;

Treasurer and Secretary, J. H. McCampbell; *General Ticket Agent*, H. H. Reynolds; *General Book-keeper*, R. J. Forsyth; *Agent at Jeffersonville*, Thomas Carse; *Agent at Indianapolis*, J. G. Whitcomb.

Freight office, 43 South street, Madison Depot.

LAFAYETTE AND INDIANAPOLIS RAILROAD.

From Indianapolis to Lafayette, in full operation. Length of Road, 64 miles.

OFFICERS.

President, W. F. Reynolds; *Superintendent*, J. O. D. Lilly; *Freight Agent*, E. Locke; *General Ticket Agent*, Jos. Livsey; *Secretary and Treasurer*, George Williams; *Master Machinist*, James L. Vruelain.

MADISON AND INDIANAPOLIS RAILROAD.

In full operation. Running from Indianapolis to Madison. Length of Road, 89 miles.

OFFICERS.

President, F. H. Smith; *Superintendent*, D. C. Branham; *Secretary*, Thomas Pollock.

Office, 45 South street, Madison Depot.

TERRE HAUTE AND RICHMOND RAILROAD.

From Terre Haute to Indianapolis, seventy-three miles. Passenger trains leave Terre Haute, three trains daily, (Sundays excepted,) making close connections with all trains at Indianapolis, also, at Terre Haute, with through trains for St. Louis.

OFFICERS.

President and Superintendent, E. J. Peck; *Secretary*, Charles Wood; *Road Master*, J. Hice; *Master Machinist*, Charles P. Peddle; *Ticket Agent*, R. A. Morris; *Freight Agent*, C. W. Mancourt.

PERU AND INDIANAPOLIS RAILROAD.

In full operation from Indianapolis to Peru, a distance of seventy-three miles. Connects at Peru, with Toledo, Wabash and Western Railroad.

OFFICERS.

Superintendent, David Macy; *Assistant Sup't.*, C. B. Robinson, *Secretary and Treasurer*, T. P. Haughey; *General Freight Agent*, L. N. Andrews; *Master Machinist*, F. Gilman.

INDIANAPOLIS GYMNASTIC ASSOCIATION.

Gymnasium 3d floor, C. A. Elliott's Building, N. W. corner Meridian and Maryland.

Organized March 9th, 1859. Number of members, 275. Tickets of membership, $5. Resident clergymen are furnished with tickets gratis.

Cost of fitting up Hall, fixtures, apparatus, &c., including four bowling alleys, $1,200.

OFFICERS.

Simon Yandes, *President;* William Wallace, *Vice President;* Thomas H. Bowles, *Secretary;* Thomas H. Sharpe, *Treasurer.* John Coburn, J. H. Vajen, Robert Meek, *Directors.*

POPULATION.

The following may be considered as approximates to the present population of our City. Males, 13,866; Females, 11,740. Total, 25,606; including Colored, 625.

Of single Men and heads of Families, there were originally from Germany, 1,889; Ireland, 686; England, 202; Scotland, 106; France, 85; Prussia, 34; Switzerland, 13; Italy, 5; Austria 2; Denmark, 2; Wales, 2; Holland, 2. *Total from Foreign Countries,* 3,028.

Of those born in the United States, there are natives of Indiana, 760; Pennsylvania, 601; Kentucky, 441; New York, 334; Virginia, 294; Maryland, 212; Ohio, 200; Massachusetts, 136; New Jersey, 126; North Carolina, 125, Connecticut, 60; Vermont, 44; New Hampshire, 38; Illinois, 34; Georgia, 34; Maine. 24; South Carolina, 16; Delaware, 14; Tennessee, 7; Louisiana, 6; D. C., 6; Alabama, 4; Iowa, 2; Wisconsin, 1. *Total born in the United States,* 3,519.

We believe the above figures to be very nearly correct, but it will be readily perceived that in the hurry of our Canvass, it would be impossible to attend to the matter with that degree of care, necessary to insure perfect accuracy.

MANUFACTURES.

It was designed to furnish a complete statement of the manufacturing interests of the city, and to this end considerable efforts were made by means of circulars, &c., to obtain the requisite materials; but, upon examination, we find that our returns are so meagre and incomplete that we could only present a *partial* view at best, and we therefore determined to defer the matter until the publication of the next edition, when we intend to take a different, and we hope more successful, method of obtaining the necessary facts and figures. However, we give below a business summary, showing at a glance the number engaged in the various professions and every department of industrial trade:

SUMMARY OF PROFESSIONS, TRADES, &c.

Accouchers	5	Dentists	7
Agents, Ale and Porter	2	Drug Stores	12
Agents, Book	1	Dry Goods (retail)	15
Agents, Insurance	12	Dry Goods (wholesale)	4
Agents, Patent Right	7	Dyers and Scourers	8
Agents, Real Estate	12	Edge Tool Manufacturers	1
Agents, Sewing Machines	7	Embroideries	3
Agricultural Implements	9	Engraver	1
Architects	6	Express Offices	4
Artists	9	Fancy Goods	11
Attorneys at Law	76	File Maker	1
Bakeries	17	Flour and Feed Dealers	10
Banking Houses	3	Flooring Mills	3
Banks	1	Foundries and Machine Shops	4
Barbers' Saloons	14	Furniture Dealers	10
Beef and Pork Packers	2	Gas and Steam Pipe Fitters	3
Bell Hanger and Locksmith	1	Gilders and Picture Frame Makers	1
Billiard Saloons	9	Grocers (wholesale)	16
Bill-posters	2	Grocers (retail)	110
Blacksmiths	13	Guns and Pistols	4
Blank Book Manufacturers	4	Hardware Stores	7
Boarding Houses	22	Hats, Caps and Furs	5
Boiler Makers	1	Hide and Leather Dealers	5
Bonnet Bleachers	3	Hosiery and Trimmings	1
Book Binders	6	Hotels	24
Book Stores	6	Ice Dealers	2
Boots and Shoes (wholesale)	4	Insurance Companies (Home)	5
Boots and Shoes (retail)	45	Insurance Companies (Foreign)	27
Bowling Alleys	3	Iron Railings	2
Brass Foundries	2	Iron and Steel	4
Breweries	3	Justices of the Peace	4
Brick Yards	6	Land, Oil, Soap and Candles	2
Brokers, (bill and note)	8	Lard and Peg Factories	2
Building Stone	1	Lightning Rod Manufacturers (copper)	1
Butchers	13	Lime and Cement Dealers	2
Butter and Egg Dealers	1	Livery Stables	9
Cancer Doctors	2	Loan Offices	3
Carpenters and Builders	28	Locksmith	1
Carpets, &c.	4	Lumber Yards	6
Carriage Shops	6	Marble Yards	7
China, Glass, &c.	3	Merchant Tailors	10
Cigar and Tobacco Stores	11	Milliners and Dressmakers	27
Clothing Stores	13	Model Builders	3
Coal Dealers	6	Money Brokers	1
Coal Oil Lamp Dealer	1	Music Stores	2
Commercial Colleges	2	News Depots	2
Commission Merchants	12	Newspapers (daily)	2
Confectioners	10	Newspapers (semi-weekly)	1
Cooperages	3	Newspapers (weekly)	9
Coppersmiths	2	Periodicals (monthly)	3
Daguerrean Rooms	7	Notaries Public	21

Nurseries 2
Oculists 1
Opticians 2
Paint and Color Works 1
Painters 13
Paper Box Makers 1
Paper Mill 1
Patent Medicines 3
Patent Solicitors 3
Physicians 60
Piano Fortes 3
Planing Mills 3
Plasterers 2
Plumbers 2
Portrait Painters 4
Professors of Music 7
Printing Offices 9
Printers (book and job) 6
Publishers (book) 5
Pump Makers 4
Real Estate Auctioneers 2
Restaurants 15
Rolling Mills 1
Saddle and Harness Manufacturers 6
Saddlery Hardware 3
Saloons 44
Sash, Doors and Blinds 4
Saw Manufacturers 1
Saw Mills 4
Stoves 2
Silversmiths 3
Stair Builders 1
Stock Brokers 1
Stoneware 1
Surveyors 6
Tanners 3
Tea Dealers 5
Tinware and Stoves 10
Trunk Manufacturers 2
Turners 1
Umbrella Manufacturers 1
Undertakers 4
Vinegar Manufacturers 2
Wagon Manufacturers 5
Wall Papers 2

Watches and Jewelry 9
Well Diggers 2
Wines and Liquors 12
Wood and Willow Ware 6
Woolen Factories 2
Yankee Notions and Toys 3

Miscellaneous.

Steam Fire Companies 3
Military Companies 3
Artillery Company 1
Company of Light Dragoons 1
Gas Light and Coke Company 1
Building and Savings Association 1
Halls and Public Buildings 12
Postoffice 1
Literary Institutes 3
Chess Club 1
Churches 30
Female Seminaries 2
Academy (Catholic) 1
Public Libraries 3
State Benevolent Institutions 3
Grand Encampment Knight Templars,
   (Masonic) 1
Grand Council 1
Grand Chapter 1
Grand Lodge 1
Subordinate Encampment 1
Subordinate Council 1
Subordinate Chapter 1
Masonic Lodges 3
Grand Encampment, I. O. O. F. 1
Grand Lodge 1
Subordinate Encampments 3
Subordinate Lodges 4
Lodge I. O. S. M. 1
Lodge (German) Haragaris 1
Railroads completed 8
Railroads under construction 2
Temperance organizations 6
Typographical Union 1
Gymnastic Association 1

NAMES

TOO LATE FOR REGULAR INSERTION, REMOVALS, &C.

Adams Wm. M., carpenter, res. 184 N. Illinois.

BARRY DR. E. H., R. W. G. Scribe, Grand encampment of the State of Indiana, I. O. O. F., office Odd Fellows' Hall.

Batty John H., 31 N. Alabama.

Bamberger Isaac, clerk H. Bamberger, bds. Tremont House.

Bobbs J. S., physician and surgeon, office removed to Harrison's Bank.

BOYD J. T., physician, (home,) removed to 28 N. Illinois, res. Ohio, bet. Illinois and Tennessee.

BRANSON MISS S., agent for J. B. Aiken's Knitting machine, 2 Ray's Building, W. Washington.

Bugby L. M., res. 118 N. Pennsylvania.

FERGUSON KILBY, attorney at law and notary public, Sentinel Building, res. S. E. cor. East and McCarty.

Fish A. A., ambrotype artist, cor. Washington and Meridian.

Gold Joseph S., traveling agent G. W. Hawes, bds. American House.

Hasket E., pump maker, Kentucky ave., below State offices.

Hoshour Samuel K., removed to W. S. New Jersey, bet. Market and Ohio.

Kellogg Henry S., wholesale iron and hardware commission store, 66 E. Washington, res. 87 N. Meridian.

Lord Julian F., teacher of piano forte and melodian, res. at Rev. A. L. Brooks, 89 E. Ohio.

McLean & Gummer, model builders, removed to cor. Maryland and Meridian, up stairs.

Moffitt & Hall, dentists, removed to C. A. Elliott's Building.

MORRISON JAMES A., clerk Palmer House.

Reynolds John, (Sulgrove & R.,) res. 30 Ohio.

PERU AND INDIANAPOLIS

COMPANY.

This road is seventy-three miles in length, runs through the center of Marion, Hamilton, Howard and Miami, and extends from Indianapolis to Peru, passing through the flourishing towns of Noblesville, Cicero, Tipton, Sharpsville and Kokomo, connecting at Peru with the Toledo, Wabash and Western Railroad, East for Toledo and Detroit, and West for Logansport, Delphi, Lafayette, and towns in Eastern Illinois. Connects with the numerous Railroads diverging from Indianapolis. This is the most direct route from Louisville and Southern towns to

Toledo, Detroit and Montreal.

Freight and passengers are carried as low as by any other route. This is 62 miles shorter to the Lakes from Indianapolis than by any other road. This Company have excellent facilities for transporting both FREIGHT and PASSENGERS, and the road is in good running condition, and a safe and reliable route.

OFFICERS.

DAVID MACY, General Agent and Superintendent.
C. B. ROBINSON, Assistant Superintendent.
THEO. P. HAUGHEY, Sec., Treas. and Gen. Ticket Agt.
L. N. ANDREWS, General Freight Agent.
F. GILMAN, Master Machinist, (Peru, Indiana.)

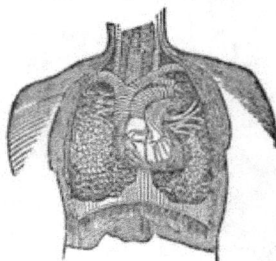